THAI

A ROUGH GUIDE PHRASEBOOK

D0950703

Credits

Compiled by Lexus with David and Somsong Smyth
Lexus Series Editor: Sally Davies
Rough Guides Phrase Book Editor: Jonathan Buckley
Rough Guides Series Editor: Mark Ellingham

This edition published in 1999 by Rough Guides Ltd,
62–70 Shorts Gardens, London WC2H 9AB.

Distributed by the Penguin Group.

Penguin Books Ltd, 27 Wrights Lane, London W8 5TZ
Penguin Books USA Inc., 375 Hudson Street, New York 10014, USA
Penguin Books Australia Ltd, 487 Maroondah Highway,
PO Box 257, Ringwood, Victoria 3134, Australia
Penguin Books Canada Ltd, Alcorn Avenue,
Toronto, Ontario, Canada M4V 1E4
Penguin Books (NZ) Ltd, 182–190 Wairau Road,
Auckland 10, New Zealand

Typeset in Bembo and Helvetica to an original design by Henry Iles.
Printed in Spain by Graphy Cems.

© Lexus Ltd 1999
288pp.

British Library Cataloguing in Publication Data
A catalogue for this book is available from the British Library.

ISBN 1-85828-608-5

HELP US GET IT RIGHT

Lexus and Rough Guides have made great efforts to be accurate and
informative in this Rough Guide Thai phrasebook. However, if you
feel we have overlooked a useful word or phrase, or have any other
comments to make about the book, please let us know. All contributors
will be acknowledged and the best letters will be rewarded with a free
Rough Guide phrasebook of your choice. Please write to 'Thai Phrasebook
Update', at either Shorts Gardens (London) or Hudson Street (New York) –
for full addresses see above. Alternatively you can email us at
mail@roughguides.co.uk

Online information about Rough Guides can be found at our website
www.roughguides.com

CONTENTS

CONTENTS

Introduction

The Rough Guide Thai phrasebook is a highly practical introduction to the contemporary language. Laid out in clear A–Z style, it uses key-word referencing to lead you straight to the words and phrases you want – so if you need to book a room, just look up 'room'. The Rough Guide gets straight to the point in every situation, in bars and shops, on trains and buses, and in hotels and banks.

The first part of the Rough Guide is a section called **Basics**, which sets out the fundamental rules of the language and its pronunciation, with plenty of practical examples. You'll also find here other essentials like numbers, dates, telling the time and basic phrases.

Forming the heart of the guide, the **English-Thai** section gives easy-to-use transliterations of the Thai words plus the text in Thai script, so that if the pronunciation proves too tricky, you can simply indicate what you want to say. To get you involved quickly in two-way communication, the Rough Guide also includes dialogues featuring typical responses on key topics – such as renting a car and asking directions. Feature boxes fill you in on cultural pitfalls as well as the simple mechanics of how to make a phone call, what to do in an emergency, where to change money, and more. Throughout this section, cross-references enable you to pinpoint key facts and phrases, while asterisked words indicate where further information can be found in the Basics.

The **Thai-English** section is in two parts: a dictionary, arranged phonetically, of all the words and phrases you're likely to hear (starting with a section of slang and colloquialisms); then a compilation, arranged by subject, of all the signs, labels, instructions and other basic words you might come across in print or in public places.

Finally the Rough Guide rounds off with an extensive **Menu Reader**. Consisting of food and drink sections arranged by subject (each starting with a list of essential terms), it's indispensable whether you're eating out, stopping for a quick drink, or browsing through a local food market.

เที่ยวให้สนุกนะ
têe-o hâi sa-nòOk ná!
have a good trip!

Basics

Pronunciation

Throughout this book Thai words have been written in a romanized system (see the Thai alphabet page 13) so that they can be read as though they were English, bearing in mind the notes on pronunciation below. There are, however, some sounds that are unlike anything in English. In this pronunciation guide, words containing these sounds are given in Thai script as well; ask a Thai to pronounce them for you.

Vowels

a	as in **a**live
e	as in t**e**n
i	as in s**i**n
o	as in **o**n
u	as in f**u**n
ah	as the **a** in r**a**ther
ai	as in Th**ai**
air	as in f**air**
ao	as in L**ao**
ay	as in h**ay**
ee	as in s**ee**
er	as in numb**er**
er-ee	as in the Thai word **ner-ee**
	เนย (butter); the **r** is not pronounced
eu	as in the Thai word **meu**
	มือ (hand); like the English exclamation **ugh!**
ew	as in f**ew**
oh	as the **o** in n**o**
oo	as in b**oo**t
oo	as in l**oo**k
oy	as in b**oy**

9

Consonants

bp   sharp **p** sound (don't pronounce the **b**). It occurs in the word **bpai** ไป (go)

dt   sharp **t** (don't pronounce the **d**). It occurs in the word **dtàir** แต (but)

g   as in **g**ate

ng   as in ri**ng**

When **k**, **p** and **t** are at the end of a word, it may sound almost as if these consonants are not being pronounced. Ask a Thai to say:

lâhk	ลาก	drag (verb)
lâhp	ลาบ	minced meat
lâht	ลาด	cover; spread (verb)

When a final **r** is followed by a vowel, the **r** is not pronounced:

ner-ee   เนย   butter

Bangkok Thai

Among some Bangkok speakers, when there are two consonants at the beginning of a word, the second consonant sound is often omitted:

bplah (fish) becomes bpah
gra-tee-um (garlic) becomes ga-tee-um

Sometimes, words beginning with a **kw** sound are pronounced as if they began with an **f** instead:

kwǎh (right) becomes fǎh
kwahm sòok (happiness) becomes fahm sòok

Tones

Thai is a tonal language which means that the pitch at which a word is pronounced determines its meaning. The same combination of letters pronounced with a different tone will produce different words. In Thai there are five different tones: mid tone (no mark), high tone (′), low tone (`), falling tone (ˆ) and rising tone (ˇ). For example:

mai	ไมล์	(mid-tone)	mile	mài	ใหม่	(low tone)	new
mái	ไม้	(high tone)	wood	mǎi	ไหม	(rising tone)	silk
mâi	ไม่	(falling tone)	not				

In Thai, the tone is as important a part of the word as the consonant and vowel sounds.

To help you get a clearer idea of how the tones sound, Thai script equivalents are given for the words in this section. Ask a Thai speaker to read the words for you so that you can hear the tonal differences.

Mid-tone: e.g. **bpai** (go). This can be thought of as normal voice pitch. The following are words pronounced with mid-tone:

mah	มา	come	mee	มี	have
bpen	เป็น	is	tum	ทำ	do
nai	ใน	in			

High tone: e.g. **rórn** (hot). The voice has to be pitched slightly higher than normal. Tones are relative, though, and a Thai with a deep voice will have no problem producing a high tone, even though it will not be as 'high' in absolute terms as a child's high tone.

The following are words pronounced with high tones:

sái	ซ้าย	left	rót	รถ	car
cháo	เช้า	morning	lék	เล็ก	little
náhm	น้ำ	water			

11

Low tone: e.g. **nèung** (one). The voice should be pitched below the normal level:

yài	ใหญ่	big		jàhk	จาก	from
bpìt	ปิด	closed		gài	ไก่	chicken
tòok	ถูก	cheap				

Falling tone: e.g. **dâi** (can). The best way to convey a falling tone is to speak very emphatically, but this doesn't mean that Thai words with falling tones have to be shouted. English speakers tend to find this the most difficult tone and do not let the voice fall sufficiently. The secret is to start at a fairly high pitch in order to achieve a distinct fall:

têe	ที่	at		mâi	ไม่	not
hâh	ห้า	five		mâhk	มาก	much
chôrp	ชอบ	like				

Rising tone: e.g. **sŏrng** (two). The rising tone is like the into-nation used when asking a question in English:

pŏm	ผม	I (said by a man)		kŏr ...	ขอ ...	may I ...
kwăh	ขวา	right		lăi	หลาย	several
mŏr	หมอ	doctor				

The relative positions of the five Thai tones can be represented graphically like this:

High Tone	Falling Tone	Mid Tone	Low Tone	Rising Tone

The Thai alphabet

Vowels

-อ	-or	เ-อะ	-er
-ะ	-a	เ-ะ	-e
-ั	-u-	เ-า	-aw
-ัว	-oo-a	เ-าะ	-or
-า	-ah	เ-	-er
-ำ	-um	เ-ีย	-ee-a
-ิ	-i	เ-ียะ	-ee-a
-ี	-ee	เ-ือ	-eu-a
-ึ	-eu	แ-	-air
-ื	-eu	แ-	-air
-ุ	-oo	แ-ะ	-air
-ู	-oo	โ-	-oh
เ-	-ay	โ-ะ	-o
เ-	-e	ใ-	-ai
เ-ย	-er-ee	ไ-	-ai

Consonants

ก	g	ฑ	t
ข	k	ฒ	t
ค	k	ณ	n
ฆ	k	ด	d
ง	ng	ต	dt
จ	j	ถ	t
ฉ	ch	ท	t
ช	ch	ธ	t
ซ	s	น	n
ฌ	ch	บ	b
ญ	y	ป	bp
ฎ	d	ผ	p
ฏ	dt	ฝ	f
ฐ	t	พ	p

13

ฟ	f		ฦๅ	leu
ภ	p		ว	w
ม	m		ศ	s
ย	y		ษ	s
ร	r		ส	s
ฤ	reu		ห	h
ฤๅ	reu		ฬ	l
ล	l		อ	consonant that is not sounded
ฦ	leu		ฮ	h

Note

When appropriate, in the **Basics** and **English–Thai** sections of this book, the phrases include two forms, the second of which is in brackets.

Where you have **pŏm (chún)** ('I' or 'me') in a phrase, **pŏm** should be used by a male speaker and **chún** by a female speaker.

There are also different polite particle forms for male and female speakers (see the **Basics** section, page 26). Where you have **krúp (kâ)** or **krúp (ká)**, the form in brackets should be used by a female speaker.

Articles

There are no definite or indefinite articles in Thai. So, for example, **rót** (car) can mean either 'a car' or 'the car'-depending on the context.

Nouns

Gender and Number

There is no gender in Thai and nouns have a single fixed form for both singular and plural. So, for example, **bâhn** means either 'house' or 'houses', depending on the context. In most cases, this is enough to make it clear whether it is a single item or more than one item that is being referred to. Even so, the Westerner has to learn to live with apparently ambiguous statements like **bpai gùp pêu-un** which can mean: 'I'm going with a friend' or 'I'm going with friends'.

You can be more specific in Thai by using a number with a noun. However, if you use a number or word denoting quantity, you also have to use a special 'counting' word known as a 'classifier'.

Classifiers

Every noun in Thai has a specific classifier which is used when counting or quantifying that noun. Some classifiers can be readily translated into English while others cannot. The classifier for all human beings, for example, is **kon** which means 'person' and the classifier for cars is **kun** which means 'vehicle'; **dtoo-a** literally means 'body' but is the classifier for animals.

The most common classifiers are:

bai	fruit, eggs, cups, bowls, small bits of paper such as tickets
cha-bùp	letters, newspapers, papers, documents
chín	pieces of cake, meat or cloth
dtoo-a	animals, chairs, tables, clothing
hàirng	places, buildings
hôrng	rooms
kon	people (excluding monks and royalty)
kòo-ut	bottles
kun	vehicles
lôok	round objects such as fruit or balls
lêm	books, knives
lŭng	houses

Uncountable nouns such as coffee, tea, beer etc are counted by the container in which they are sold. So food can be counted by the 'plate', coffee by the 'cup', beer by the 'bottle' etc.

When referring to more than one item the word order is as follows:

noun	number	classifier	
dtŏo-a	**hâh**	**bai**	five tickets
dtôm yum gài	**săhm**	**chahm**	three bowls of chicken 'tom yam'
cháhng	**sŏrng**	**dtoo-a**	two elephants
gairng néu-a	**sŏrng**	**jahn**	two plates of beef curry
pôo-yĭng	**săhm**	**kon**	three girls
bee-a	**sèe**	**kòo-ut**	four bottles of beer
rót	**sèe**	**kun**	four cars

When only one item is being counted the order of number and classifier is reversed:

noun	classifier	number	
dtǒo-a	bai	nèung	one/a ticket
mǎh	dtoo-a	nèung	one/a dog
pôo-chai	kon	nèung	one/a man
bee-a	koo-ùt	nèung	one/a bottle of beer
gah-fair	tôo-ay	nèung	one/a cup of coffee

For some nouns, the classifier is the same as the noun itself. For example, **hôrng** means 'room', and is also the classifier for rooms. However, the word **hôrng** is not repeated and only the classifier is used with the number:

sèe hôrng
four rooms

hôrng nèung
a room

Similarly, **kon** means 'person' and is also the classifier for people:

mee sǎhm kon
there were three people

kon nèung
a person, one person

Units of time and measurement are used in the same way as **hôrng** above; that is, the unit of time or measurement is the same as the classifer and is not repeated:

hâh wun
five days

sǒrng ah-tít
two weeks

deu-un nèung
one month

bpra-mahn yêe-sìp gi-loh-met
it's about 20 kilometres

Words such as 'all', 'every', 'many', 'several' and 'some' are also used with classifiers:

pêu-un
friend

tóok
every/all

kon
classifier

all my friends

17

kon ung-grìt	lǎi	kon
English person	many	classifier
many English people		

rohng rairm	bahng	hàirng
hotel	some	classifier
some hotels		

If you can't think of the right classifier for something, use the general classifier **un**:

pǒm (chún) mâi dâi kǒr ao un née
I didn't ask for this (thing)

un la tâo-rài?
how much are they each?

èek un nèung
another one, the other one, the other thing

Adjectives and adverbs

Adjectives are always placed after the noun to which they refer:

pôo-yǐng sǒo-ay	rót yài	ngern deu-un dee
a beautiful girl	a large car	a good salary

Thai adjectives also function as verbs: **sǒo-ay** thus means both 'beautiful' and 'to be beautiful' and **yài** means both 'big' and 'to be big'. The above examples might therefore just as readily have been translated as 'the girl is beautiful', 'the car is big', and 'the salary is good'.

Note, however, that the Thai verb **bpen** (to be) cannot be used with adjectives and you cannot say:

pôo-yǐng bpen sǒo-ay* or **rót bpen yài***

*incorrect sentences

Comparatives

To form the comparative (more ..., ...-er), add **gwàh** after the adjective:

yài	large	**sŏo-ay**	beautiful
yài gwàh	larger	**sŏo-ay gwàh**	more beautiful
dee	good, nice		
dee gwàh	better, nicer		

To say 'more ... than ...' or '...-er than ...', the word order is as follows:

adjective + **gwàh** ...

grOOng-tâyp yài gwàh chee-ung mài
Bangkok is bigger than Chiangmai

dee gwàh un née rĕu bplào?
is it better than this one?

bpai rót fai tòok gwàh bpai krêu-ung bin
going by train is cheaper than going by plane

Superlatives

To form the superlative, add **têe sòot** after the adjective:

yài	large	**dee**	good
yài têe sòot	(the) largest	**dee têe sòot**	(the) best
wút sŭm-kun têe sòot		**tahng ray-o têe sòot**	
the most important temple		the quickest route	

Adverbs

Adverbs are placed after the verb as in English. The adverb is the same as the adjective in Thai:

rót ray-o	**káo wîng ray-o**
a fast car	he runs quickly
pêu-un dee	**kăi dee**
a good friend	(it) sells well

19

Demonstrative Adjectives

The English demonstrative adjective 'this' is translated by née. 'That' is translated either by nún or nóhn. nún refers to something near the speaker and nóhn refers to something further away. Classifiers are also used with Thai demonstrative adjectives (see the section on Classifiers page 15):

noun	classifier	demonstrative	
dtó	dtoo-a	née	this table
gah-fair	tôo-ay	nún	that cup of coffee
dtum-ròo-ut	kon	nóhn	that policeman over there

Pronouns

Personal pronouns

There are many more personal pronouns in Thai than there are in English. The most useful pronouns are listed below. There is no distinction between subject and object pronouns in Thai:

pǒm (said by a man)	I, me
chún (said by a woman)	I, me
dee-chún (said by a woman)	I, me (more formal)
koOn	you
káo	he, him; she, her; they, them
ráo	we, us
mun*	it

*Thais tend to avoid this as it is regarded as impolite in formal spoken Thai.

When appropriate, in the **Basics** and **English-Thai** sections of this book, the phrases show both the male and female forms. Where you have pǒm (chún) ('I' or 'me') in a phrase, pǒm should be used by a male speaker and chún by a female speaker.

Frequently, pronouns are omitted altogether and it is only from the context that you will know who or what is being referred to. This sentence, for example,

doo nǔng láir-o glùp bâhn
see film already return home

could mean, 'after seeing a film, I/we/he/she/they went home'.

If you know a person's name, the polite way to address them or to speak about them is to use their first name and to place the word **kOOn** in front of it:

kOOn Chârt-chai mah jàhk nǎi?
where are you from?
where is Chartchai from?

kOOn Sǒm-chai séu a-rai?
what did you buy?
what did Somchai buy?

Possessives

The equivalent of possessive pronouns and adjectives in Thai is as follows:

noun + **kǒrng** + pronoun

The word **kǒrng** (of), however, is optional and frequently omitted:

pêu-un kǒrng káo or **pêu-un káo**
his/her/their friend

nûn kǒrng káo
that's his/hers/theirs

bâhn kǒrng pǒm or **bâhn pǒm**
my house

kǒrng chún
it's mine

Relative pronouns

There is only one relative pronoun in Thai – **têe** – which translates as either 'who', 'which', 'that' or 'where'. Here are some examples of how it is used:

kroo têe sŏrn pah-săh tai
the teacher, who teaches Thai

pŏn-la-mái têe rao séu
the fruit which we bought

órp-fit têe káo tum ngahn
the office where he works

Verbs

Verbs in Thai have a single fixed form. That is, unlike European languages, the form of the verb does not change according to the person or the tense. So, for example, **káo bpai** can mean 'he goes', 'he will go', 'he went' or 'he has gone'. Usually, the context in which you hear the verb will make it clear whether the speaker is referring to the past, present or future. But when it is important to be more specific, the context can be made clearer by placing a 'time-marker' word in front of or after the verb.

The most common and useful of these time-marker words are as follows:

ja

ja is placed immediately in front of the verb to indicate the future tense. For example:

chún ja bpai prôong née
I shall go tomorrow

rao ja séu rót mài
we shall buy a new car

ker-ee

ker-ee is placed in front of the verb to indicate the fact of having done something at least once in the past. It can also mean 'used to (do something)':

rao ker-ee bpai têe-o Chee-ung-mài
we have been to (visit) Chiangmai

káo ker-ee ree-un pah-săh tai
he used to study Thai

pŏm mâi ker-ee gin
I have never eaten it

láir-o
láir-o is placed at the end of a clause or sentence to indicate a completed action in the past:

káo gin kâo láir-o
he has eaten

chún doo láir-o
I've seen (it)

gum-lung
gum-lung is placed in front of the verb to indicate the continuous present or past:

káo gum-lung doo tee wee
he is watching TV or he was watching TV

These time-marker words are often omitted when the time context is specified or is otherwise obvious:

pŏm séu bpee gòrn
I bought (it) last year

rao bpai bpee nâh
we are going next year

Negatives

To form a negative sentence, place the word **mâi** in front of the main verb:

ah-hăhn a-ròy
the food is tasty

pŏm (chún) mee way-lah wâhng
I have some free time

ah-hăhn mâi a-ròy
the food is not tasty

pŏm (chún) mâi mee way-lah wâhng
I don't have any free time

Imperative

To make the imperative or command form, add **si** (pronounced **sí, see** or **sée**) after the verb:

doo sí
look!

ra-wung sí
look out!

bpìt bpra-dtoo sí
close the door!

For negative commands (don't ...), the word **yàh** is placed in front of the verb:

yàh tum	don't do it
yàh bpai	don't go
yàh gin	don't eat

Questions, answers, yes and no

... mái? questions

A statement can be made into a question by adding the question particle **mái** at the end of the sentence:

jèp	jèp mái?
(it) hurts	does it hurt?
bâhn yài	**bâhn yài mái?**
the house is big	is the house big?

To answer 'yes' to this type of question, you simply repeat the verb:

jèp mái?	jèp
does it hurt?	yes
bâhn yài mái?	**yài**
is the house big?	yes

If you want to say 'no', place the negative word **mâi** in front of the verb:

jèp mái?	mâi jèp
does it hurt?	no
bâhn yài mái?	**mâi yài**
is the house big?	no

... châi mái? questions

To form tag-questions in Thai, equivalent to the English 'isn't it?' or 'aren't they?' etc, add **châi mái?** to the end of a sentence:

| **káo mâi mah, châi mái?** | **soy săhm sìp săhm, châi mái?** |
| he's not coming, is he? | soi 33, isn't it? |

The **châi mái** question form is extremely useful for checking that you have understood what is going on. A 'yes' answer to a **châi mái?** question is **châi**. A 'no' answer is **mâi châi**:

bpai láir-o, châi mái?   **châi/mâi châi**
he's gone, hasn't he?   yes/no

... rěu bplào? questions

Another common question form tags **rěu blpào?** on to the end of a statement. Literally it means '... or not?', but it is not nearly as abrupt as such a translation suggests; it simply demands a straight answer:

kOOn bpai doo rěu bplào?   **mee rěu bplào?**
are you going to see (it) or not?   are there (any) or not?

If you want to say 'yes' to this, repeat the main verb – that is **bpai** in the first example, and **mee** in the second; if you want to say 'no', the answer is **bplào**.

Other question words: who? what? where? why? how? how much? how many?

Here are the remaining question words with examples; note that in almost every example the question word occurs at the end of the sentence.

krai	**kOOn bpai gùp krai?**
who?	who are you going with?
	krai mâi bpai?
	who isn't going?
a-rai	**nêe arai?**
what?	what's this?
	kOOn pôot arai?
	what did you say?
têe năi	**káo púk yòo têe năi?**
where?	where is he staying?
	hôrng náhm yòo têe năi?
	where's the toilet?

25

tum-mai?	káo bpai tum-mai?
why?	why is he going?
yung-ngai?	kOOn ja tum yung-ngai?
how?	how will you do (it)?
tâo-rài?	nêe tâo-rài?
how much?	how much is this?
gèe	bpai gèe krúng?
how many?	how many times did (you) go?

Polite particles: krúp, kâ, ká

An important way of making your speech sound polite in Thai is to use polite particles, which are untranslatable words placed at the end of a sentence. A male speaker should add the particle **krúp** to the end of both statements and questions to make them sound more polite, while a female speaker should add the particle **kâ** to the end of a statement and **ká** to the end of a question:

pŏm bpai prôOng née krúp
I am going tomorrow (said by a man)

chún mâi bpai kâ
I am not going (said by a woman)

káo bpai năi krúp?
where is he going? (said by a man)

kOOn tum a-rai ká?
what are you doing? (said by a woman)

It is important to get into the habit of using the appropriate polite particle at the end of every sentence and question. In the English-Thai section, most of the phrases have been given without these particles and the appropriate one should be added. Sometimes, depending on the situation and person addressed, it is acceptable to omit the polite particles, but, until you are more familiar with the Thai language, it is better to use them all the time.

Dates

Dates are expressed using the pattern:

wun (day)   + ordinal number
                    + month

Ordinal numbers are formed by placing **têe** in front of the cardinal number. A list of numbers is given on pages 30-31.

the first of July wun têe nèung ga-rúk-ga-dah-kom
วันที่หนึ่งกรกฎาคม
the twentieth of March wun têe yêe sìp mee-nah-kom
วันที่ยี่สิบมีนาคม
the twenty first of June wun têe yêe sìp èt mí-tOO-nah-yon
วันที่ยี่สิบเอ็ดมิถุนายน

Thais use both the Western Gregorian calendar and a Buddhist calendar – Buddha is said to have attained enlightenment in the year 543BC, so Thai dates start from that point: thus 1996 AD becomes 2539 BE (Buddhist Era).

Days

Monday wun jun วันจันทร์
Tuesday wun ung-kahn วันอังคาร
Wednesday wun pÓOt วันพุธ
Thursday wun pá-réu-hùt วันพฤหัส
Friday wun sùk วันศุกร์
Saturday wun sǎo วันเสาร์
Sunday wun ah-tít วันอาทิตย์

Months

January mók-ga-rah-kom มกราคม
February gOOm-pah-pun กุมภาพันธ์
March mee-nah-kom มีนาคม

April may-sǎh-yon เมษายน
May préut-sa-pah-kom พฤษภาคม
June mí-tOO-nah-yon มิถุนายน
July ga-rúk-ga-dah-kom กรกฎาคม
August sǐng-hǎh-kom สิงหาคม
September gun-yah-yon กันยายน
October dtOO-lah-kom ตุลาคม
November préut-sa-ji-gah-yon พฤศจิกายน
December tun-wah-kom ธันวาคม

Time

The Thai system of telling the time seems rather complicated at first because it uses different words for 'o'clock'
depending on what time of day it is:

from 1 a.m. to 5 a.m.	dtee
from 6 a.m. to midday	mohng cháo
from 1 p.m. to 4 p.m.	bài
from 5 p.m. to 6 p.m	yen
from 7 p.m. to midnight	tÔOm

Here, then, is how the hours are expressed in Thai:

1 a.m. dtee nèung ตีหนึ่ง
2 a.m. dtee sǒrng ตีสอง
3 a.m. dtee sǎhm ตีสาม
4 a.m. dtee sèe ตีสี่
5 a.m. dtee hâh ตีห้า
6 a.m. hòk mohng cháo หกโมงเช้า
7 a.m. jèt mohng cháo เจ็ดโมงเช้า
  or mohng cháo โมงเช้า
8 a.m. bpàirt mohng cháo แปดโมงเช้า
  or sǒrng mohng cháo สองโมงเช้า
9 a.m. gâo mohng cháo เก้าโมงเช้า
  or sǎhm mohng cháo สามโมงเช้า

10 a.m. sìp mohng cháo สิบโมงเช้า
  or sèe mohng cháo สี่โมงเช้า
11 a.m. sìp èt mohng cháo สิบเอ็ดโมงเช้า
  or hâh mohng cháo ห้าโมงเช้า
midday têe-ung wun เที่ยงวัน
1 p.m. bài mohng บ่ายโมง
2 p.m. bài sŏrng mohng บ่ายสองโมง
3 p.m. bài săhm mohng บ่ายสามโมง
4 p.m. bài sèe mohng บ่ายสี่โมง
5 p.m. hâh mohng yen ห้าโมงเย็น
6 p.m. hòk mohng yen หกโมงเย็น
7 p.m. tÔOm nèung ทุ่มหนึ่ง
8 p.m. sŏrng tÔOm สองทุ่ม
9 p.m. săhm tÔOm สามทุ่ม
10 p.m. sèe tÔOm สี่ทุ่ม
11 p.m. hâh tÔOm ห้าทุ่ม
midnight têe-ung keun เที่ยงคืน

Note: There is no equivalent of 'it is ...' in Thai when stating the time; **săhm tôom** means both '9 p.m.' and 'it is 9 p.m.'.

To say 'half-past', use the word **krêung** (half). There is no special word for 'quarter past' or 'quarter to' the hour; these are translated by 'fifteen minutes (past)' and 'fifteen minutes (to)' the hour:

11.30 a.m sìp-èt mohng krèung สิบเอ็ดโมงครึ่ง
3.30 p.m bài săhm mohng krèung บ่ายสามโมงครึ่ง
11.30 p.m hâh tÔOm krèung ห้าทุ่มครึ่ง
1.15 p.m bài mohng síp hâh nah-tee บ่ายโมงสิบห้านาที
1.45 p.m èek sìp hâh nah-tee bài sŏrng mohng
  อีกสิบห้านาทีบ่ายสองโมง

Note that when expressing minutes past the hour, the word order is:

hour time	number of minutes	**nah-tee** (minutes)

2.10 p.m bài sŏrng mohng sìp nah-tee บ่ายสองโมงสิบนาที
8.25 p.m sŏrng tÔOm yêe sìp hâh nah-tee สองทุ่มยี่สิบห้านาที

To express minutes to the hour, the word order is as follows:

èek (further, more)	number of minutes	hour time

4.50 p.m èek sìp nah-tee hâh mohng yen อีกสิบนาทีห้าโมงเย็น
10.55 p.m èek hâh nah-tee hâh tÔOm อีกห้านาทีห้าทุ่ม

what time is it? gèe mohng láir-o? กี่โมงแล้ว
hour chôo-a-mohng ชั่วโมง
minute nah-tee นาที
two minutes sŏrng nah-tee สองนาที
second wí-nah-tee วินาที
a quarter of an hour sìp hâh nah-tee สิบห้านาที
half an hour krêung chôo-a-mohng ครึ่งชั่วโมง
three quarters of an hour sèe sìp hâh nah-tee สี่สิบห้านาที

Numbers

0	sŏon ๐ ศูนย์	14	sìp-sèe ๑๔ สิบสี่
1	nèung ๑ หนึ่ง	15	sìp-hâh ๑๕ สิบห้า
2	sŏrng ๒ สอง	16	sìp-hòk ๑๖ สิบหก
3	sǎhm ๓ สาม	17	sìp-jèt ๑๗ สิบเจ็ด
4	sèe ๔ สี่	18	sìp-bpàirt ๑๘ สิบแปด
5	hâh ๕ ห้า	19	sìp-gâo ๑๙ สิบเก้า
6	hòk ๖ หก	20	yêe-sìp ๒๐ ยี่สิบ
7	jèt ๗ เจ็ด	21	yêe-sìp-èt ๒๑ ยี่สิบเอ็ด
8	bpàirt ๘ แปด	22	yêe-sìp-sŏrng ๒๒
9	gâo ๙ เก้า		ยี่สิบสอง
10	sìp ๑๐ สิบ	30	sǎhm-sìp ๓๐ สามสิบ
11	sìp-èt ๑๑ สิบเอ็ด	31	sǎhm-sìp-èt ๓๑
12	sìp-sŏrng ๑๒ สิบสอง		สามสิบเอ็ด
13	sìp-sǎhm ๑๓ สิบสาม	40	sèe-sìp ๔๐ สี่สิบ

50	hâh-sìp ๕๐
	ห้าสิบ
60	hòk-sìp ๖๐
	หกสิบ
70	jèt-sìp ๗๐ เจ็ดสิบ
80	bpàirt-sìp
	๘๐ แปดสิบ
90	gâo-sìp
	๙๐ เก้าสิบ
100	nèung róy
	๑๐๐ หนึ่งร้อย
101	nèung róy nèung
	๑๐๑ หนึ่งร้อยหนึ่ง
102	nèung róy sŏrng
	๑๐๒ หนึ่งร้อยสอง
110	nèung róy sìp
	๑๑๐ หนึ่งร้อยสิบ
200	sŏrng róy
	๒๐๐ สองร้อย
201	sŏrng róy nèung
	๒๐๑ สองร้อยหนึ่ง
202	sŏrng róy sŏrng
	๒๐๒ สองร้อยสอง
210	sŏrng róy sìp
	๒๑๐ สองร้อยสิบ
1,000	nèung pun
	๑๐๐๐ หนึ่งพัน
2,000	sŏrng pun
	๒๐๐๐ สองพัน
10,000	nèung mèun
	๑๐๐๐๐ หนึ่งหมื่น
100,000	nèung săirn
	๑๐๐๐๐๐ หนึ่งแสน
1,000,000	nèung láhn
	๑๐๐๐๐๐๐ หนึ่งล้าน

| 100,000,000 | nèung róy láhn |
| | ๑๐๐๐๐๐๐๐๐ หนึ่งร้อยล้าน |

Ordinals

1st	têe nèung ที่หนึ่ง
2nd	têe sŏrng ที่สอง
3rd	têe săhm ที่สาม
4th	têe sèe ที่สี่
5th	têe hâh ที่ห้า
6th	têe hòk ที่หก
7th	têe jèt ที่เจ็ด
8th	têe bpàirt ที่แปด
9th	têe gâo ที่เก้า
10th	têe sìp ที่สิบ

Basic phrases

yes
krúp (kâ); châi
ครับ(คะ) ใช่

no
mâi
ไม่

OK
oh-kay
โอเค

hello
sa-wùt dee
สวัสดี

hi!
bpai nǎi?
ไปไหน

good morning
sa-wùt dee krúp (kâ)
สวัสดีครับ(คะ)

good evening
sa-wùt dee krúp (kâ)
สวัสดีครับ(คะ)

good night
sa-wùt dee krúp (kâ)
สวัสดีครับ(คะ)

goodbye
lah gòrn ná
ลาก่อนนะ

bye
lah gòrn
ลาก่อน

see you!
jer gun mài ná!
เจอกันใหม่นะ

see you later
děe-o jer gun èek
เดี๋ยวเจอกันอีก

please
(requesting something)
kǒr ...
ขอ ...

(offering)
chern krúp (kâ)
เชิญครับ(คะ)

(could you) please ...?
chôo-ay ... nòy dâi mái?
ช่วย ... หน่อยได้ไหม

yes please
ao krúp (kâ)
เอาครับ(คะ)

thanks, thank you
kòrp-kOOn
ขอบคุณ

no thanks, no thank you
mâi ao kòrp-kOOn
ไม่เอาขอบคุณ

32

thank you very much
kòrp-kOOn mâhk
ขอบคุณมาก

don't mention it
mâi bpen rai
ไม่เป็นไร

how do you do?
sa-wùt dee krúp (kâ)
สวัสดีครับ(ค่ะ)

how are you?
bpen yung-ngai bâhng?
เป็นอย่างไรบ้าง

fine, thanks
sa-bai dee krúp (kâ)
สบายดีครับ(ค่ะ)

nice to meet you
yin dee têe dâi róo-jùk gun
ยินดีที่ได้รู้จักกัน

excuse me
(to get past, to say sorry) kŏr-tôht
ขอโทษ

(to get attention) kOOn krúp (kâ)
คุณครับ (ค่ะ)

(to say pardon?) a-rai ná?
อะไรนะ

I'm sorry
pŏm (chún) sĕe-a jai
ผม(ฉัน)เสียใจ

sorry?/pardon (me)?
(didn't understand) a-rai ná krúp (ká)?
อะไรนะครับ(คะ)

I see/I understand
kâo jai láir-o
เข้าใจแล้ว

I don't understand
pŏm (chún) mâi kâo jai
ผม(ฉัน)ไม่เข้าใจ

do you speak English?
kOOn pôot pah-sǎh ung-grìt bpen mái?
คุณพูดภาษาอังกฤษเป็นไหม

I don't speak Thai
pŏm (chún) pôot pah-sǎh tai mâi bpen
ผม(ฉัน)พูดภาษาไทยไม่เป็น

could you speak more slowly?
pôot cháh cháh nòy!
พูดช้า ๆ หน่อย

could you repeat that?
pôot èek tee dâi mái?
พูดอีกทีได้ไหม

33

could you write it down?
chôo-ay kĕe-un long hâi
  nòy, dâi mái?
ช่วยเขียนลงให้หน่อยได้ไหม

I'd like a ...
pŏm (chún) ao ...
ผม(ฉัน)เอา ...

I'd like to ...
pŏm (chún) yàhk ...
ผม(ฉัน)อยาก ...

can I have ...?
kŏr ... dâi mái?
ขอ ... ได้ไหม

how much is it?
tâo-rài?
เท่าไร

it is ...
bpen ...
เป็น ...

where is it?
yòo têe năi?
อยู่ที่ไหน

is it far?
yòo glai mái?
อยู่ไกลไหม

Conversion Tables

1 centimetre = 0.39 inches   1 inch = 2.54 cm

1 metre = 39.37 inches = 1.09 yards   1 foot = 30.48 cm

1 kilometre = 0.62 miles = 5/8 mile   1 yard = 0.91 m

1 mile = 1.61 km

km	1	2	3	4	5	10	20	30	40	50	100
miles	0.6	1.2	1.9	2.5	3.1	6.2	12.4	18.6	24.8	31.0	62.1

miles	1	2	3	4	5	10	20	30	40	50	100
km	1.6	3.2	4.8	6.4	8.0	16.1	32.2	48.3	64.4	80.5	161

1 gram = 0.035 ounces   1 kilo = 1000 g = 2.2 pounds

g	100	250	500
oz	3.5	8.75	17.5

1 oz = 28.35 g
1 lb = 0.45 kg

kg	0.5	1	2	3	4	5	6	7	8	9	10
lb	1.1	2.2	4.4	6.6	8.8	11.0	13.2	15.4	17.6	19.8	22.0

kg	20	30	40	50	60	70	80	90	100
lb	44	66	88	110	132	154	176	198	220

lb	0.5	1	2	3	4	5	6	7	8	9	10	20
kg	0.2	0.5	0.9	1.4	1.8	2.3	2.7	3.2	3.6	4.1	4.5	9.0

1 litre = 1.75 UK pints / 2.13 US pints

1 UK pint = 0.57 l   1 UK gallon = 4.55 l
1 US pint = 0.47 l   1 US gallon = 3.79 l

centigrade / Celsius $°C = (°F - 32) \times 5/9$

°C	-5	0	5	10	15	18	20	25	30	36.8	38
°F	23	32	41	50	59	64	68	77	86	98.4	100.4

Fahrenheit $°F = (°C \times 9/5) + 32$

°F	23	32	40	50	60	65	70	80	85	98.4	101
°C	-5	0	4	10	16	18	21	27	29	36.8	38.3

English

→

Thai

A

a, an*

about: about 20 **bpra-mahn**
yêe-sìp
ประมาณยี่สิบ

it's about 5 o'clock **bpra-mahn** hâh mohng yen
ประมาณห้าโมงเย็น

a film about Thailand nǔng rêu-ung meu-ung tai
หนังเรื่องเมืองไทย

above kâhng bon
ข้างบน

abroad dtàhng bpra-tâyt
ต่างประเทศ

absolutely (I agree) nâir-norn
แน่นอน

absorbent cotton sǔm-lee
สำลี

accelerator kun rêng
คันเร่ง

accept rúp
รับ

accident OO-bùt-dti-hàyt
อุบัติเหตุ

there's been an accident mee
OO-bùt-dti-hàyt
มีอุบัติเหตุ

accommodation têe púk
ที่พัก

see **room** and **hotel**

accurate tòok-dtôrng
ถูกต้อง

ache bpòo-ut
ปวด

my back aches bpòo-ut lǔng
ปวดหลัง

across: across the ...
kâhm ...
ข้าม ...

adapter (for voltage) krêu-ung
bplairng fai fáh
เครื่องแปลงไฟฟ้า

(plug) bplúk
ปลั๊ก

address têe-yòo
ที่อยู่

what's your address? kOOn
púk yòo têe-nǎi?
คุณพักอยู่ที่ไหน

 Thai addresses can be confusing, mainly because property is often numbered twice, firstly to show which real estate lot it stands in, and then to distinguish where it is on that lot. In large cities a minor road running off a major road is often numbered as a **soi** ('lane' or 'alley', although it may be a sizeable thoroughfare), rather than given its own street name.

Sukhumwit Road for example –
Bangkok's longest – has minor roads
numbered Soi 1 to Soi 103, with odd
numbers on one side of the road and
even on the other. Addresses are
written as follows:

215/3 Sukhumwit 31

Bangkok 10110

which means no.3 on lot 215 on soi
31.

address book sa-mÒOt têe-
yòo
สมุดที่อยู่

admission charge kâh kâo
ค่าเข้า

adult pôo-yài
ผู้ใหญ่

advance: in advance lôo-ung
nâh
ล่วงหน้า

aeroplane krêu-ung bin
เครื่องบิน

after lǔng
หลัง

after you chern gòrn
เชิญก่อน

after lunch lǔng ah-hǎhn
glahng wun
หลังอาหารกลางวัน

afternoon dtorn bài
ตอนบ่าย

in the afternoon dtorn bài
ตอนบ่าย

this afternoon bài née
บ่ายนี้

aftershave yah tah lǔng gohn
nòo-ut
ยาทาหลังโกนหนวด

aftersun cream yah tah lǔng
àhp dàirt
ยาทาหลังอาบแดด

afterwards tee lǔng
ทีหลัง

again èek
อีก

against: I'm against it pǒm
(chún) mâi hěn dôo-ay
ผม(ฉัน)ไม่เห็นด้วย

age ah-yÓO
อายุ

ago: a week ago ah-tít nèung
mah láir-o
อาทิตย์หนึ่งมาแล้ว

an hour ago chôo-a mohng
nèung mah láir-o
ชั่วโมงหนึ่งมาแล้ว

agree: I agree pǒm (chún)
hěn dôo-ay
ผม(ฉัน)เห็นด้วย

AIDS rôhk áyd
โรคเอดส์

air ah-gàht
อากาศ

by air tahng ah-gàht
ทางอากาศ

air-conditioning krêu-ung air
เครื่องแอร์

airmail: by airmail sòng tahng
ah-gàht
ส่งทางอากาศ

airmail envelope sorng jòt-
mǎi ah-gàht
ซองจดหมายอากาศ

airport sa-nǎhm bin
สนามบิน

to the airport, please bpai sa-
nǎhm bin
ไปสนามบิน

airport bus rót sa-nǎhm
bin
รถสนามบิน

aisle seat têe nûng dtìt tahng
dern
ที่นั่งติดทางเดิน

alarm clock nah-li-gah
bplòok
นาฬิกาปลุก

alcohol lâo
เหล้า

alcoholic kon kêe lâo mao
yah
คนขี้เหล้าเมายา

all: all the boys pôo-chai
tóok kon
ผู้ชายทุกคน

all the girls pôo-yǐng tóok
kon
ผู้หญิงทุกคน

all of it túng mòt
ทั้งหมด

all of them tóok kon
ทุกคน

that's all, thanks sèt láir-o
kòrp-kOOn
เสร็จแล้วขอบคุณ

allergic: I'm allergic to ... pǒm
(chún) páir ...
ผม(ฉัน)แพ้ ...

allowed: is it allowed? un-
nÓO-yâht mái?
อนุญาตไหม

all right mâi bpen rai
ไม่เป็นไร

I'm all right pǒm (chún)
sa-bai dee
ผม(ฉัน)สบายดี

are you all right? bpen yung-
ngai bâhng?
เป็นอย่างไรบ้าง

almost gèu-up
เกือบ

alone kon dee-o
คนเดียว

alphabet dtoo-a uk-sǒrn
ตัวอักษร

already ... láir-o
... แล้ว

also dôo-ay
ด้วย

although máir wâh
แม้ว่า

altogether túng mòt
ทั้งหมด

always sa-mĕr
เสมอ

am*: I am ... pŏm (chún)
bpen ...
ผม(ฉัน)เป็น ...

a.m.: at six/seven a.m.
hòk/jèt mohng cháo
หก/เจ็ดโมงเช้า

amazing (surprising) mâi nâh
chêu-a
ไม่น่าเชื่อ

(very good) wi-sàyt
วิเศษ

ambulance rót pa-yah-bahn
รถพยาบาล

call an ambulance! rêe-uk
rót pa-yah-bahn!
เรียกรถพยาบาล

see police

America a-may-ri-gah
อเมริกา

American (adj) a-may-ri-gun
อเมริกัน

I'm American pŏm (chún)
bpen kon a-may-ri-gun
ผม(ฉัน)เป็นคนอเมริกัน

among nai ra-wàhng
ในระหว่าง

amount jum-noo-un
จำนวน

amp: a 13-amp fuse few sìp
săhm airm
ฟิวส์สิบสามแอมป์

and láir
และ

angry gròht
โกรธ

animal sùt
สัตว์

ankle kôr táo
ข้อเท้า

anniversary (wedding) wun
cha-lŏrng króp rôrp
วันฉลองครบรอบ

**annoy: this man's annoying
me** kon née tum hâi pŏm
(chún) rum-kahn
คนนี้ทำให้ผม(ฉัน)รำคาญ

annoying nâh
rum-kahn
น่ารำคาญ

another èek
อีก

can we have another room?
kŏr bplèe-un hôrng nòy dâi
mái?
ขอเปลี่ยนห้องหน่อยได้ไหม

another beer, please kŏr bee-

a èek kòo-ut nèung
ขอเบียร์อีกขวดหนึ่ง

antibiotics yah bpùti-chee-wa-ná
ยาปฏิชีวนะ

antihistamines yah airn-dtee hít-dta-meen
ยาแอนตีฮีสตะมีน

antique: is it an antique? bpen kǒrng gào taîr táir rěu bplào?
เป็นของเก่าแท้ ๆ หรือเปล่า

antique shop rúhn kǎi kǒrng gào
ร้านขายของเก่า

antiseptic yah kâh chéu-a
ยาฆ่าเชื้อ

any: have you got any bread/tomatoes? mee ka-nǒm-bpung/ma-kěu-a-tâyt mái?
มีขนมปัง/มะเขือเทศไหม

do you have any change? mee sàyt sa-dtahng mái?
มีเศษสตางค์ไหม

sorry, I don't have any kǒr-tôht pǒm (chún) mâi mee
ขอโทษผม(ฉัน)ไม่มี

anybody krai gôr dâi
ใครก็ได้

does anybody speak English? mee **krai** pôot pah-sǎh ung-grìt dâi?
มีใครพูดภาษาอังกฤษได้

there wasn't anybody there mâi mee **krai** yòo têe nûn
ไม่มีใครอยู่ที่นั่น

anything a-rai gôr dâi
อะไรก็ได้

dialogues

anything else? ao a-rai èek mái?
nothing else, thanks mâi ao krúp (kâ)

would you like anything to drink? dèum a-rai mái?
I don't want anything, thanks mâi krúp (kâ)

apart from nôrk jàhk
นอกจาก

apartment a-páht-mén
อพาร์ตเม้นท์

apartment block dtèuk a-páht-mén
ตึกอพาร์ตเม้นท์

apologize kǒr-tôht
ขอโทษ

appendicitis rôhk sâi dtìng
โรคไส้ติ่ง

apple air-bpêrn
แอปเปิล
appointment nút
นัด

dialogue

good morning, how can I
help you? sa-wùt dee
krúp mee a-rai ja hâi
chôo-ay mái krúp?
I'd like to make an
appointment with ... yàhk
nút póp gùp ...
what time would you like?
yàhk dâi way-lah tâo-rài?
three o'clock bài săhm
mohng
I'm afraid that's not
possible, is four o'clock all
right? kít wâh kong mâi
dâi ao bpen way-lah sèe
mohng dâi mái?
yes, that will be fine krúp
dtòk-long
the name was? chêu a-rai
krúp?

apricot ay-pri-kort
เอพริคอท
April may-săh-yon
เมษายน

are*: we are rao bpen
เราเป็น
you are kOOn bpen
คุณเป็น
they are káo bpen
เขาเป็น
area bor-ri-wayn
บริเวณ
area code ra-hùt
รหัส
arm kăirn
แขน
arrange: will you arrange it for
us? chôo-ay jùt gahn hâi
nòy dâi mái?
ช่วยจัดการให้หน่อยได้ไหม
arrival gahn mah těung
การมาถึง
arrive mah těung
มาถึง
when do we arrive? rao ja
těung mêu-a rài?
เราจะถึงเมื่อไร
has my fax arrived yet? fairks
kŏrng pŏm (chún) **mah** rěu
yung?
แฟกซ์ของผม(ฉัน)มาหรือยัง
we arrived today rao **mah**
těung wun née
เรามาถึงวันนี้
art sĭn-la-bpà
ศิลป

44

art gallery ráhn kǎi pâhp kěe-un

ร้านขายภาพเขียน

artist sǐn-la-bpin

ศิลปิน

as: as big as yài tâo gùp

ใหญ่เท่ากับ

as soon as possible yàhng ray-o têe sÒOt têe ja ray-o dâi

อย่างเร็วที่สุดที่จะเร็วได้

ashtray têe kèe-a bOO-rèe

ที่เขี่ยบุหรี่

Asia ay-see-a

เอเชีย

ask tǎhm

ถาม

I didn't ask for this pǒm (chún) mâi dâi kǒr ao un née

ผม(ฉัน)ไม่ได้ขอเอาอันนี้

could you ask him to ...? chôo-ay bòrk hâi káo ... dâi mái?

ช่วยบอกให้เขา ... ได้ไหม

asleep: she's asleep káo norn lùp yòo

เขานอนหลับอยู่

aspirin airt-pai-rin

แอสไพริน

asthma rôhk hèut

โรคหืด

astonishing nâh bpra-làht jai

น่าประหลาดใจ

at: at the hotel têe rohng rairm

ที่โรงแรม

at the station têe sa-tǎh-nee rót fai

ที่สถานีรถไฟ

at six o'clock way-lah hòk mohng

เวลาหกโมง

at Noi's têe bâhn kOOn nói

ที่บ้านคุณน้อย

athletics gree-tah

กรีฑา

attractive sǒo-ay

สวย

aubergine ma-kěu-a

มะเขือ

August sǐng-hǎh-kom

สิงหาคม

aunt (elder sister of mother/father) bpâh

ป้า

(younger sister of father) ah

อา

(younger sister of mother) náh

น้า

Australia órt-sa-tray-lee-a

ออสเตรเลีย

Australian (adj) órt-sa-tray-

lee-a
ออสเตรเลีย
I'm Australian pŏm (chún)
bpen kon órt-sa-tray-lee-a
ผม(ฉัน)เป็นคนออสเตรเลีย
automatic ùt-dta-noh-mút
อัตโนมัติ
(car) rót ùt-dta-noh-mút
รถอัตโนมัติ
automatic teller bor-ri-gahn
ngern dòo-un
บริการเงินด่วน
autumn réu-doo bai-mái
rôo-ung
ฤดูใบไม้ร่วง
in the autumn dtorn réu-doo
bai-mái rôo-ung
ตอนฤดูใบไม้ร่วง
average tum-ma-dah
ธรรมดา
on average doy-ee cha-
lèe-a
โดยเฉลี่ย
awake: is he awake? káo
dtèun láir-o rěu yung?
เขาตื่นแล้วหรือยัง
away: go away! bpái!
ไป
is it far away? yòo glai mái?
อยู่ไกลไหม
awful yâir mâhk
แย่มาก

axle plao
เพลา

B

baby dèk òrn
เด็กอ่อน
baby food ah-hǎhn dèk
อาหารเด็ก
baby's bottle kòo-ut nom
ขวดนม
baby-sitter kon fâo dèk
คนเฝ้าเด็ก
back (of body) lǔng
หลัง
(back part) kâhng lǔng
ข้างหลัง
at the back kâhng lǔng
ข้างหลัง
can I have my money back?
kŏr ngern keun dâi mái?
ขอเงินคืนได้ไหม
to come/go back glùp
mah/glùp bpai
กลับมา/กลับไป
backache bpòo-ut lǔng
ปวดหลัง
bacon mǒo bay-korn
หมูเบคอน
bad mâi dee
ไม่ดี

a bad headache bpòo-ut hǒo-a mâhk
ปวดหัวมาก

badly mâi dee
ไม่ดี

bag tǒOng
ถุง

(handbag) gra-bpǎo tĕu
กระเป๋าถือ

(suitcase) gra-bpǎo dern tahng
กระเป๋าเดินทาง

baggage gra-bpǎo
กระเป๋า

baggage check têe fàhk gra-bpǎo
ที่ฝากกระเป๋า

baggage claim sǎi pahn lum-lee-ung gra-bpǎo
สายพานลำเลียงกระเป๋า

bakery ráhn tum ka-nǒm-bpung
ร้านทำขนมปัง

balcony ra-bee-ung
ระเบียง

a room with a balcony hôrng mee ra-bee-ung
ห้องมีระเบียง

ball lôok born
ลูกบอล

ballpoint pen bpàhk-gah lôok lêun
ปากกาลูกลื่น

bamboo mái pài
ไม้ไผ่

bamboo shoot(s) nòr mái
หน่อไม้

banana glôo-ay
กล้วย

band (musical) wong don-dtree
วงดนตรี

bandage pâh pun plǎir
ผ้าพันแผล

Bandaids® plah-sa-dter
พลาสเตอร์

Bangkok grOOng-tâyp
กรุงเทพฯ

bank (money) ta-nah-kahn
ธนาคาร

 Banking hours are Monday to Friday from 8.30 a.m. to 3.30 p.m., but exchange kiosks are always open till at least 5 p.m., sometimes 10 p.m. Upmarket hotels will change money 24 hours a day and the Don Muang airport exchange counter also operates 24 hours, so there's little point in buying **baht** before you arrive, especially as it takes seven working days to order from most banks outside Thailand. Anyone entering Thailand is officially required to bring a minimum amount of foreign currency with them, a sum that varies with the class of visa. If you import Thai money, you're restricted to a paltry B2000 cash per person or B4000 per family; when you leave you're supposed to export no more than B500/B1000 without prior authorization.

bank account bun-chee
ngern fàhk ta-nah-kahn
ปัญชีเงินฝากธนาคาร
bar bah
บาร์

'Bars' to most Thais are places where foreign men go for alcohol and hired female company. In Bangkok, however, there are several 'yuppie' bars, where young, affluent Thai professionals drink expensive foreign whisky and brandy to a background of sentimental music, as well as a fair number of Western-style bars catering to serious drinkers of all backgrounds. Beer and whisky can be ordered at virtually any time of the day in food shops, coffee shops, guesthouses and restaurants.

barber's châhng dtùt pǒm
ช่างตัดผม
bargaining gahn dtòr rah-kah
การต่อราคา

Bargaining or haggling over the price of goods is essential in markets or at pavement stalls, but in most shops it is inappropriate. When travelling by **tuk-tuk** (three-wheeled motorized pedicab) it is important to negotiate a price before the journey begins. Most taxis in Bangkok have meters, but in provincial towns be prepared to haggle. It is important to remember, however, that bargaining should be carried out in a good-humoured manner. Losing your temper, or trying to drive an unreasonably hard bargain will not help to seal a deal, while an offended tuk-tuk driver will be only too willing to give the tight-fisted the scariest ride of their life.

dialogue

how much is this? nêe
tâo-rài?
500 baht hâh ròy bàht

that's too expensive
pairng bpai nòy
how about 400? sèe róy
dâi mái?
I'll let you have it for 450
kít sèe róy hâh sìp gôr
láir-o gun
**can't you reduce it a bit
more?/OK, it's a deal** lót
èek mâi dâi lěu?/oh kay,
dtòk long

basket dta-grâh
ตะกร้า
bath àhng àhp náhm
อ่างอาบน้ำ
can I have a bath? kŏr àhp
náhm dâi mái?
ขออาบน้ำได้ไหม
bathroom hôrng náhm
ห้องน้ำ
with a private bathroom
hôrng norn têe mee hôrng
náhm dôo-ay
ห้องนอนที่มีห้องน้ำด้วย
bath towel pâh chét
dtoo-a
ผ้าเช็ดตัว
bathtub àhng àhp náhm
อ่างอาบน้ำ
battery bair-dta-rêe
แบตเตอรี

bay ào
อ่าว
be* bpen
เป็น
beach chai hàht
ชายหาด
on the beach tee chai
haht
ที่ชายหาด

 Topless bathing/
sunbathing is not
something that will win a
great deal of respect from Thais.
Indeed, sunbathing is not to be
recommended at all in Thailand
because of the heat. Wearing
protective clothing is a good idea
when swimming, snorkelling or
diving: a T-shirt will stop you from
getting sunburnt in the water, while
long trousers can guard against
coral grazes. Thailand's seas are
home to a few dangerous creatures,
such as jellyfish, poisonous sea
snakes, sea urchins, stingrays and
stone fish, whose potentially lethal
venomous spikes are easily stepped
on because the fish look like stones.
If stung or bitten you should always
seek medical advice as soon as
possible.

beach mat sèu-a bpoo chai-
hàht
เสื่อปูชายหาด

beach umbrella rôm gun dàirt
ร่มกันแดด

beans tòo-a
ถั่ว

beansprouts tòo-a ngôrk
ถั่วงอก

beard krao
เครา

beautiful sŏo-ay
สวย

because prór
เพราะ

because of ... neû-ung
jàhk ...
เนื่องจาก ...

bed dtee-ung
เตียง

I'm going to bed now pŏm
(chún) bpai norn
ผม(ฉัน)ไปนอน

bedroom hôrng norn
ห้องนอน

beef néu-a woo-a
เนื้อวัว

beer bee-a
เบียร์

two beers, please kŏr bee-a
sŏrng kòo-ut
ขอเบียร์สองขวด

Beer is one of the few
consumer items in
Thailand that's not a
bargain: it works out roughly the
same as what you'd pay in the West.
The most popular beers are the
locally-brewed **Singha**, and **Kloster**
and **Carlsberg**, which are brewed in
Thailand under German licence and
cost slightly more than Singha. Some
places also stock a lighter version of
Singha called **Singha Gold** and
another beer called **Amarit**, though
that's not widely available.

before gòrn
ก่อน

begin rêrm
เริ่ม

when does it begin? rêrm
mêu-a rài?
เริ่มเมื่อไร

beginner pôo rêrm ree-un
ผู้เริ่มเรียน

beginning: at the beginning
dtorn dtôn
ตอนต้น

behind kâhng lŭng
ข้างหลัง

behind me kâhng lŭng pŏm
(chún)
ข้างหลังผม(ฉัน)

Belgian (adj) bayl-yee-um
เบลเยียม

Belgium bpra-tâyt bayl-yee-um
ประเทศเบลเยียม

below dtâi
ใต้

belt kěm kùt
เข็มขัด

bend (in road) tahng kóhng
ทางโค้ง

berth (on ship) têe-norn
ที่นอน

beside: beside the ... kâhng kâhng ...
ข้างๆ ...

best dee têe sÒOt
ดีที่สุด

better dee gwàh
ดีกว่า

are you feeling better? kôy yung chôo-a mái?
ค่อยยังชั่วไหม

between ra-wàhng
ระหว่าง

beyond ler-ee bpai
เลยไป

bicycle jùk-gra-yahn
จักรยาน

big yài
ใหญ่

too big yài gern bpai
ใหญ่เกินไป

it's not big enough yài mâi por
ใหญ่ไม่พอ

bike jùk-gra-yahn
จักรยาน

(motorbike) jùk-gra-yahn-yon
จักรยานยนตร์

bikini bi-gi-nee
บิกินี

bill bin
บิล

(US) bai báirng
ใบแบ๊งค์

could I have the bill, please? chék bin
เช็คบิล

If you go out for a meal with a group of people, it is normal for the host or the most senior person present to pick up the bill. It is not usual to split the bill.

bin tǔng ka-yà
ถังขยะ

bin liners tǒOng ka-yà
ถุงขยะ

bird nók
นก

birthday wun gèrt
วันเกิด

happy birthday! oo-ay-porn
wun gèrt!
อวยพรวันเกิด

biscuit kÓOk-gêe
คุกกี้

bit: a little bit nít-nòy
นิดหน่อย

a big bit chín yài
ชิ้นใหญ่

a bit of ... ... chín
nèung
... ชิ้นหนึ่ง

a bit expensive pairng bpai
nòy
แพงไปหน่อย

bite (by insect, dog) gùt
กัด

bitter (taste etc) kǒm
ขม

black sěe dum
สีดำ

blanket pâh hòm
ผ้าห่ม

bleach (for toilet) yah láhng
hôrng náhm
ยาล้างห้องน้ำ

blind dtah bòrt
ตาบอด

blinds môo-lêe
มู่ลี่

blister plǎir porng
แผลพอง

blocked (road, pipe, sink) dtun
ตัน

blond (adj) pǒm sěe torng
ผมสีทอง

blood lêu-ut
เลือด

high blood pressure kwahm
dun loh-hìt sǒong
ความดันโลหิตสูง

blouse sêu-a pôo-yǐng
เสื้อผู้หญิง

blow-dry bpào pǒm
เป่าผม

I'd like a cut and blow-dry
yàhk hâi dtùt láir bpào pǒm
อยากให้ตัดและเป่าผม

blue sěe núm ngern
สีน้ำเงิน

boarding pass bùt têe-nûng
บัตรที่นั่ง

boat reu-a
เรือ

body râhng-gai
ร่างกาย

boiled egg kài dtôm
ไข่ต้ม

boiled rice kâo sǒo-ay
ข้าวสวย

boiler môr náhm
หม้อน้ำ

bone gra-dòok
กระดูก

bonnet (of car) gra-bprohng rót
กระโปรงรถ

book (noun) núng-sěu
หนังสือ

(verb) jorng
จอง

can I book a seat? kŏr jorng têe-nûng dâi mái?
ขอจองที่นั่งได้ไหม

dialogue

I'd like to book a table for two yàhk jorng dtó sǔm-rùp sŏrng kon

what time would you like it booked for? ja jorng way-lah tâo-rài?

half past seven tÔOm krêung

that's fine dâi krúp

and your name? chêu a-rai krúp?

bookshop, bookstore ráhn kǎi núng-sěu
ร้านขายหนังสือ

boot (footwear) rorng-táo
รองเท้า

(of car) gra-bprohng tái rót
กระโปรงท้ายรถ

border (of country) chai-dairn
ชายแดน

bored: I'm bored pǒm (chún) bèu-a
ผม(ฉัน)เบื่อ

boring nâh bèu-a
น่าเบื่อ

born: I was born in Manchester pǒm (chún) gèrt têe Manchester
ผม(ฉัน)เกิดที่ Manchester

I was born in 1960 pǒm (chún) gèrt bpee nèung pun gâo róy hòk sìp
ผม(ฉัน)เกิดปีหนึ่งพันเก้าร้อยหกสิบ

borrow yeum
ยืม

may I borrow ...? kŏr yeum ... dâi mái?
ขอยืม ... ได้ไหม

both túng sŏrng
ทั้งสอง

bother: sorry to bother you kŏr-tôht têe róp-goo-un
ขอโทษที่รบกวน

bottle kòo-ut
ขวด

bottle-opener têe bpèrt kòo-ut
ที่เปิดขวด

bottom (of person) gôn
ก้น

at the bottom of the hill
cherng kǎo
เชิงเขา

at the bottom of the street
bplai ta-nǒn
ปลายถนน

bowl chahm
ชาม

box hèep
หีบ

box office hôrng kǎi
dtǒo-a
ห้องขายตั๋ว

boy pôo-chai
ผู้ชาย

boyfriend fairn
แฟน

bra sêu-a yók song
เสื้อยกทรง

bracelet gum-lai meu
กำไลมือ

brake bràyk
เบรค

brandy lâo brùn-dee
เหล้าบรั่นดี

bread ka-nǒm-bpung
ขนมปัง

break (verb) dtàirk
แตก

I've broken the ... pǒm

(chún) tum ... dtàirk
ผม(ฉัน)ทำ ... แตก

I think I've broken my wrist
pǒm (chún) kít wâh kôr
meu **hùk**
ผม(ฉัน)คิดว่าข้อมือหัก

break down sěe-a
เสีย

I've broken down (car) rót
pǒm (chún) sěe-a
รถผม(ฉัน)เสีย

breakdown service bor-ri-
gahn sôrm
บริการซ่อม

breakfast ah-hǎhn cháo
อาหารเช้า

**break-in: I've had a
break-in** mee ka-moy-ee
kâo bâhn
มีขโมยเข้าบ้าน

breast nom
นม

breathe hǎi jai
หายใจ

breeze lom òrn òrn
ลมอ่อนๆ

bridge (over river) sa-pahn
สะพาน

brief sûn
สั้น

briefcase gra-bpǎo
กระเป๋า

bright (light etc) sa-wàhng
สว่าง

bright red dairng jùt
แดงจัด

brilliant (idea) yêe-um
เยี่ยม

bring ao ... mah
เอา ... มา

I'll bring it back later ja keun
hâi tee lǔng
จะคืนให้ทีหลัง

Britain bpra-tâyt ung-grìt
ประเทศอังกฤษ

British ung-grìt
อังกฤษ

brochure rai la-èe-ut
รายละเอียด

broken dtàirk láir-o
แตกแล้ว

bronchitis lòrt lom ùk-sàyp
หลอดลมอักเสบ

brooch kěm glùt sêu-a
เข็มกลัดเสื้อ

broom mái gwàht
ไม้กวาด

brother (older) pêe chai
พี่ชาย

(younger) nórng chai
น้องชาย

brother-in-law (older) pêe
kěr-ee
พี่เขย

(younger) nórng kěr-ee
น้องเขย

brown sěe núm dtahn
สีน้ำตาล

bruise fók-chúm
ฟกช้ำ

brush (for hair) bprairng pǒm
แปรงผม

(artist's) bprairng
แปรง

(for cleaning) mái gwàht
ไม้กวาด

bucket tǔng
ถัง

Buddha prá-pÓOt-ta-jâo
พระพุทธเจ้า

Buddhism sàh-sa-nǎh
pÓOt
ศาสนาพุทธ

 Buddhism plays an essential part in the lives of most Thais, and Buddhist monuments should be treated accordingly – which means wearing long trousers or knee-length skirts, covering your arms, and removing your shoes whenever you visit one. All Buddha images are sacred, however small, and should never be used as a backdrop for a portrait photo, clambered over, or treated in any manner that could be construed as disrespectful.

Buddhist (noun) chao pÓOt
ชาวพุทธ

buffet car rót sa-bee-ung
รถเสบียง

buggy (for child) rót kěn dèk
รถเข็นเด็ก

building ah-kahn
อาคาร

bulb (light bulb) lòrt fai fáh
หลอดไฟฟ้า

bumper gun chon
กันชน

bungalow bung-gah-loh
บังกาโล

bureau de change bor-ri-
gahn lâirk ngern
บริการแลกเงิน
see bank

burglary ka-moy-ee kâo bâhn
ขโมยเข้าบ้าน

Burma bpra-tâyt pa-mâh
ประเทศพม่า

Burmese pa-mâh
พม่า

burn (noun) plǎir mâi
แผลไหม้

burnt: this is burnt un née
mâi
อันนี้ไหม้

burst: a burst pipe tôr dtàirk
ท่อแตก

bus rót may
รถเมล์

what number bus is it to ...?
rót bpai ... ber tâo-rài?
รถไป ... เบอร์เท่าไร

when is the next bus to ...?
rót têe-o nâh bpai ... òrk gèe
mohng?
รถเที่ยวหน้าไป ... ออกกี่โมง

what time is the last bus? rót
têe-o sÒOt tái òrk gèe
mohng?
รถเที่ยวสุดท้ายออกกี่โมง

Buses, overall the fastest
way of getting around the
country, come in two
categories: ordinary (**rót tum-ma-
dah**) and air-conditioned (**rót air**),
with an additional 'air-con'
subsection misleadingly known as
tour buses (**rót too-a**), which are
privately owned and ply the most
popular long-distance routes. The
orange-coloured ordinary buses are
incredibly cheap and cover most
short-range routes between main
towns, but they have frequent stops.
'Air-con' buses stop a lot less often
(if at all) and cover the distances

faster and more comfortably. On the downside, they cost almost twice as much, depart less frequently, and don't cover nearly as many routes. In rural areas, the bus network is supplemented by **songthaews** (literally: two rows), which are open-ended vans with two facing benches, onto which the drivers squash as many passengers as possible. (In the deep south they do things with a little more style – the longer-distance songthaews there are known as 'share taxis', and are usually old limousines.) Songthaews ply set routes within and between towns; to pick one up between destinations just flag it down. As a general rule, the cost of inter-town songthaews is comparable to that of 'air-con' buses.

dialogue

does this bus go to ...? rót kun née bpai ... mái?
no, you need a number ... mái bpai kOOn dtòrng kêun măi-lâyk ...

business tÓO-rá
ธุระ

bus station sa-tăh-nee rót may
สถานีรถเมล์
bus stop bpâi rót may
ป้ายรถเมล์
bust nâh òk
หน้าอก
busy (restaurant etc) nâirn
แน่น
I'm busy tomorrow prÔOng née mee tÓO-rá
พรุ่งนี้มีธุระ
but dtàir
แต่
butcher's ráhn néu-a
ร้านเนื้อ
butter ner-ee sòt
เนยสด
button gra-dOOm
กระดุม
buy séu
ซื้อ
where can I buy ...? pŏm (chún) séu ... dâi têe năi?
ผม(ฉัน)ซื้อ ... ได้ที่ไหน
by: by bus/car doy-ee rót may/rót yon
โดยรถเมล์/รถยนต์
written by ... kĕe-un doy-ee ...
เขียนโดย ...
by the window glâi

nâh-dtàhng
ใกล้หน้าต่าง

by the sea chai ta-lay
ชายทะเล

by Monday gòrn wun jun
ก่อนวันจันทร์

bye lah gòrn
ลาก่อน

C

cabbage ga-lùm-bplee
กะหล่ำปลี

café see **coffee shop** and
restaurant

cake ka-nŏm káyk
ขนมเค้ก

call (verb) rêe-uk
เรียก

(to phone) toh-ra-sùp, toh
โทรศัพท์, โทร

what's it called? rêe-uk wâh
a-rai?
เรียกว่าอะไร

he/she is called ... káo
chêu ...
เขาชื่อ ...

please call the doctor chôo-
ay rêe-uk mŏr hâi nòy
ช่วยเรียกหมอให้หน่อย

please give me a call at 7.30

a.m. chôo-ay **toh mah**
way-lah jèt mohng
krêung
ช่วยโทรมาเวลาเจ็ดโมงครึ่ง

please ask him to call me
chôo-ay hâi káo **toh mah**
ช่วยให้เขาโทรมา

call back: I'll call back later
dĕe-o ja **toh mah mài**
เดี๋ยวจะโทรมาใหม่

call round: I'll call round
tomorrow prÔOng née ja
wáir mah hăh
พรุ่งนี้จะแวะมาหา

Cambodia bpra-tâyt gum-
poo-cha
ประเทศกัมพูชา

Cambodian (adj) ka-mǎyn
เขมร

camcorder glôrng bun-téuk
pâhp
กล้องบันทึกภาพ

camera glôrng tài rôop
กล้องถ่ายรูป

camera shop ráhn kǎi glôrng
tài rôop
ร้านขายกล้องถ่ายรูป

Camping
You can usually camp in a
national park for a
minimal fee and some national parks

also rent out tents. Unless you're
planning an extensive tour of national
parks though, there's little point in
lugging a tent around Thailand:
accommodation everywhere else is
too cheap to make camping a
necessity, and anyway there are no
campsites inside town perimeters.
Few travellers bother to bring tents
for beaches either, opting for cheap
bungalow accommodation or simply
sleeping out under the stars. But
camping is allowed on nearly all
islands and beaches, many of which
are national parks in their own right.

can gra-bpǒrng
กระป๋อง
a can of beer bee-a gra-
bpǒrng
เบียร์กระป๋อง
can*: can you ...? kOOn ... dâi
mái?
คุณ ... ได้ไหม
can I have ...? kǒr ... dâi mái?
ขอ ... ได้ไหม
I can't ... pǒm (chún) ... mâi
dâi
ผม(ฉัน) ... ไม่ได้
Canada bpra-tâyt kairn-nah-
dah
ประเทศแคนาดา

Canadian (adj) kair-nah-dah
แคนาดา
I'm Canadian pǒm (chún)
bpen kon kair-nah-dah
ผม(ฉัน)เป็นคนแคนาดา
canal klorng
คลอง
cancel ngót
งด
candies tórp-fêe
ท็อฟฟี่
candle tee-un
เทียน
can-opener têe bpèrt
gra-bpǒrng
ที่เปิดกระป๋อง
cap (hat) mòo-uk
หมวก
car rót yon
รถยนต์
by car doy-ee rót yon
โดยรถยนต์
carburettor
kah-ber-ret-dtêr
คาร์บูเรเตอร์
card (business) nahm bùt
นามบัตร
here's my card nêe nahm
bùt pǒm (chún)
นี่นามบัตรผม(ฉัน)
cardigan sêu-a nǎo
เสื้อหนาว

careful ra-mút ra-wung
ระมัดระวัง

be careful! ra-wung ná!
ระวังนะ

caretaker kon fâo bâhn
คนเฝ้าบ้าน

car ferry pair chái bun-tÓOk
rót-yon kâhm fâhk
แพใช้บรรทุกรถยนต์ข้ามฟาก

car hire bor-ri-gahn rót châo
บริการรถเช่า

see driving and rent

carnival ngahn
งาน

car park têe jòrt rót
ที่จอดรถ

carpet prom
พรม

car rental bor-ri-gahn rót châo
บริการรถเช่า

see driving and rent

carriage (of train) dtôo rót fai
ตู้รถไฟ

carrier bag tǒOng hêw
ถุงหิ้ว

carrot hǒo-a pùk-gàht
dairng
หัวผักกาดแดง

carry (something in the hands) těu
ถือ

(something by a handle) hêw
หิ้ว

(a heavy load on the back or
shoulder) bàirk
แบก

(a child, in one's arms) ÔOm
อุ้ม

carry-cot dta-grâh sài
dèk
ตะกร้าใส่เด็ก

carton glòrng
กล่อง

carwash bor-ri-gahn láhng
rót
บริการล้างรถ

case (suitcase) gra-bpǎo dern
tahng
กระเป๋าเดินทาง

cash (noun) ngern sòt
เงินสด

(verb) kêun ngern
ขึ้นเงิน

will you cash this for me?
chôo-ay bpai kêun ngern
hâi nòy dâi mái?
ช่วยไปขึ้นเงินให้หน่อยได้ไหม

cash desk dtó jài ngern
โต๊ะจ่ายเงิน

cash dispenser bor-ri-gahn
ngern dòo-un
บริการเงินด่วน

cassette móo-un táyp
kah-sèt
ม้วนเทปคาสเซ็ท

cassette recorder krêu-ung
lên tâyp kah-set
เครื่องเล่นเทปคาสเซ็ท

castle bprah-sàht
ปราสาท

casualty department pa-nàirk
OO-bùt-dti-hàyt chÒOk
chérn
แผนกอุบัติเหตุฉุกเฉิน

cat mair-o
แมว

catch (verb) jùp
จับ

where do we catch the bus
to ...? rao kêun rót may bpai
... têe nǎi?
เราขึ้นรถเมล์ไป ... ที่ไหน

Catholic (adj) káirt-oh-lík
แคโทลิค

cauliflower dòrk ga-lùm-
bplee
ดอกกะหล่ำปลี

cave tûm
ถ้ำ

ceiling pay-dahn
เพดาน

cemetery bpàh cháh
ป่าช้า

centigrade* sen-dti-gràyd
เซ็นติเกรด

centimetre* sen-dti-mét
เซ็นติเมตร

central glahng
กลาง

centre sǒon glahng
ศูนย์กลาง

how do we get to the city
centre? bpai sǒon glahng
meu-ung yung-ngai?
ไปศูนย์กลางเมืองอย่างไร

certainly nâir-norn
แน่นอน

certainly not! mâi ròrk!
ไม่หรอก

chair gâo êe
เก้าอี้

champagne chairm-bpayn
แชมเปญ

change (noun: money) sàyt sa-
dtahng
เศษสตางค์

change (verb: money) bplèe-un
เปลี่ยน

can I change this for ...? kǒr
lâirk âi nêe bpen ... dâi mái?
ขอแลกไอ้นี่เป็น ... ได้ไหม

I don't have any change pǒm
(chún) mâi mee **báirnk
yôy yôy**
ผม(ฉัน)ไม่มีแบงค์ย่อยๆ

can you give me change for a
100 baht note? kǒr dtàirk bai
la róy nòy, dâi mái?
ขอแตกใบละร้อยหน่อยได้ไหม

dialogue

do we have to change (trains)? dtôrng **bplèe-un** rót fai rĕu bplào?

เปลี่ยน

yes, change at Bang Krathum/no it's a direct train dtôrng, dtôrng **bplèe-un** têe bahng gra-tOOm/mâi dtôrng, bpen rót dtrong

changed: to get changed bplèe-un sêu-a

เปลี่ยนเสื้อ

charge (noun) kâh

ค่า

(verb) kít kâh

คิดค่า

charge card see credit card

cheap tòok

ถูก

do you have anything cheaper? mee a-rai tòok gwàh rĕu bplào?

มีอะไรถูกกว่าหรือเปล่า

check (verb) chék doo

เช็คดู

could you check the ..., please? chôo-ay chék doo ... nòy, dâi mái?

ช่วยเช็คดู ... หน่อยได้ไหม

check (US: noun) chék

เช็ค

(US: bill) bin

บิล

see **cheque** and **bill**

check book sa-mÒOt chék

สมุดเช็ค

check-in dtròo-ut chûng núm-nùk

ตรวจชั่งน้ำหนัก

check in: where do we have to check in? rao dtôrng 'check in' têe năi?

เราต้อง 'check in' ที่ไหน

cheek (on face) gâirm

แก้ม

cheerio! wùt dee hâ!

วัสดีฮ่ะ

cheese ner-ee kăirng

เนยแข็ง

chemist's ráhn kăi yah

ร้านขายยา

see **pharmacy**

cheque chék

เช็ค

do you take cheques? jai bpen chék, dâi mái?

จ่ายเป็นเช็คได้ไหม

 The safest and most economical way to carry your money is in traveller's

cheques. Sterling and dollar cheques
issued by American Express or Visa are
accepted by banks, exchange booths
and upmarket hotels in every sizeable
town, and most places also deal in a
variety of other currencies. Everyone
offers better rates for cheques than for
cash and they generally charge a
minimal commission per cheque –
though kiosks and hotels in isolated
places may charge extra.

cheque book sa-mÒOt chék
สมุดเช็ค
cheque card bùt chék
บัตรเช็ค
cherry cher-rêe
เชอร์รี่
chess màhk róOk
หมากรุก
chest nâh òk
หน้าอก
chewing gum màhk fa-rùng
หมากฝรั่ง
Chiangmai chee-ung mài
เชียงใหม่
chicken gài
ไก่
chickenpox ee-sÒOk ee-săi
อีสุกอีใส
child dèk
เด็ก

child minder kon lée-ung doo
dèk
คนเลี้ยงดูเด็ก
children's pool sà wâi náhm
dèk
สระว่ายน้ำเด็ก
chilli prík
พริก
chin kahng
คาง
Chinese (adj) jeen
จีน
chips mun fa-rùng tôrt
มันฝรั่งทอด
chocolate chork-goh-lairt
ช็อกโกเลต
choose lêu-uk
เลือก
chopsticks dta-gèe-up
ตะเกียบ
Christian name chêu
ชื่อ
Christmas krít-sa-maht
คริสต์มาส
church bòht
โบสถ์
cigar si-gah
ซิการ์
cigarette bOO-rèe
บุหรี่
cigarette lighter fai cháirk
ไฟแช็ค

cinema rohng nǔng
โรงหนัง

Cinemas in Bangkok will often have four or five showings of a film in one day. Tickets can be booked in advance from the box office in the foyer. In the capital it is often possible to catch the latest American and European films with English soundtracks and Thai subtitles. The national anthem is played at the beginning and end of each showing; everyone stands to attention during this.

circle wong glom
วงกลม

city meu-ung
เมือง

city centre jai glahng meu-ung
ใจกลางเมือง

clean (adj) sa-àht
สะอาด

can you clean these for me?
tum kwahm sa-àht nêe hâi nòy dâi mái?
ทำความสะอาดนี้ให้หน่อยได้ไหม

cleaning solution (for contact lenses) núm yah tum kwahm sa-àht
น้ำยาทำความสะอาด

cleansing lotion núm yah tum kwahm sa-àht
น้ำยาทำความสะอาด

clear chút
ชัด

(obvious) hěn dâi chút
เห็นได้ชัด

clever cha-làht
ฉลาด

cliff nâh pǎh
หน้าผา

clinic klee-ník
คลีนิค

cloakroom têe fàhk kǒrng
ที่ฝากของ

clock nah-li-gah
นาฬิกา

close (verb) bpìt
ปิด

dialogue

what time do you close?
kOOn bpìt gèe mohng?
we close at 8 p.m. on weekdays and 6 p.m. on Saturdays rao bpìt way-lah sǒrng tÔOm ra-wàhng wun jun wun

64

sÒOk láir hòk mohng
wun sǎo
do you close for lunch?
bpìt way-lah ah-hǎhn
glahng wun rěu bplào?
**yes, between 1 and 3.30
p.m.** krúp ra-wàhng way-
lah bài mohng tĕung
sǎhm mohng krêung

closed bpìt
ปิด

cloth (fabric) pâh
ผ้า
(for cleaning etc) pâh kêe
réw
ผ้าขี้ริ้ว

clothes sêu-a pâh
เสื้อผ้า

clothes line rao dtàhk pâh
ราวตากผ้า

clothes peg mái nèep pâh
ไม้หนีบผ้า

clothing
The Western liberalism
embraced by the Thai sex
industry is very unrepresentative of
the general Thai attitude to the body.
Clothing – or the lack of it – is what
bothers Thais most about tourist
behaviour. Stuffy and sweaty as it

sounds, you need to dress modestly
at all times, keeping shorts and
singlets for the real tourist resorts,
and be especially diligent about
covering up in rural areas. Baring
your flesh on beaches is very much
a Western practice: when Thais go
swimming they often do so fully
clothed, and they find topless and
nude bathing extremely unpalatable.
It's not illegal, but it won't win you
many friends.

cloud mâyk
เมฆ

cloudy mâyk kréum
เมฆครึ้ม

clutch klút
คลัทช์

coach (bus) rót too-a
รถทัวร์
(on train) dtôo rót fai
ตู้รถไฟ

coach station sa-tǎhn-nee rót
may
สถานีรถเมล์

coach trip rót num têe-o
รถนำเที่ยว

coast chai ta-lay
ชายทะเล

on the coast chai ta-lay
ชายทะเล

coat (long coat) sêu-a klOOm
เสื้อคลุม
(jacket) sêu-a nôrk
เสื้อนอก

coathanger mái kwǎirn sêu-a
ไม้แขวนเสื้อ

cockroach ma-lairng sàhp
แมลงสาบ

cocoa goh-gôh
โกโก้

coconut ma-práo
มะพร้าว

coconut milk núm ma-práo
น้ำมะพร้าว

code (for phoning) ra-hùt
รหัส

what's the (dialling) code for Chiangmai? ra-hùt chee-ung mài ber a-rai?
รหัสเชียงใหม่เบอร์อะไร?

coffee gah-fair
กาแฟ

two coffees, please kǒr gah-fair sǒrng tôo-ay
ขอกาแฟสองถ้วย

coffee shop kòrp-fêe chórp
คอฟฟี่ช้อบ

Although coffee shops do sell coffee, the term covers a range of

establishments: some of the more upmarket ones are in effect restaurants and others are places where you can go for a quick beer and a bowl of noodles. Many are open 24 hours.

coin ngern rěe-un
เงินเหรียญ

Coke® koh-lâh
โคล่า

cold (adj) nǎo
หนาว

I'm cold pǒm (chún) nǎo
ผม(ฉัน)หนาว

I have a cold pǒm (chún) bpen wùt
ผม(ฉัน)เป็นหวัด

collapse: he's collapsed káo mòt sa-dtì
เขาหมดสติ

collar kor bpòk sêu-a
คอปกเสื้อ

collect gèp
เก็บ

I've come to collect ... pǒm (chún) mah gèp ...
ผม(ฉัน)มาเก็บ ...

collect call toh-ra-sùp gèp ngern bplai tahng
โทรศัพท์เก็บเงินปลายทาง

co

66

college wít-ta-yah-lai
วิทยาลัย
colour sěe
สี
do you have this in other
colours? mee sěe èun mái?
มีสีอื่นไหม
colour film feem sěe
ฟิล์มสี
comb (noun) wěe
หวี
come mah
มา

dialogue

where do you come from?
kOOn mah jàhk nǎi krúp
(ká)?
I come from Edinburgh
pǒm (chún) mah jàhk
Edinburgh

come back glùp mah
กลับมา
I'll come back tomorrow
prôOng née glùp mah mài
พรุ่งนี้กลับมาใหม่
come in chern kâo mah
เชิญเข้ามา
comfortable sa-dòo-uk
สะดวก

compact disc pàirn see dee
แผ่นซีดี
company (business)
bor-ri-sùt
บริษัท
compartment (on train) hôrng
pôo doy-ee sǎhn
ห้องผู้โดยสาร
compass kěm-tít
เข็มทิศ
complain bòn
บ่น
complaint rêu-ung rórng ree-
un
เรื่องร้องเรียน
I have a complaint pǒm
(chún) mee rêu-ung rórng
ree-un
ผม(ฉัน)มีเรื่องร้องเรียน
completely túng mòt
ทั้งหมด
computer korm-pew-dter
คอมพิวเตอร์
concert gahn sa-dairng don-
dtree
การแสดงดนตรี
concussion sa-mǒrng tòok
gra-tóp gra-teu-un
สมองถูกกระทบกระเทือน
conditioner (for hair) kreem
nôo-ut pǒm
ครีมนวดผม

condom tŏOng yahng
ถุงยาง

conference gahn bpra-chOOm
การประชุม

confirm rúp-rorng
รับรอง

congratulations! kŏr sa-dairng
kwahm yin dee!
ขอแสดงความยินดี

connecting flight têe-o bin
dtòr
เที่ยวบินต่อ

connection dtòr
ต่อ

conscious mee sa-dtì
มีสติ

constipation tórng pòok
ท้องผูก

consulate sa-tăhn gong-
sŏOn
สถานกงสุล

contact (verb) dtìt dtòr
ติดต่อ

contact lenses korn-táirk
layn
คอนแทคเล็นซ์

contraceptive krêu-ung
kOOm gum-nèrt
เครื่องคุมกำเนิด

convenient sa-dòo-uk
สะดวก

that's not convenient nûn
mâi kôy sa-dòo-uk
นั่นไม่ค่อยสะดวก

cook (verb) tum ah-hăhn
ทำอาหาร

not cooked dìp dìp
ดิบๆ

cooker dtao
เตา

cookie kÓOk-gêe
คุกกี้

cooking utensils krêu-ung
chái nai kroo-a
เครื่องใช้ในครัว

cool yen
เย็น

cork jòOk kòo-ut
จุกขวด

corkscrew têe bpèrt kòo-ut
ที่เปิดขวด

corner: on the corner têe
mOOm
ที่มุม

in the corner yòo dtrong
hŏo-a mum
อยู่ตรงหัวมุม

correct (right) tòok
ถูก

corridor tahng dern
ทางเดิน

cosmetics krêu-ung sŭm-
ahng
เครื่องสำอาง

cost (noun) rah-kah
ราคา
how much does it cost? rah-
kah tâo-rài?
ราคาเท่าไร
cot bplay
เปล
cotton fâi
ผ้าย
cotton wool sǔm-lee
สำลี
couch (sofa) têe nûng rúp
kàirk
ที่นั่งรับแขก
cough ai
ไอ
cough medicine yah gâir
ai
ยาแก้ไอ
could: could you ...? kOOn ...
dâi mái?
คุณ ... ได้ไหม
could I have ...? kŏr ... dâi
mái?
ขอ ... ได้ไหม
I couldn't ... pŏm (chún) ...
mâi dâi
ผม(ฉัน) ... ไม่ได้
country (nation) bpra-tâyt
ประเทศ
countryside chon-na-bòt
ชนบท

couple (two people) kôo
คู่
a couple of ... sŏrng sǎhm ...
สองสาม ...
courier múk-kOO-tâyt
มัคคุเทศก์
course (main course etc) chÓOt
ah-hǎhn
ชุดอาหาร
of course nâir-norn
แน่นอน
of course not mâi ròrk
ไม่หรอก
cousin lôok pêe lôok
nórng
ลูกพี่ลูกน้อง
cow woo-a
วัว
crab bpoo
ปู
crash (noun) rót chon
รถชน
I've had a crash pŏm (chún)
gèrt rót chon
ผม(ฉัน)เกิดรถชน
crazy bâh
บ้า
cream kreem
ครีม
credit card bùt kray-dìt
บัตรเครดิต
can I pay by credit card? jài

doy-ee bùt kray-dìt dâi mái?
จ่ายโดยบัตรเครดิตได้ไหม

 Visa, Access/Mastercard, American Express and Diners Club credit cards and charge cards are accepted at top hotels as well as in some posh restaurants, department stores, tourist shops and travel agents, but surcharging of up to 5 per cent is rife, and theft and forgery are major industries – always demand the carbon copies and destroy them immediately, and never leave cards in baggage storage. The most useful cards are Visa and Access/Mastercard, because with these you can also withdraw cash on your bank account from 650 cashpoints/ATMs around the country – most provincial capitals have at least one cashpoint/ATM.

dialogue

can I pay by credit card? jài doy-ee bùt kray-dìt dâi mái?
which card do you want to use? ja chái bùt a-rai krúp?

Access/Visa
yes, sir dâi krúp
what's the number? ber a-rai krúp?
and the expiry date? láir-o bùt mòt ah-yÓO mêu-rai?

crisps mun fa-rùng tôrt
มันฝรั่งทอด

crockery tôo-ay chahm
ถ้วยชาม

crossing (by sea) kâhm ta-lay
ข้ามทะเล

crossroads sèe yâirk
สี่แยก

crowd fŏong kon
ฝูงคน

crowded kon nâirn
คนแน่น

crown (on tooth) lèe-um fun
เหลี่ยมฟัน

cruise lôrng reu-a
ล่องเรือ

crutches mái yun rúk ráir
ไม้ยันรักแร้

cry (verb) rórng hâi
ร้องไห้

cucumber dtairng gwah
แตงกวา

cup tôo-ay
ถ้วย

a cup of ..., please kŏr ...
tôo-ay nèung
ขอ ... ถ้วยหนึ่ง

cupboard dtôo
ตู้

cure (verb) gâir
แก้

curly pŏm yìk
ผมหยิก

current (electrical) gra-săir fai
fáh
กระแสไฟฟ้า
(in water) gra-săir náhm
กระแสน้ำ

curtains mâhn
ม่าน

cushion mŏrn
หมอน

custom bpra-pay-nee
ประเพณี

Customs sŎOn-la-gah-gorn
ศุลกากร

Thai embassies and
consulates can provide
up-to-date information on
Customs regulations. Rules
governing the export of antiques are
particularly strict and permission
from the Department of Fine Arts
(through Bangkok's National
Museum) may have to be obtained.

cut (noun) dtùt
ตัด
(verb) roy bàht
รอยบาด

I've cut myself pŏm (chún)
mee roy bàht
ผม(ฉัน)มีรอยบาด

cutlery chórn sôrm
ช้อนส้อม

cycling gahn tèep jùk-ra-
yahn
การถีบจักรยาน

cyclist kon tèep
jùk-ra-yahn
คนถีบจักรยาน

D

dad pôr
พ่อ

daily bpra-jum wun
ประจำวัน

damage (verb) kwahm sĕe-a
hăi
ความเสียหาย

damaged sĕe-a láir-o
เสียแล้ว

I'm sorry, I've damaged this
kŏr-tôht pŏm (chún) tum
hăi sĕe-a
ขอโทษผม(ฉัน)ทำให้เสีย

damn! chìp-hǎi!
ฉิบหาย

damp (adj) chéun
ชื้น

dance (noun) ra-bum
ระบำ

(verb) dtên rum
เต้นรำ

would you like to dance?
yàhk dtên rum mái?
อยากเต้นรำไหม

dangerous un-dta-rai
อันตราย

Danish den-mahk
เดนมาร์ก

dark (adj: colour) gàir
แก่

(hair) dum
ดำ

it's getting dark mêut láir-o
มืดแล้ว

date*: what's the date today?
wun née wun têe tâo-rài?
วันนี้วันที่เท่าไร

**let's make a date for next
Monday** nút póp gun wun
jun nâh
นัดพบกันวันจันทร์หน้า

Thais use both the
Western Gregorian
calendar and the

Buddhist calendar – Buddha is said
to have attained enlightenment
in the year 543 BC, so Thai
dates start from that point: thus
1996 AD becomes 2539 BE
(Buddhist Era).

dates (fruit) in-ta-pa-lǔm
อินทผลัม

daughter lôok sǎo
ลูกสาว

daughter-in-law lôok
sa-pái
ลูกสะใภ้

dawn (noun) rôOng
รุ่ง

at dawn rôOng cháo
รุ่งเช้า

day wun
วัน

the day after tomorrow wun
ma-reun née
วันมะรืนนี้

the day before wun gòrn
วันก่อน

the day before yesterday
mêu-a wun seun née
เมื่อวานวันซืนนี้

every day tóOk wun
ทุกวัน

all day túng wun
ทั้งวัน

in two days' time èek sŏrng wun
อีกสองวัน

day trip bpai glùp wun dee-o
ไปกลับวันเดียว

dead dtai
ตาย

deaf hŏo nòo-uk
หูหนวก

deal (business) tÓO-ra-gìt
ธุรกิจ

it's a deal dtòk long láir-o
ตกลงแล้ว

death gahn dtai
การตาย

decaffeinated coffee gah-fair mâi mee kah-fay-in
กาแฟไม่มีคาเฟอิน

December tun-wah-kom
ธันวาคม

decide dtùt sĭn jai
ตัดสินใจ

we haven't decided yet rao yung mâi dâi dtùt sĭn jai
เรายังไม่ได้ตัดสินใจ

decision gahn dtùt sĭn jai
การตัดสินใจ

deck (on ship) dàht fáh
ดาดฟ้า

deckchair gâo êe pâh bai
เก้าอี้ผ้าใบ

deep léuk
ลึก

definitely nâir-norn
แน่นอน

definitely not! mâi ròrk!
ไม่หรอก

degree (qualification) bpa-rin-yah
ปริญญา

delay (noun) kwahm chúk cháh
ความชักช้า

deliberately doy-ee ay-dta-nah
โดยเจตนา

delicatessen ráhn kǎi ah-hǎhn sŭm-rèt rôop
ร้านขายอาหารสำเร็จรูป

delicious a-ròy
อร่อย

deliver sòng
ส่ง

delivery (of mail) gahn sòng jòt-mǎi
การส่งจดหมาย

Denmark bpra-tâyt den-mahk
ประเทศเดนมาร์ก

dentist mŏr fun
หมอฟัน

dialogue

it's this one here un nêe
ná

this one? un née, châi
mái?

no that one mâi châi, un
nún

here? un nêe, châi mái?

yes châi

dentures chóOt fun
tee-um
ชุดฟันเทียม

deodorant yah dùp glìn
dtoo-a
ยาดับกลิ่นตัว

department pa-nàirk
แผนก

department store hâhng
ห้าง

departure kǎh òrk
ขาออก

departure lounge hôrng pôo
doy-ee sǎhn kǎh òrk
ห้องผู้โดยสารขาออก

depend: it depends láir-o
dtàir
แล้วแต่

it depends on ... láir-o
dtàir ...
แล้วแต่ ...

deposit (as security) ngern
fàhk
เงินฝาก

(as part payment) kâh mút-jum
ค่ามัดจำ

description kum ùt-ti-bai
คำอธิบาย

dessert kǒrng wǎhn
ของหวาน

destination jÒOt-mǎi bplai
tahng
จุดหมายปลายทาง

develop (film) láhng
ล้าง

dialogue

**could you develop these
films?** láhng feem née dâi
mái?

yes, certainly dâi krúp

when will they be ready?
sèt mêu-rai? :

tomorrow afternoon
prÔOng née bài

**how much is the four-hour
service?** bor-ri-gahn sèe
chôo-a mohng tâo-rài?

diabetic (noun) bpen rôhk bao
wǎhn
เป็นโรคเบาหวาน

dial (verb) mŎOn
หมุน

dialling code ra-hùt toh-ra-sùp
รหัสโทรศัพท์

 If you're dialling from abroad, the international code for Thailand is 66. When calling abroad from Thailand, dial 001 and then the relevant country code:

Australia	61	Ireland	353
New Zealand	64	USA	1
Canada	1	UK	44

diamond pét
เพชร

diaper pâh ôrm
ผ้าอ้อม

diarrhoea tórng sěe-a
ท้องเสีย

do you have something for diarrhoea? mee yah gâir tórng sěe-a mái?
มียาแก้ท้องเสียไหม

diary sa-mÒOt bun-téuk bpra-jum wun
สมุดบันทึกประจำวัน

dictionary pót-ja-nah-nÓOgrom
พจนานุกรม

didn't* mâi dâi …
ไม่ได้ …

see **not**

die dtai
ตาย

diesel núm mun rót dee-sen
น้ำมันรถดีเซล

diet ah-hǎhn pi-sàyt
อาหารพิเศษ

I'm on a diet pǒm (chún) gum-lung lót núm nùk
ผม(ฉัน)กำลังลดน้ำหนัก

I have to follow a special diet pǒm (chún) dtôrng tahn ah-hǎhn pi-sàyt
ผม(ฉัน)ต้องทานอาหารพิเศษ

difference kwahm dtàirk dtàhng
ความแตกต่าง

what's the difference? dtàirk dtàhng gun yung-ngai?
แตกต่างกันอย่างไร

different dtàhng
ต่าง

this one is different un née **dtàhng gun**
อันนี้ต่างกัน

a different table/room èek dtó/hôrng nèung
อีกโต๊ะ/ห้องหนึ่ง

difficult yâhk
ยาก

difficulty bpun-hǎh
ปัญหา

dinghy reu-a bòt
เรือบด

dining room hôrng
rúp-bpra-tahn ah-hǎhn
ห้องรับประทานอาหาร

dinner (evening meal) ah-hǎhn
yen
อาหารเย็น

to have dinner tahn ah-hǎhn
yen
ทานอาหารเย็น

direct (adj) dtrong
ตรง

is there a direct train? mee
rót fai dtrong bpai mái?
มีรถไฟตรงไปไหม

direction tahng
ทาง

which direction is it? yòo
tahng nǎi?
อยู่ทางไหน

is it in this direction? bpai
tahng née, châi mái?
ไปทางนี้ใช่ไหม

directory enquiries
bor-ri-gahn sòrp tǎhm ber
toh-ra-sùp
บริการสอบถามเบอร์โทรศัพท์

For international directory
enquiries dial 100.

dirt kêe fòOn
ขี้ฝุ่น

dirty sòk-ga-bpròk
สกปรก

disabled pí-gahn
พิการ

disappear hǎi bpai
หายไป

it's disappeared mun hǎi
bpai nǎi gôr mâi róo
มันหายไปไหนก็ไม่รู้

disappointed pìt wǔng
ผิดหวัง

disappointing mâi dee tâo têe
kít wái
ไม่ดีเท่าที่คิดไว้

disaster hǎi-ya-ná
หายนะ

disco dit-sa-gôh
ดิสโก้

discount lót rah-kah
ลดราคา

is there a discount? lót rah-
kah nòy dâi mái?
ลดราคาหน่อยได้ไหม

disease rôhk
โรค

disgusting nâh glèe-ut
น่าเกลียด

dish (meal) gùp kâo
กับข้าว

(bowl) chahm
ชาม

dishcloth pâh chét jahn
ผ้าเช็ดจาน

disinfectant yah kâh chéu-a
rôhk
ยาฆ่าเชื้อโรค

disk (for computer) jahn
bun-téuk
จานบันทึก

disposable diapers/
nappies pâh òrm
sǔm-rèt rôop chái krúng
dee-o
ผ้าอ้อมสำเร็จรูปใช้ครั้งเดียว

distance ra-yá tahng
ระยะทาง

in the distance yòo nai ra-yá
glai
อยู่ในระยะไกล

district kàyt
เขต

disturb róp-goo-un
รบกวน

diversion (detour) bplèe-un sên
tahng dern
เปลี่ยนเส้นทางเดิน

diving board têe gra-dòht
náhm
ที่กระโดดน้ำ

divorced yàh gun láir-o
หย่ากันแล้ว

dizzy: I feel dizzy pǒm (chún)
wee-un hǒo-a
ผม(ฉัน)เวียนหัว

do (verb) tum
ทำ

what shall we do? rao ja tum
yung-ngai?
เราจะทำอย่างไร

how do you do it? tum
yung-ngai?
ทำอย่างไร

will you do it for me? chôo-
ay tum hâi nòy, dâi mái?
ช่วยทำให้หน่อยได้ไหม

dialogues

how do you do? sa-wùt
dee krúp (kâ)
nice to meet you yin dee
têe dâi róo-jùk gun
what do you do? (work)
kOOn tum ngahn a-rai
krúp (ká)?
I'm a teacher, and you?
bpen kroo, láir-o kOOn
lâ?
I'm a student bpen núk
sèuk-sǎh
what are you doing this

evening? yen née bpai
năi?
we're going out for a drink,
do you want to join us?
rao bpai gin lâo, bpai
dôo-ay gun mái?

do you want fish sauce?
sài núm bplah mái?
I do, but she doesn't mâi
sài dtàir káo gôr sài

doctor mŏr
หมอ
we need a doctor rao dtôrng
gahn hăh mŏr
เราต้องการหาหมอ
please call a doctor chôo-ay
rêe-uk mŏr
ช่วยเรียกหมอ

  Hospital cleanliness and
efficiency varies, but
generally hygiene and
health care standards are good and
the ratio of medical staff to patients
considerably higher than in most
parts of the West. Most doctors
speak English. All provincial capitals
have at least one hospital: ask at
your hotel for advice on and possibly
transport to the nearest or most

suitable. In the event of a major
health crisis, get someone to contact
your embassy or insurance company
– it may be best to get yourself
flown home. If you do have to
undergo hospital treatment you'll
have to pay, so taking out travel
insurance is definitely worth it.

dialogue

where does it hurt? jèp
dtrong năi?
right here dtrong née
does that hurt now? yung
jèp yòo rĕu bplào?
yes jèp
take this to the pharmacy
ao née bpai ráhn kăi yah

document àyk-ga-săhn
เอกสาร
dog măh
หมา
doll dtÓOk-ga-dtah
ตุ๊กตา
domestic flight têe-o bin pai
nai
เที่ยวบินภายใน
don't!* yàh!
อย่า
don't do that! yàh tum yàhng

nún!
อย่าทำอย่างนั้น

door bpra-dtoo
ประตู

doorman kon fâo bpra-dtoo
คนเฝ้าประตู

double kôo
คู่

double bed dtee-ung yày
เตียงใหญ่

double room hôrng kôo
ห้องคู่

doughnut doh-nút
โดนัท

down: down here yòo têe nêe
อยู่ที่นี่

put it down over there wahng
bpai têe nôhn
วางไปที่โน่น

it's down there on the right
ler-ee bpai kâhng nâh tahng
dâhn kwǎh meu
เลยไปข้างหน้าทางด้านขวามือ

it's further down the road
bpai dtahm ta-nǒn kâhng
nâh
ไปตามถนนข้างหน้า

downmarket (restaurant etc)
rah-kah tòok
ราคาถูก

downstairs kâhng lâhng
ข้างล่าง

dozen lǒh
โหล

half a dozen krêung lǒh
ครึ่งโหล

drain (in sink, in street) tôr ra-bai
ท่อระบาย

draughty: it's draughty mee
lom yen kâo
มีลมเย็นเข้า

draw wâht
วาด

drawer lín-chúk
ลิ้นชัก

drawing rôop wâht
รูปวาด

dreadful yâir
แย่

dream (noun) kwahm fǔn
ความฝัน

dress (noun) sêu-a chóOt
เสื้อชุด

dressed: to get dressed
dtàirng dtoo-a
แต่งตัว

dressing (for cut) pâh pun plǎir
ผ้าพันแผล

salad dressing núm (râht)
sa-lùt
น้ำ(ราด)สลัด

dressing gown sêu-a klOOm
chóOt norn
เสื้อคลุมชุดนอน

drink (noun) krêu-ung dèum
เครื่องดื่ม
(verb) dèum
ดื่ม
a cold drink krêu-ung dèum
yen yen
เครื่องดื่มเย็นๆ
can I get you a drink? kOOn
ja dèum a-rai mái?
คุณจะดื่มอะไรไหม
what would you like (to
drink)? kOOn ja dèum a-rai?
คุณจะดื่มอะไร
no thanks, I don't drink mâi
krúp (kâ) pǒm (chún) mâi
dèum
ไม่ครับ(ค่ะ)ผม(ฉัน)ไม่ดื่ม
I'll just have a drink of water
kǒr náhm bplào tâo-nún
ขอน้ำเปล่าเท่านั้น
see bar
drinking water náhm dèum
น้ำดื่ม
is this drinking water? náhm
née gin dâi mái?
น้ำนี้กินได้ไหม

Thais don't drink water
straight from the tap, and
nor should you: plastic
bottles of drinking water are sold
countrywide, even in the smallest
villages. Cheap restaurants and
hotels generally serve free jugs of
boiled water which should be fine to
drink, though not as foolproof as the
bottles.

drive (verb) kùp
ขับ
we drove here rao kùp rót
mah
เราขับรถมา
I'll drive you home pǒm
(chún) kùp rót bpai sòng
ผม(ฉัน)ขับรถไปส่ง
driver kon kùp
คนขับ

driving
Take a look at the general
standard of driving
(dangerously reckless) and state of
the roads (poor) before deciding to
rent a car or motorbike, and then
take time to get used to the more
eccentric conventions. Of these,
perhaps the most notable is the fact
that a major road doesn't
necessarily have right of way over a
minor, but that the bigger vehicle
always has right of way. The
published rules of the road state
that everyone drives on the left

(which they do) and that they should keep to the speed limit of 60kmh within built-up areas and 80kmh outside them (which they don't). Theoretically, foreigners need an international driver's licence to rent any kind of vehicle, but some companies accept national licences, and the smaller operations (especially bike rentals) may not ask for any kind of proof. If you decide to rent a car, go to an international company or a rental company recommended by TAT (Tourist Authority of Thailand), and make sure you get insurance from them. If appropriate, consider the safer option of hiring a driver along with the car, which you can often do for the same price on day rentals. see rent

driving licence bai kùp kèe
ใบขับขี่
drop: just a drop, please (of drink) nít dee-o tâo-nún
นิดเดียวเท่านั้น
drug yah
ยา
drugs (narcotics) yah-sàyp-dtìt
ยาเสพติด

Only an idiot would try to take drugs through Thai Customs. On no account agree to take a package through Customs that you haven't inspected yourself. Drug smuggling carries a maximum penalty of death and will almost certainly get you from five to twenty years in a Thai prison. Don't expect special treatment as a foreigner.

drunk (adj) mao
เมา
drunken driving kùp rót ka-nà mao
ขับรถขณะเมา
dry (adj) hâirng
แห้ง
dry-cleaner ráhn súk hâirng
ร้านซักแห้ง
duck bpèt
เป็ด
due: he was due to arrive yesterday káo koo-un ja mah mêu-a wahn née
เขาควรจะมาเมื่อวานนี้
when is the train due? rót fai mah gèe mohng?
รถไฟมากี่โมง
dull (pain) mâi rOOn rairng
ไม่รุนแรง

Du

81

(weather) mêut moo-a
มืดมัว

dummy (baby's) hŏo-a nom
lòrk
หัวนมหลอก

during nai ra-wàhng
ในระหว่าง

dust fÒOn
ฝุ่น

dustbin tǔng ka-yà
ถังขยะ

dusty mee fÒOn yér
มีฝุ่นเยอะ

Dutch horl-lairn
ฮอลแลนด์

duty-free (goods) mâi dtôrng
sěe-a pah-sěe
ไม่ต้องเสียภาษี

duty-free shop ráhn káh sǐn-
káh bplòrt pah-sěe ah-gorn
ร้านค้าสินค้าปลอดภาษีอากร

E

each (every) tÓOk
ทุก

how much are they each? un
la tâo-rài?
อันละเท่าไร

ear hŏo
หู

earache: I have earache pǒm
(chún) bpòo-ut hŏo
ผม(ฉัน)ปวดหู

early ray-o
เร็ว

early in the morning cháo
dtròo
เช้าตรู่

I called by earlier pǒm
(chún) mah hǎh mêu-a gòrn
née
ผม(ฉัน)มาหาเมื่อก่อนนี้

earrings dtÔOm hŏo
ตุ้มหู

east dta-wun òrk
ตะวันออก

in the east tahng dta-wun
òrk
ทางตะวันออก

Easter ee-sa-dtêr
อีสเตอร์

easy ngâi
ง่าย

eat gin kâo
กินข้าว

we've already eaten, thanks
rao gin kâo láir-o
เรากินข้าวแล้ว

eating habits
Thais normally eat three
meals a day. Typically,

each meal will consist of rice with a number of side dishes, such as curry, fried meat and vegetables and fish. Thais use a spoon and fork (although chopsticks are used in the thousands of Chinese noodle shops) and the meal is a constant 'dipping-in' process, taking a spoonful or two at a time from the side dishes.

eau de toilette núm òp
น้ำอบ

egg kài
ไข่

egg noodles ba-mèe
บะหมี่

either: either ... or ... ... rěu ... ... หรือ ...

either of them un nǎi gôr dâi
อันไหนก็ได้

elastic (noun) sǎi yahng yêut
สายยางยืด

elastic band yahng rút
ยางรัด

elbow kôr sòrk
ข้อศอก

electric fai fáh
ไฟฟ้า

electrical appliances krêu-ung fai fáh
เครื่องไฟฟ้า

electrician châhng fai fáh
ช่างไฟฟ้า

electricity fai fáh
ไฟฟ้า

see **voltage**

elephant cháhng
ช้าง

elevator líf
ลิฟท์

else: something else a-rai èek
อะไรอีก

somewhere else têe èun
ที่อื่น

dialogue

would you like anything else? ao a-rai èek mái?
no, nothing else, thanks mâi krúp (kâ), kòrp-kOOn

embassy sa-tǎhn tôot
สถานทูต

emergency chÒOk chěrn
ฉุกเฉิน

this is an emergency! bpen pah-wá chÒOk chěrn!
เป็นภาวะฉุกเฉิน

emergency exit tahng òrk chÒOk chěrn
ทางออกฉุกเฉิน

empty wâhng
ว่าง

end (noun) jòp
จบ

(verb) sîn sòOt, jòp
สิ้นสุด, จบ

at the end of the soi sòOt soy
สุดซอย

when does it end? jòp mêu-rài?
จบเมื่อไร

engaged (toilet, telephone) mâi wâhng
ไม่ว่าง

(to be married) mûn
หมั้น

engine (car) krêu-ung yon
เครื่องยนต์

England bpra-tâyt ung-grìt
ประเทศอังกฤษ

English (adj) ung-grìt
อังกฤษ

(language) pah-săh ung-grìt
ภาษาอังกฤษ

I'm English pǒm (chún) bpen kon ung-grìt
ผม(ฉัน)เป็นคนอังกฤษ

do you speak English? kOOn pôot pah-săh ung-grìt bpen mái?
คุณพูดภาษาอังกฤษเป็นไหม

enjoy: to enjoy oneself
sa-nÒOk
สนุก

dialogue

how did you like the film?
nǔng sa-nÒOk mái?
I enjoyed it very much, did
you enjoy it? sa-nÒOk
mâhk, kOOn kít wâh sa-
nÒOk mái?

enjoyable sa-nÒOk dee
สนุกดี

enlargement (of photo) pâhp ka-yǎi
ภาพขยาย

enormous yài bêr-rêr
ใหญ่เบ้อเร่อ

enough por
พอ

there's not enough mâi por
ไม่พอ

it's not big enough yài mâi por
ใหญ่ไม่พอ

that's enough por láir-o
พอแล้ว

entrance (noun) tahng kâo
ทางเข้า

envelope sorng jòt-măi
ซองจดหมาย

epileptic bpen rôhk lom bâh
mŏo
เป็นโรคลมบ้าหมู

equipment
Òop-bpa-gorn
อุปกรณ์

error têe pìt
ที่ผิด

especially doy-ee cha-pòr
โดยเฉพาะ

essential jum-bpen
จำเป็น

it is essential that ...
jum-bpen têe ...
จำเป็นที่ ...

Europe yOO-rohp
ยุโรป

European (adj) yOO-rohp
ยุโรป

even máir dtàir
แม้แต่

even if ... máir wâh ...
แม้ว่า ...

evening (early evening) dtorn
yen
ตอนเย็น

(late evening) dtorn glahng
keun
ตอนกลางคืน

this evening (early evening) yen

née
เย็นนี้

(late evening) keun née
คืนนี้

in the evening (early evening)
dtorn yen
ตอนเย็น

(late evening) dtorn glahng
keun
ตอนกลางคืน

evening meal ah-hăhn yen
อาหารเย็น

eventually nai têe sòOt
ในที่สุด

ever ker-ee
เคย

dialogue

have you ever been to
Phuket? kOOn ker-ee
bpai poo-gèt mái?
yes, I was there two years
ago ker-ee, ker-ee bpai
mêu-a sŏrng bpee gòrn

every tóOk
ทุก

every day tóOk wun
ทุกวัน

everyone tóOk kon
ทุกคน

everything tÓOk yàhng
ทุกอย่าง

everywhere tôo-a bpai
ทั่วไป

exactly! châi láir-o!
ใช่แล้ว

exam gahn sòrp
การสอบ

example dtoo-a yàhng
ตัวอย่าง

for example chên ...
เช่น ...

excellent yêe-um
เยี่ยม

excellent! yêe-um ler-ee!
เยี่ยมเลย

except yók wáyn
ยกเว้น

excess baggage núm nùk
gern
น้ำหนักเกิน

exchange rate ùt-dtrah lâirk
bplèe-un
อัตราแลกเปลี่ยน

exciting nâh dtèun dtên
น่าตื่นเต้น

excuse me (to get past, to say
sorry) kǒr-tôht
ขอโทษ
(to get attention) kOOn krúp
(kâ)
คุณครับ (คะ)

(to say pardon?) a-rai ná?
อะไรนะ

exhaust (pipe) tôr ai sěe-a
ท่อไอเสีย

exhausted (tired) nèu-ay
เหนื่อย

exhibition ní-tá-sa-gahn
นิทรรศการ

exit tahng òrk
ทางออก

where's the nearest exit?
tahng òrk glâi têe sÒOt yòo
têe năi?
ทางออกใกล้ที่สุดอยู่ที่ไหน

expect kâht
คาด

expensive pairng
แพง

experienced mee
bpra-sòp-ba-gahn
มีประสบการณ์

explain ùt-ti-bai
อธิบาย

can you explain that?
chôo-ay ùt-ti-bai hâi nòy,
dâi mái?
ช่วยอธิบายให้หน่อยได้ไหม

express (mail) bprai-sa-nee
dòo-un
ไปรษณีย์ด่วน
(train) rót fai dòo-un
รถไฟด่วน

extension (telephone) dtòr
ต่อ

extension 341, please kŏr
dtòr ber săhm sèe nèung
ขอต่อเบอร์สามสี่หนึ่ง

extension lead săi pôo-ung
สายพ่วง

extra: can we have an extra
one? kŏr èek un nèung
ขออีกอันหนึ่ง

do you charge extra for that?
kít dtàhng hàhk rĕu
bplào?
คิดต่างหากหรือเปล่า

extraordinary bplàirk mâhk
แปลกมาก

extremely mâhk lĕu-a gern
มากเหลือเกิน

eye dtah
ตา

will you keep an eye on my
suitcase for me? chôo-ay fâo
gra-bpăo hâi nòy, dâi mái?
ช่วยเฝ้ากระเป๋าให้หน่อยได้
ไหม

eyebrow pencil din-sŏr kĕe-
un kéw
ดินสอเขียนคิ้ว

eye drops yah yòrt dtah
ยาหยอดตา

eyeglasses (US) wâirn dtah
แว่นตา

eyeliner têe kĕe-un kòrp dtah
ที่เขียนขอบตา

eye make-up remover núm
yah láhng têe kĕe-un kòrp
dtah
น้ำยาล้างที่เขียนขอบตา

eye shadow kreem tah năng
dtah
ครีมทาหนังตา

F

face nâh
หน้า

factory rohng ngahn
โรงงาน

Fahrenheit* fah-ren-háit
ฟาเรนไฮท์

faint (verb) bpen lom
เป็นลม

she's fainted káo bpen
lom
เขาเป็นลม

I feel faint pŏm (chún) róo-
sèuk bpen lom
ผม(ฉัน)รู้สึกเป็นลม

fair (funfair) ngahn òrk ráhn
งานออกร้าน

(trade) ngahn sa-dairng sĭn-
káh
งานแสดงสินค้า

(adj) yÓOt-dti-tum
ยุติธรรม

fairly kôrn-kâhng
ค่อนข้าง

fake kŏrng bplorm
ของปลอม

fall (US) réu-doo bai-mái
rôo-ung
ฤดูใบไม้ร่วง

in the fall dtorn réu-doo
bai-mái rôo-ung
ตอนฤดูใบไม้ร่วง

fall (verb) hòk lóm
หกล้ม

she's had a fall káo hòk
lóm
เขาหกล้ม

false mâi jing
ไม่จริง

family krôrp-kroo-a
ครอบครัว

famous mee chêu sěe-ung
มีชื่อเสียง

fan (electrical) pút lom
พัดลม

(handheld) pút
พัด

(sports) kon chôrp doo
gee-lah
คนชอบดูกีฬา

fan belt sǎi pahn
สายพาน

fantastic yêe-um yôrt
เยี่ยมยอด

far glai
ไกล

dialogue

is it far from here? yòo
glai mái?
no, not very far mâi
glai
well, how far? gèe
gi-loh-met?
it's about 20 kilometres
bpra-mahn yêe-sìp
gi-loh-met

fare kâh doy-ee sǎhn
ค่าโดยสาร

farm fahm
ฟาร์ม

fashionable tun sa-mǎi
ทันสมัย

fast ray-o
เร็ว

fat (person) ôo-un
อ้วน

(on meat) mun
มัน

father pôr
พ่อ

father-in-law (of a man) pôr

dtah
พ่อตา

(of a woman) pôr pǒo-a
พ่อผัว

faucet górk náhm
ก๊อกน้ำ

fault kwahm pìt
ความผิด

sorry, it was my fault
kǒr-tôht **kwahm pìt** kǒrng
pǒm (chún)
ขอโทษ ความผิดของผม(ฉัน)

it's not my fault mâi châi
kwahm pìt kǒrng pǒm
(chún)
ไม่ใช่ความผิดของผม(ฉัน)

faulty pìt
ผิด

favourite bpròht
โปรด

fax (machine) krêu-ung
toh-ra-sǎhn
เครื่องโทรสาร

(verb: person) sòng toh-ra-sǎhn
bpai hâi
ส่งโทรสารไปให้

(document) bun-téuk
toh-ra-sǎhn, fáirks
บันทึกโทรสาร, แฟกซ์

February
gOOm-pah-pun
กุมภาพันธ์

feel róo-sèuk
รู้สึก

I feel hot pǒm (chún) róo-
sèuk rórn
ผม(ฉัน)รู้สึกร้อน

I feel unwell pǒm (chún)
róo-sèuk mâi sa-bai
ผม(ฉัน)รู้สึกไม่สบาย

I feel like going for a walk
pǒm (chún) yàhk ja bpai
dern lên
ผม(ฉัน)อยากจะไปเดินเล่น

how are you feeling? kOOn
róo-sèuk bpen yung-ngai
bâhng?
คุณรู้สึกเป็นอย่างไรบ้าง

I'm feeling better pǒm (chún)
róo-sèuk kôy yung chôo-a
ผม(ฉัน)รู้สึกค่อยยังชั่ว

felt-tip (pen) bpàhk-gah
may-jik
ปากกาเมจิก

fence róo-a
รั้ว

fender gun chon
กันชน

ferry reu-a kâhm fâhk
เรือข้ามฟาก

Regular ferries connect all
major islands with the
mainland, and for the vast

majority of crossings you simply buy your ticket on board. Boats generally operate a reduced service during the monsoon season – from May till September along the east coast and Andaman coast and from November through April on the Gulf coast – while the more remote spots become inaccessible in these periods. Wherever there's a decent public waterway, there'll be a longtailed boat ready to ferry you along it. Longtailed boats carry from ten to twenty passengers: in Bangkok most follow fixed routes, but elsewhere most are for rent.

festival ngahn
งาน

fetch rúp
รับ

I'll fetch him pǒm (chún) ja bpai rúp káo
ผม(ฉัน)จะไปรับเขา

will you come and fetch me later? mah rúp pǒm (chún) tee lǔng dâi mái?
มารับผม(ฉัน)ทีหลังได้ไหม

feverish bpen kâi
เป็นไข้

few: a few sǒrng sǎhm
สองสาม

a few days sǒrng sǎhm wun
สองสามวัน

fiancé(e) kôo mûn
คู่หมั้น

field sa-nǎhm
สนาม

fight (noun) gahn chók dtòy
การชกต่อย

fill dterm
เติม

fill in gròrk
กรอก

do I have to fill this in? dtôrng gròrk un née rěu bplào?
ต้องกรอกอันนี้หรือเปล่า

fill up tum hâi dtem
ทำให้เต็ม

fill it up, please dterm núm mun hâi dtem
เติมน้ำมันให้เต็ม

filling (in tooth) ÒOt fun
อุดฟัน

film (movie) nǔng
หนัง

(for camera) feem
ฟิล์ม

dialogue

do you have this kind of film? mee feem bàirp née mái?
yes, how many exposures?

mee, ao gèe rôop?

36 sǎhm sìp

film processing láhng feem
ล้างฟิล์ม

filthy sòk-ga-bpròk
สกปรก

find (verb) jer
เจอ

I can't find it pǒm (chún)
hǎh mâi jer
ผม(ฉัน)หาไม่เจอ

I've found it pǒm (chún) jer
láir-o
ผม(ฉัน)เจอแล้ว

find out hǎh rai la-êe-ut
หารายละเอียด

could you find out for me?
chôo-ay hǎh rai la-êe-ut hâi
nòy dâi mái?
ช่วยหารายละเอียดให้หน่อย
ได้ไหม

fine (weather) dee
ดี

(punishment) kâh bprùp
ค่าปรับ

dialogues

how are you? bpen yung-
ngai bâhng?
I'm fine, thanks sa-bai dee

kòrp-kOOn mâhk

is that OK? oh kay mái?
that's fine thanks dee láir-
o kòrp-kOOn

finger néw meu
นิ้วมือ

finish (verb) jòp
จบ

I haven't finished yet pǒm
(chún) yung mâi sèt
ผม(ฉัน)ยังไม่เสร็จ

when does it finish? jòp gèe
mohng?
จบกี่โมง

fire: fire! fai mâi!
ไฟไหม้

can we light a fire here? gòr
fai dtrong née dâi mái?
ก่อไฟตรงนี้ได้ไหม

fire alarm sǔn-yahn fay
mâi
สัญญาณไฟไหม้

fire brigade gorng
dtum-ròo-ut dùp plerng
กองตำรวจดับเพลิง
see police

fire escape bun-dai sǔm-rùp
něe fai
บรรไดสำหรับหนีไฟ

fire extinguisher krêu-ung

dùp plerng
เครื่องดับเพลิง

first râirk
แรก

I was first pŏm (chún) bpen
kon râirk
ผม(ฉัน)เป็นคนแรก

at first tee râirk
ที่แรก

the first time krúng râirk
ครั้งแรก

first on the left lée-o sái
tée tahng yâirk kâhng
nâh
เลี้ยวซ้ายที่ทางแยกข้างหน้า

first aid gahn bpa-tŏm
pa-yah-bahn
การปฐมพยาบาล

first-aid kit chÓOt bpa-thŏm
pa-yah-bahn
ชุดปฐมพยาบาล

first class (travel etc) chún
nèung
ชั้นหนึ่ง

first floor chún sŏrng
ชั้นสอง

(US) chún nèung
ชั้นหนึ่ง

first name chêu
ชื่อ

fish (noun) bplah
ปลา

fisherman kon jùp bplah
คนจับปลา

fishing gahn jùp bplah
การจับปลา

fishing boat reu-a bpra-mong
เรือประมง

fishing village mòo bâhn
bpra-mong
หมู่บ้านประมง

fishmonger's ráhn kăi bplah
ร้านขายปลา

fit (attack) ah-gahn bpen lom
อาการเป็นลม

fit: it doesn't fit me sài mâi dâi
ใส่ไม่ได้

fitting room hôrng lorng
sêu-a pâh
ห้องลองเสื้อผ้า

fix (verb: arrange) jùt
จัด

can you fix this? (repair) un
née gâir dâi mái?
อันนี้แก้ได้ไหม

fizzy sâh
ซ่า

flag tong
ธง

flannel (facecloth) pâh chét
nâh
ผ้าเช็ดหน้า

flash (for camera) fláirt
แฟลช

flat (noun: apartment) fláirt
แฟลต

(adj) bairn
แบน

I've got a flat tyre yahng
bairn
ยางแบน

flavour rót
รส

flea mùt
หมัด

flight têe-o bin
เที่ยวบิน

flight number têe-o bin
mǎi-lâyk
เที่ยวบินหมายเลข

flippers rorng táo ma-nóOt
gòp
รองเท้ามนุษย์กบ

floating market dta-làht
náhm
ตลาดน้ำ

flood núm tôo-um
น้ำท่วม

floor (of room) péun
พื้น

(storey) chún
ชั้น

on the floor yòo bon péun
อยู่บนพื้น

florist ráhn kǎi dòrk-mái
ร้านขายดอกไม้

flour bpâirng sǎh-lee
แป้งสาลี

flower dòrk-mái
ดอกไม้

flu kâi wùt
ไข้หวัด

fluent: John speaks fluent Thai
John pôot pah-sǎh tai dâi
khlôrng
จอห์นพูดภาษาไทยได้คล่อง

fly (noun) ma-lairng wun
แมลงวัน

(verb) bin
บิน

can we fly there? bpai
krêu-ung bin dâi mái?
ไปเครื่องบินได้ไหม

fly in bin kâo mah
บินเข้ามา

fly out bin òrk bpai
บินออกไป

fog mòrk long
หมอกลง

foggy: it's foggy mòrk
long
หมอกลง

folk dancing gahn fórn rum
péun meu-ung
การฟ้อนรำพื้นเมือง

folk music don-dtree péun
meu-ung
ดนตรีพื้นเมือง

follow dtahm
ตาม

follow me dtahm pǒm
(chún) mah
ตามผม(ฉัน)มา

food ah-hǎhn
อาหาร

food poisoning ah-hǎhn bpen
pít
อาหารเป็นพิษ

food shop/store ráhn kǎi
kǒrng chum
ร้านขายของชำ

foot* (of person) táo
เท้า

on foot dern bpai
เดินไป

football (game) fóOt-born
ฟุตบอล

(ball) lôok fóOt-born
ลูกฟุตบอล

football match gahn
kàirng kǔn
fóOt-born
การแข่งขันฟุตบอล

for: do you have something
for ...? (headache/diarrhoea
etc) mee a-rai gâir ...
mái?
มีอะไรแก้ ... ไหม

dialogue

who's the fried rice for?
kâo pùt **sǔm-rùp** krai?

that's for me **sǔm-rùp**
pǒm

and this one? láir-o nêe
lâ?

that's for her **sǔm-rùp**
káo

where do I get the bus for
Bangsaen? kêun rót bpai
bahng-sǎirn têe-nǎi?

the bus for Bangsaen
leaves from the central
market rót bpai bahng-
sǎirn òrk jàhk dta-làht
glahng

how long have you been
here for? kOOn yòo têe
nêe nahn tâo-rài?

I've been here for two days,
how about you? yòo sǒrng
wun, láir-o kOOn lâ?

I've been here for a week
pǒm (chún) yòo têe nêe
ah-tít nèung láir-o

forehead nâh pàhk
หน้าผาก

foreign dtàhng bpra-tâyt
ต่างประเทศ

foreigner chao dtàhng
bpra-tâyt
ชาวต่างประเทศ

forest bpàh
ป่า

forget leum
ลืม

I forget, I've forgotten pǒm
(chún) leum láir-o
ผม(ฉัน)ลืมแล้ว

fork sôrm
ส้อม

(in road) tahng yâirk
ทางแยก

form (document) bàirp form
แบบฟอร์ม

formal (dress) bpen tahng
gahn
เป็นทางการ

fortnight sǒrng ah-tít
สองอาทิตย์

fortunately chôhk dee
โชคดี

forward: could you forward
my mail? chôo-ay sòng
jòt-mǎi dtòr bpai hâi
dôo-ay
ช่วยส่งจดหมายต่อไปให้ด้วย

forwarding address têe yòo
sǔm-rùp sòng jòt-mǎi bpai

hâi
ที่อยู่สำหรับส่งจดหมายไปให้

foundation cream kreem
rorng péun
ครีมรองพื้น

fountain núm pÓO
น้ำพุ

foyer (of hotel) hôrng tǒhng
glahng sǔm-rùp rúp kàirk
ห้องโถงกลางสำหรับรับแขก

(of theatre) bor-ri-wayn nûng
púk ror
บริเวณนั่งพักรอ

fracture (noun) gra-dòok hùk
กระดูกหัก

France bpra-tâyt
fa-rùng-sàyt
ประเทศฝรั่งเศส

free ì-sa-rá
อิสระ

(no charge) free
ฟรี

is it free (of charge)? free rěu
bplào?
ฟรีหรือเปล่า

freeway tahng dòo-un
ทางด่วน

freezer dtôo châir kǎirng
ตู้แช่แข็ง

French (adj) fa-rùng-sàyt
ฝรั่งเศส

(language) pah-sǎh

fa-rùng-sàyt
ภาษาฝรั่งเศส

French fries mun fa-rùng tôrt
มันฝรั่งทอด

frequent bòy bòy
บ่อย ๆ

how frequent is the bus to
Pattaya? mee rót bpai pút-
ta-yah bòy kâir nǎi?
มีรถไปพัทยาบ่อยแค่ไหน

fresh (weather, breeze) sòt chêun
สดชื่น

(fruit etc) sòt
สด

fresh orange núm sôm kún
น้ำส้มคั้น

Friday wun sÒOk
วันศุกร์

fridge dtôo yen
ตู้เย็น

fried pùt
ผัด

fried egg kài dao
ไข่ดาว

fried noodles (Thai-style) pùt tai
ผัดไทย

(Chinese-style) pùt see éw
ผัดซีอิ๊ว

fried rice kâo pùt
ข้าวผัด

friend pêu-un
เพื่อน

friendly bpen pêu-un
เป็นเพื่อน

frog gòp
กบ

from jàhk
จาก

when does the next train
from Ubon arrive? rót fai
jàhk OO-bon têe-o nâh
mah těung gèe mohng?
รถไฟจากอุบลเที่ยวหน้ามา
ถึงกี่โมง

from Monday to Friday
dtûng dtàir wun jun jon
těung wun sÒOk
ตั้งแต่วันจันทร์จนถึงวันศุกร์

from next Thursday dtûng
dtàir wun pa-réu-hùt
ตั้งแต่วันพฤหัส

dialogue

where are you from?
kOOn mah jàhk nǎi?
I'm from Slough pǒm
(chún) mah jàhk
Slough

front nâh
หน้า

in front kâhng nâh
ข้างหน้า

in front of the hotel kâhng
nâh rohng rairm
ข้างหน้าโรงแรม

at the front kâhng nâh
ข้างหน้า

frozen châir kǎirng
แช่แข็ง

frozen food ah-hǎhn châir
kǎirng
อาหารแช่แข็ง

fruit pǒn-la-mái
ผลไม้

fruit juice núm pǒn-la-mái
น้ำผลไม้

fry (deep-fry) tôrt
ทอด

(stir-fry) pùt
ผัด

frying pan ga-tá
กะทะ

full dtem
เต็ม

it's full of ... dtem bpai
dôo-ay ...
เต็มไปด้วย ...

I'm full pǒm (chún) ìm
láir-o
ผม(ฉัน)อิ่มแล้ว

full board gin yòo prórm
กินอยู่พร้อม

fun: it was fun sa-nÒOk dee
สนุกดี

funeral ngahn sòp
งานศพ

funny (strange) bplàirk
แปลก

(amusing) dta-lòk
ตลก

furniture krêu-ung reu-un
เครื่องเรือน

further ler-ee bpai
เลยไป

it's further down the road
bpai dtahm ta-nǒn kâhng
nâh
ไปตามถนนข้างหน้า

dialogue

**how much further is it to
Hua Hin?** bpai hǒo-a hǐn
èek glai mái?
about 5 kilometres bpra-
mahn hâh gi-loh-met

fuse few
ฟิวส์

the lights have fused few
kàht
ฟิวส์ขาด

fuse box glòrng few
กล่องฟิวส์

fuse wire sǎi few
สายฟิวส์

future a-nah-kót
อนาคต
in future nai a-nah-kót
ในอนาคต

G

game (cards etc) gaym
เกม
(match) gahn lên
การเล่น
(meat) néu-a sùt bpàh
เนื้อสัตว์ป่า
garage (for fuel) bpúm núm
mun
ปั๊มน้ำมัน
(for repairs) òo sôrm rót
อู่ซ่อมรถ
(for parking) rohng rót
โรงรถ
see petrol
garbage (waste) ka-yà
ขยะ
garden sŏo-un
สวน
garlic gra-tee-um
กระเทียม
gas gáirt
แก๊ส
(US) núm mun
น้ำมัน

see petrol
gas cylinder (camping gas) tǔng
gáirt
ถังแก๊ส
gasoline núm mun
น้ำมัน
see petrol
gas station bpúm núm mun
ปั๊มน้ำมัน
gate bpra-dtoo
ประตู
(at airport) chôrng kâo
ช่องเข้า
gay gra-ter-ee
กระเทย
gay bar bah sǔm-rùp gra-ter-
ee
บาร์สำหรับกระเทย
gearbox glòrng gee-a
กล่องเกียร์
gear lever kun gee-a
คันเกียร์
gears gee-a
เกียร์
general (adj) tôo-a bpai
ทั่วไป
gents (toilet) bOO-ròOt
บุรุษ
genuine (antique etc) táir
แท้
German (adj) yer-ra-mun
เยอรมัน

(language) pah-săh yer-ra-
mun

ภาษาเยอรมัน

German measles rôhk hùt
yer-ra-mun

โรคหัดเยอรมัน

Germany bpra-tâyt yer-ra-mun

ประเทศเยอรมัน

get (fetch) dâi

ได้

will you get me another one,
please? kŏr ao èek un
nèung dâi mái?

ขอเอาอีกอันหนึ่งได้ไหม

how do I get to ...? bpai ...
yung-ngai?

ไป ... อย่างไร

do you know where I can get
them? sâhp mái wâh ja séu
dâi têe năi?

ทราบไหมว่าจะซื้อได้ที่ไหน

get back (return) glùp

กลับ

get in (arrive) tĕung

ถึง

get off long

ลง

where do I get off? pŏm
(chún) long têe năi?

ผม(ฉัน)ลงที่ไหน

get on (to train etc) kêun

ขึ้น

get out (of car etc) long

ลง

get up (in the morning)
dtèun

ตื่น

gift kŏrng kwǔn

ของขวัญ

gin lâo yin

เหล้ายิน

a gin and tonic, please kŏr
yin toh-nik

ขอยินโทนิค

girl pôo-yǐng

ผู้หญิง

girlfriend fairn

แฟน

give hâi

ให้

can you give me some
change? kŏr lâirk sàyt
sa-dtahng dâi mái?

ขอแลกเศษสตางค์ได้ไหม

I gave it to him pŏm
(chún) hâi káo bpai
láir-o

ผม(ฉัน)ให้เขาไปแล้ว

will you give this to ...?
chôo-ay ao née bpai hâi ...
nòy, dâi mái?

ช่วยเอานี้ไปให้ ...
หน่อยได้ไหม

dialogue

how much do you want for
this? nêe kít tâo-rài?

200 baht sŏrng róy bàht

I'll give you 150 baht pŏm
(chún) ja hâi kOOn róy
hâh sìp bàht

give back keun
คืน

glad yin dee
ยินดี

glass gâir-o
แก้ว

glasses (spectacles) wâirn
dtah
แว่นตา

gloves tŏOng meu
ถุงมือ

glue (noun) gao
กาว

go bpai
ไป

we'd like to go to the
waterfalls rao yàhk ja bpai
têe-o núm dtòk
เราอยากจะไปเที่ยวน้ำตก

where are you going? kOOn
bpai nǎi?
คุณไปไหน

where does this bus go? rót

may sǎi née bpai nǎi?
รถเมล์สายนี้ไปไหน

let's go! bpai tèr!
ไปเถอะ

she's gone (left) káo bpai
láir-o
เขาไปแล้ว

where has he gone? káo bpai
nǎi?
เขาไปไหน

I went there last week
pŏm (chún) bpai têe
nûn mêu-a ah-tít têe
láir-o
ผม(ฉัน)ไปที่นั่นเมื่อ
อาทิตย์ที่แล้ว

go away bpai
ไป

go away! bpai hâi pón!
ไปให้พ้น

go back (return) glùp
กลับ

go down (the stairs etc) long
bpai
ลงไป

go in (enter) kâo bpai
เข้าไป

go out (in the evening) têe-o
bpai
ไปเที่ยว

do you want to go out
tonight? keun née yàhk bpai

têe-o mái?
คืนนี้อยากไปเที่ยวไหม

go through pàhn bpai
ผ่านไป

go up (the stairs etc) kêun bpai
ขึ้นไป

goat pâir
แพะ

God pra-jâo
พระเจ้า

goggles wâirn dtah dum náhm
แว่นตาดำน้ำ

gold torng
ทอง

Golden Triangle sǎhm lèe-um torng kum
สามเหลี่ยมทองคำ

goldsmith châhng torng
ช่างทอง

golf górp
กอล์ฟ

golf course sa-nǎhm górp
สนามกอล์ฟ

good dee
ดี

good! dee láir-o!
ดีแล้ว

goodbye lah gòrn ná
ลาก่อนนะ

good evening sa-wùt dee

krúp (kâ)
สวัสดีครับ(ค่ะ)

good morning sa-wùt dee krúp (kâ)
สวัสดีครับ(ค่ะ)

good night sa-wùt dee krúp (kâ)
สวัสดีครับ(ค่ะ)

goose hàhn
ห่าน

got: we've got to leave rao dtôrng bpai
เราต้องไป

have you got any ...? mee ... mái?
มี ... ไหม

government rút-ta-bahn
รัฐบาล

gradually tee la nòy
ทีละหน่อย

grammar wai-yah-gorn
ไวยากรณ์

gram(me) grum
กรัม

granddaughter lǎhn sǎo
หลานสาว

grandfather (maternal) dtah
ตา
(paternal) bpòo
ปู่

grandmother (maternal) yai
ยาย

(paternal) yâh
ย่า

grandson lǎhn chai
หลานชาย

grapefruit sôm oh
ส้มโอ

grapes a-ngÒOn
องุ่น

grass yâh
หญ้า

grateful róo-sèuk kòrp-kOOn
รู้สึกขอบคุณ

great (excellent) yôrt
ยอด

that's great! yôrt!
ยอด

Great Britain bpra-tâyt ung-grìt
ประเทศอังกฤษ

Greece bpra-tâyt greet
ประเทศกรีซ

greedy dta-glà
ตะกละ

green sěe kěe-o
สีเขียว

greengrocer's ráhn kǎi pùk
ร้านขายผัก

greeting people
Thais very rarely shake
hands, using instead the
wai – a prayer-like gesture made
with raised hands – to greet and say
goodbye and to acknowledge
respect, gratitude or apology. The
wai changes according to the
relative status of the two people
involved: Thais can instantaneously
assess which wai to use, but as a
foreigner your safest bet is to go for
the 'stranger's' wai, which requires
that your hands be raised close to
your chest and your fingertips
placed just below your chin. If
someone makes a wai at you, you
should definitely wai back, but it's
generally wise not to initiate.

grey sěe tao
สีเทา

grill (noun) dtao bpîng
เตาปิ้ง

grilled yâhng
ย่าง

grocer's ráhn kǎi kǒrng chum
ร้านขายของชำ

ground péun din
พื้นดิน

on the ground bon péun din
บนพื้นดิน

ground floor chún nèung
ชั้นหนึ่ง

group glòOm
กลุ่ม

guarantee (noun) bai rúp-rorng
ใบรับรอง

is it guaranteed? mee bai rúp bpra-gun mái?
มีใบรับประกันไหม

guest kàirk
แขก

guesthouse gáyt háot
เกสต์เฮาส์

Any place calling itself a guesthouse – which could be anything from a bamboo hut to a three-storey concrete block – is almost certain to provide cheap, basic accommodation specifically aimed at Western travellers, usually consisting of a sparse double room with a fan and (usually shared) bathroom. You'll find them in all major tourist centres, on beaches, where they're also called bungalows, and even in the most unlikely remote spots.
see **hotel**

guide (noun: person) múk-kOO-tâyt
มัคคุเทศก์

guidebook kôo meu num têe-o
คู่มือนำเที่ยว

guided tour rai-gahn num têe-o
รายการนำเที่ยว

guitar gee-dtah
กีตาร์

Gulf of Thailand ào tai
อ่าวไทย

gum (in mouth) ngèu-uk
เหงือก

gun (pistol) bpeun pók
ปืนพก

(rifle) bpeun yao
ปืนยาว

gym rohng yim
โรงยิม

H

hair pŏm
ผม

hairbrush bprairng pŏm
แปรงผม

haircut dtùt pŏm
ตัดผม

hairdresser's (men's) ráhn dtàirng pŏm chai
ร้านแต่งผมชาย

(women's) ráhn tum pŏm

sa-dtree
ร้านทำผมสตรี

hairdryer krêu-ung bpào
pŏm
เครื่องเป่าผม

hair gel kreem sài pŏm
ครีมใส่ผม

hairgrips gíp nèep pŏm
กิ๊บหนีบผม

hair spray sa-bpray chèet
pŏm
สเปรย์ฉีดผม

half* krêung
ครึ่ง

half an hour krêung chôo-a
mohng
ครึ่งชั่วโมง

half a litre krêung lít
ครึ่งลิตร

about half that bpra-mahn
krêung nèung
ประมาณครึ่งหนึ่ง

half-price krêung rah-kah
ครึ่งราคา

ham mŏo hairm
หมูแฮม

hamburger hairm-ber-gèr
แฮมเบอร์เกอร์

hammer (noun) kórn
ฆ้อน

hand meu
มือ

holding hands
Public displays of
physical affection in
Thailand are much more acceptable
between friends of the same sex
than between lovers of opposite
sexes. Holding hands and hugging is
as common among male friends as
with females, so if you're given fairly
intimate caresses by a Thai
acquaintance of the same sex, don't
assume you're being propositioned.

handbag gra-bpǎo tĕu
กระเป๋าถือ

handbrake brayk meu
เบรคมือ

handkerchief pâh chét nâh
ผ้าเช็ดหน้า

handle (on door, suitcase)
dâhm
ด้าม

hand luggage gra-bpǎo tĕu
กระเป๋าถือ

hang-gliding gahn hŏhn rôrn
การโหนร่อน

hangover bpòo-ut hŏo-a
ปวดหัว

I've got a hangover pŏm
(chún) bpòo-ut hŏo-a

happen gèrt kêun
เกิดขึ้น

what's happening? gèrt a-rai
kêun?
เกิดอะไรขึ้น

what has happened? mee
a-rai gèrt kêun?
มีอะไรเกิดขึ้น

happy dee jai
ดีใจ

I'm not happy about this
rêu-ung née pǒm (chún)
mâi sa-bai jai
เรื่องนี้ผม(ฉัน)ไม่สบายใจ

harbour tâh reu-a
ท่าเรือ

hard kǎirng
แข็ง
(difficult) yâhk
ยาก

hard-boiled egg kài dtôm
kǎirng
ไข่ต้มแข็ง

hardly mâi kôy ...
ไม่ค่อย ...

hardly ever mâi kôy ...
ไม่ค่อย ...

hardware shop ráhn kǎi
krêu-ung lèk
ร้านขายเครื่องเหล็ก

hat mòo-uk
หมวก

hate (verb) glèe-ut
เกลียด

have* mee
มี

can I have a ...? kǒr ... nòy
ขอ ... หน่อย

do you have ...? mee ...
mái?
มี ... ไหม

what'll you have? (drink)
kOOn ja dèum a-rai?
คุณจะดื่มอะไร

I have to leave now pǒm
(chún) **dtôrng** bpai děe-o
née
ผม(ฉัน)ต้องไปเดี๋ยวนี้

do I have to ...? pǒm (chún)
dtôrng ... rěu bplào?
ผม(ฉัน)ต้อง ... หรือเปล่า

can we have some ...? kǒr ...
nòy dâi mái?
ขอ ... หน่อยได้ไหม

hayfever rôhk hèut
โรคหืด

he* káo
เขา

head hǒo-a
หัว

headache bpòo-ut hǒo-a
ปวดหัว

headlights fai nâh rót
ไฟหน้ารถ

headphones hǒo fung
หูฟัง

healthy (person) mee sÒOk-
ka-pâhp dee
มีสุขภาพดี
(food) bpen bpra-yòht gàir
râhng-gai
เป็นประโยชน์แก่ร่างกาย
hear dâi yin
ได้ยิน

dialogue

can you hear me? dâi yin
mái?
I can't hear you, could you
repeat that? pŏm (chún)
mâi dâi yin, pôot èek tee
dâi mái?

hearing aid krêu-ung
chôo-ay fung
เครื่องช่วยฟัง
heart hŏo-a jai
หัวใจ
heart attack hŏo-a jai wai
หัวใจวาย
heat kwahm rórn
ความร้อน
heating krêu-ung tum
kwahm rórn
เครื่องทำความร้อน
heavy nùk
หนัก

106

heel (of foot) sôn táo
ส้นเท้า
(of shoe) sôn rorng táo
ส้นรองเท้า
could you heel these? bplèe-
un sôn mài hâi nòy, dâi mái?
เปลี่ยนส้นใหม่ให้หน่อยได้ไหม
height kwahm sŏong
ความสูง
helicopter hay-li-korp-dter
เฮลิคอปเตอร์
hello sa-wùt dee
สวัสดี
(answer on phone) hun-loh
ฮัลโล
helmet (for motorbike) mòo-uk
gun chon
หมวกกันชน
help (noun) kwahm chôo-ay
lěu-a
ความช่วยเหลือ
(verb) chôo-ay
ช่วย
help! chôo-ay dôo-ay!
ช่วยด้วย
can you help me? chôo-ay
pŏm (chún) nòy, dâi mái?
ช่วยผม(ฉัน)หน่อยได้ไหม
thank you very much for your
help kòrp-kOOn têe dâi
chôo-ay lěu-a
ขอบคุณที่ได้ช่วยเหลือ

helpful bpen bpra-yòht mâhk
เป็นประโยชน์มาก

hepatitis dtùp ùk-sàyp
ตับอักเสบ

her*: I haven't seen her pŏm
(chún) mâi dâi hĕn káo
ผม(ฉัน)ไม่ได้เห็นเขา

to her gàir káo
แก่เขา

with her gùp káo
กับเขา

for her sŭm-rùp káo
สำหรับเขา

that's her nûn káo
นั่นเขา

that's her towel bpen pâh
chét dtoo-a kŏrng káo
เป็นผ้าเช็ดตัวของเขา

herbs (for cooking) krêu-ung
tâyt
เครื่องเทศ

(medicinal) sa-mŎOn prai
สมุนไพร

here têe-nêe
ที่นี่

here is/are ... nêe ...
นี่ ...

here you are (offering) nêe
ngai
นี่ไง

hers* kŏrng káo
ของเขา

that's hers nûn kŏrng káo
นั่นของเขา

hey! háy!
เฮ้

hi! (hello) bpai nǎi?
ไปไหน

hide (verb) sôrn
ซ่อน

high sŏong
สูง

highchair gâo êe sŏong
เก้าอี้สูง

highway tahng dòo-un
ทางด่วน

hill kǎo
เขา

him*: I haven't seen him pŏm
(chún) mâi dâi hĕn káo
ผม(ฉัน)ไม่ได้เห็นเขา

to him gàir káo
แก่เขา

with him gùp káo
กับเขา

for him sŭm-rùp káo
สำหรับเขา

that's him nûn káo
นั่นเขา

hip sa-pôhk
สะโพก

hire châo
เช่า

for hire hâi châo
ให้เช่า

where can I hire a bike?
(bicycle) châo jùk-ra-yahn dâi
têe năi?
เช่าจักรยานได้ที่ไหน
see rent

his*: it's his car bpen rót
kŏrng káo
เป็นรถของเขา
that's his nûn kŏrng káo
นั่นของเขา

hit (verb) dtee
ตี

hitch-hike bòhk rót
โบกรถ

hobby ngahn a-di-râyk
งานอดิเรก

hold (verb) tĕu
ถือ

hole roo
รู

holiday wun yÒOt
วันหยุด
on holiday yÒOt púk pòrn
หยุดพักผ่อน

Holland bpra-tâyt hor-lairn
ประเทศฮอลแลนด์

home bâhn
บ้าน
at home (in my house etc) têe
bâhn
ที่บ้าน
(in my country) nai bpra-tâyt

pŏm (chún)
ในประเทศผม(ฉัน)
we go home tomorrow (to
country) rao glùp bâhn
prÔOng née
เรากลับบ้านพรุ่งนี้

honest sêu dtrong
ซื่อตรง

honey núm pêung
น้ำผึ้ง

honeymoon hun-nee-moon
ฮันนีมูน

hood (US: car) gra-bprohng rót
กระโปรงรถ

hope wŭng
หวัง
I hope so wŭng wâh yung
ngún
หวังว่าอย่างนั้น
I hope not wŭng wâh kong
mâi
หวังว่าคงไม่
hopefully wŭng wâh …
หวังว่า …

horn (of car) dtrair
แตร

horrible nâh glèe-ut
น่าเกลียด

horse máh
ม้า

horse riding kèe máh
ขี่ม้า

hospital rohng pa-yah-bahn
โรงพยาบาล

hospitality gahn dtôrn rúp
kùp sôo
การต้อนรับขับสู้

thank you for your hospitality
kòrp-kOOn têe dtôrn rúp
kùp sôo
ขอบคุณที่ตอนรับขับสู้

hostess (in bar) pôo-yĭng
bah
ผู้หญิงบาร์

hot rórn
ร้อน

(spicy) pèt
เผ็ด

I'm hot pŏm (chún) rórn
ผม(ฉัน)ร้อน

it's hot today wun née
ah-gàht rórn jung ler-ee
วันนี้อากาศร้อนจังเลย

hotel rohng rairm
โรงแรม

 Few Thais use
guesthouses, opting
instead for hotels. Beds in
single rooms (**hôrng dèe-o**) are
large enough for a couple, and it's
quite acceptable for two people to
ask and pay for a single. Usually run
by Chinese-Thais, you'll find three-
or four-storey budget hotels in every
sizeable town, often near the bus
station. They are generally clean and
usually come with an en-suite
bathroom, fan (or air- conditioning)
and boiled water, which makes them
good value in terms of facilities.
Moderate hotels are sometimes
good value, offering many of the
trimmings of a top-end hotel (TV,
fridge, air-conditioning, pool) but
none of the prestige.
Many of Thailand's upmarket hotels
belong to international chains,
maintaining top-quality standards in
Bangkok and major resorts at rates
far lower than you'd pay for luxury
accommodation in the West. Some
of the best home-grown upmarket
hotels are up to B1000 cheaper for
equally fine service, rooms equipped
with TV, minibar and balcony, and
full use of the hotel sports facilities
and swimming pools.

hotel room hôrng nai rohng
rairm
ห้องในโรงแรม

hour chôo-a mohng
ชั่วโมง

house bâhn
บ้าน

how? yung-ngai?
อย่างไร

how many? gèe?
กี่

how do you do? sa-wùt dee krúp (kâ)
สวัสดีครับ(ค่ะ)

dialogues

how are you? bpen yung-ngai bâhng?
fine, thanks, and you? sa-bai dee krúp (kâ) láir-o kOOn lâ?

how much is it? tâo-rài?
50 baht hâh sìp baht
I'll take it ao

humid chéun
ชื้น

hungry hěw kâo
หิวข้าว

are you hungry? hěw kâo mái?
หิวข้าวไหม

hurry (verb) rêep
รีบ

I'm in a hurry pǒm (chún) dtôrng rêep
ผม(ฉัน)ต้องรีบ

there's no hurry mâi dtôrng rêep
ไม่ต้องรีบ

hurry up! ray-o ray-o kâo!
เร็ว ๆ เข้า

hurt (verb) jèp
เจ็บ

it really hurts jèp jing jing
เจ็บจริง ๆ

husband sǎh-mee
สามี

I

I* (male) pǒm
ผม
(female) chún; dee-chún
ฉัน; ดิฉัน

ice núm kǎirng
น้ำแข็ง

with ice sài núm kǎirng
ใส่น้ำแข็ง

no ice, thanks mâi sài núm kǎirng
ไม่ใส่น้ำแข็ง

ice cream ait-greem
ไอศกรีม

ice-cream cone groo-ay sài ait-greem
กรวยใส่ไอศกรีม

iced coffee gah-fair yen
กาแฟเย็น

ice lolly ait-greem tâirng
ไอศครีมแท่ง

idea kwahm kít
ความคิด

idiot kon bâh
คนบ้า

if tâh
ถ้า

ignition fai krêu-ung yon
ไฟเครื่องยนตร์

ill mâi sa-bai
ไม่สบาย

I feel ill pŏm (chún) mâi sa-bai
ผม(ฉัน)ไม่สบาย

illness kwahm jèp bpòo-ay
ความเจ็บป่วย

imitation (leather etc) tee-um
เทียม

immediately tun-tee
ทันที

important sŭm-kun
สำคัญ

it's very important sŭm-kun mâhk
สำคัญมาก

it's not important mâi sŭm-kun
ไม่สำคัญ

impossible bpen bpai mâi dâi
เป็นไปไม่ได้

impressive nâh têung
น่าทึ่ง

improve dee kêun
ดีขึ้น

I want to improve my Thai pŏm (chún) yàhk ja pôot pah-sǎh tai hâi dee kêun
ผม(ฉัน)อยากจะพูดภาษาไทยให้ดีขึ้น

in: it's in the centre nai jai glahng meu-ung
ในใจกลางเมือง

in my car nai rót pŏm (chún)
ในรถผม(ฉัน)

in Chiangmai têe chee-ung-mài
ที่เชียงใหม่

in two days from now èek sŏrng wun dtòr jàhk née
อีกสองวันต่อจากนี้

in five minutes èek hâh nah-tee
อีกห้านาที

in May deu-un préut-sa-pah-kom
เดือนพฤษภาคม

in English bpen pah-sǎh ung-grìt
เป็นภาษาอังกฤษ

in Thai bpen pah-săh tai
เป็นภาษาไทย

is he in? káo **yòo** mái?
เขาอยู่ไหม

inch* néw
นิ้ว

include roo-um
รวม

does that include meals?
roo-um ah-hăhn dôo-ay rĕu
bplào?
รวมอาหารด้วยหรือเปล่า

is that included? roo-um
yòo dôo-ay rĕu bplào?
รวมอยู่ด้วยหรือเปล่า

inconvenient mâi sa-dòo-uk
ไม่สะดวก

incredible mâi nâh chêu-a
ไม่น่าเชื่อ

India bpra-tâyt in-dee-a
ประเทศอินเดีย

Indian (adj) kàirk
แขก

indicator (on car) fai lée-o
ไฟเลี้ยว

indigestion ah-hăhn mâi yôy
อาหารไม่ย่อย

Indonesia bpra-tâyt in-doh-
nee-see-a
ประเทศอินโดนีเซีย

indoors kâhng nai
ข้างใน

inexpensive mâi pairng, tòok
ไม่แพง, ถูก

infection ah-gahn ùk-sàyp
อาการอักเสบ

infectious rôhk dtìt dtòr
โรคติดต่อ

inflammation ah-gahn bpòo-
ut boo-um
อาการปวดบวม

informal bpen gun ayng
เป็นกันเอง

information kào-săhn
ข่าวสาร

do you have any information
about ...? mee **rai la-èe-ut**
gèe-o gùp ... mái?
มีรายละเอียดเกี่ยวกับ ... ไหม

information desk têe sòrp
tăhm
ที่สอบถาม

injection chèet yah
ฉีดยา

injured bàht jèp
บาดเจ็บ

she's been injured káo bàht
jèp
เขาบาดเจ็บ

inner tube (for tyre) yahng
nai
ยางใน

innocent bor-ri-sòOt
บริสุทธิ์

insect ma-lairng
แมลง

insect bite ma-lairng gùt
แมลงกัด

do you have anything for
insect bites? mee yah tah
gâir ma-lairng gùt mái?
มียาทาแก้แมลงกัดไหม

insect repellent yah gun
ma-lairng
ยากันแมลง

inside kâhng nai
ข้างใน

inside the hotel kâhng nai
rohng rairm
ข้างในโรงแรม

let's sit inside bpai nûng
kâhng nai tèr
ไปนั่งข้างในเถอะ

insist ka-yún ka-yor
คะยั้นคะยอ

I insist pǒm (chún) ka-yún
ka-yor
ผม(ฉัน)คะยั้นคะยอ

insomnia norn mâi lùp
นอนไม่หลับ

instant coffee gah-fair
pǒng
กาแฟผง

instead tairn
แทน

give me that one instead ao

un nún tairn
เอาอันนั้นแทน

instead of ... tairn têe ja ...
แทนที่จะ ...

insulin in-soo-lin
อินซูลิน

insurance gahn bpra-gun pai
การประกันภัย

intelligent cha-làht
ฉลาด

interested: I'm interested in ...
pǒm (chún) sǒn jai ...
ผม(ฉัน)สนใจ ...

interesting nâh sǒn jai
น่าสนใจ

that's very interesting nâh
sǒn jai mâhk
น่าสนใจมาก

international sǎh-gon
สากล

interpret bplair
แปล

interpreter lâhm
ล่าม

intersection sèe yâirk
สี่แยก

interval (at theatre) púk
krêung
พักครึ่ง

into nai
ใน

I'm not into ... pǒm (chún)

English → Thai

113

mâi chôrp ...

ผม(ฉัน)ไม่ชอบ ...

introduce náir-num

แนะนำ

may I introduce ...? pǒm
(chún) kǒr náir-num hâi
róo-jùk gùp ...

ผม(ฉัน)ขอแนะนำให้รู้จักกับ ...

invitation kum chern

คำเชิญ

invite chern choo-un

เชิญชวน

Ireland ai-lairn

ไอร์แลนด์

iron (for ironing) dtao rêet

เตารีด

can you iron these for me?
chôo-ay **rêet** hâi nòy dâi
mái?

ช่วยรีดให้หน่อยได้ไหม

is* bpen

เป็น

island gòr

เกาะ

it mun

มัน

it is ... bpen ...

เป็น ...

is it ...? ... châi mái?

... ใช่ไหม

where is it? yòo têe nǎi?

อยู่ที่ไหน

it's him káo nûn làir

เขานั่นแหละ

it was ... bpen ...

เป็น ...

Italy bpra-tâyt ì-dtah-lee

ประเทศอิตาลี

itch: it itches kun

คัน

J

jack (for car) mâir rairng

แม่แรง

jacket sêu-a nôrk

เสื้อนอก

jam yairm

แยม

jammed: it's jammed mun dtìt
nâirn

มันติดแน่น

January
mók-ga-rah-kom

มกราคม

Japan yêe-bpÒOn

ญี่ปุ่น

Japanese yêe-bpÒOn

ญี่ปุ่น

jar (noun) hǎi

ไห

jaw kǎh-gun-grai

ขากรรไกร

jazz jáirt
แจ๊ส

jealous hěung
หึง

jeans yeen
ยีนส์

jellyfish mairng ga-prOOn
แมงกะพรุน

jersey sêu-a sa-wét-dtêr
เสื้อสเวตเตอร์

jetty tâh reu-a
ท่าเรือ

jeweller's ráhn kǎi krêu-ung
pét ploy
ร้านขายเครื่องเพชรพลอย

jewellery pét ploy
เพชรพลอย

Jewish yew
ยิว

job ngahn
งาน

jogging jórk-gîng
จ็อกกิ้ง

to go jogging bpai jórk-gîng
ไปจ็อกกิ้ง

joke dta-lòk
ตลก

journey gahn dern tahng
การเดินทาง

have a good journey! dern
tahng dôo-ay dee ná!
เดินทางด้วยดีนะ

jug yèu-uk
เหยือก

a jug of water yèu-uk
náhm
เหยือกน้ำ

juice náhm pǒn-la-mái
น้ำผลไม้

July ga-rúk-ga-dah-kom
กรกฎาคม

jump (verb) gra-dòht
กระโดด

jumper sêu-a sa-wét-dtêr
เสื้อสเวตเตอร์

junction tahng yâirk
ทางแยก

June mí-tOO-nah-yon
มิถุนายน

jungle bpàh
ป่า

just (only) tâo-nún
เท่านั้น

just two sǒrng un
tâo-nún
สองอันเท่านั้น

just for me sǔm-rùp pǒm
(chún) kon dee-o
สำหรับผม(ฉัน)คนเดียว

just here dtrong née
ตรงนี้

not just now mâi ao děe-o
née
ไม่เอาเดี๋ยวนี้

JU

we've just arrived rao pêrng
mah mêu-a gêe née ayng
เราเพิ่งมาเมื่อกี้นี้เอง

K

keep gèp
เก็บ

keep the change mâi dtôrng
torn
ไม่ต้องทอน

can I keep it? pǒm (chún)
gèp wái dâi mái?
ผม(ฉัน)เก็บไว้ได้ไหม

please keep it ao wái ler-ee
เอาไว้เลย

ketchup sórt ma-kěu-a tâyt
ซอสมะเขือเทศ

kettle gah náhm
กาน้ำ

key gOOn-jair
กุญแจ

the key for room 201, please
kǒr gOOn-jair hôrng sǒrng
sǒon sèe
ขอกุญแจห้องสองศูนย์สี่

keyring hòo-ung
gOOn-jair
ห่วงกุญแจ

kidneys (in body) dtai
ไต

(food) krêu-ung nai
เครื่องใน

kill kâh
ฆ่า

kilo* gi-loh
กิโล

kilometre* gi-loh-mét
กิโลเมตร

how many kilometres is it
to ...? bpai ... gèe gi-loh?
ไป ... กี่กิโล

kind (generous) jai dee
ใจดี

that's very kind kOOn jai dee
mâhk
คุณใจดีมาก

dialogue

which kind do you want?
ao bàirp nǎi?
I want this/that kind ao
bàirp née/nún

king nai lǒo-ung
ในหลวง

kiosk dtôo
ตู้

kiss jòop
จูบ

kitchen hôrng kroo-a
ห้องครัว

knee hŏo-a kào
หัวเข่า

knickers gahng gayng nai
sa-dtree
กางเกงในสตรี

knife mêet
มีด

knock (verb) kór
เคาะ

knock down (road accident) rót
chon
รถชน

he's been knocked down káo
tòok rót chon
เขาถูกรถชน

knock over (object, pedestrian)
chon lóm
ชนล้ม

know (somebody) róo-jùk
รู้จัก
(something) róo; (formal) sâhp
รู้; ทราบ
(a place) róo-jùk
รู้จัก

I don't know pŏm (chún)
mâi róo/sâhp
ผม(ฉัน)ไม่รู้/ทราบ

I didn't know that pŏm
(chún) mâi róo/sâhp mah
gòrn
ผม(ฉัน)ไม่รู้/ทราบมาก่อน

do you know where I can

find ...? sâhp mái wâh ja hăh
... dâi tée năi?
ทราบไหมว่าจะหา ... ได้ที่ไหน

L

label bpâi
ป้าย

ladies' (room) sa-dtree
สตรี

ladies' wear krêu-ung dtàirng
gai sa-dtree
เครื่องแต่งกายสตรี

lady pôo-yĭng
ผู้หญิง

lager lah-ger
ลาเกอร์
see beer

lake ta-lay sàhp
ทะเลสาบ

lamb (meat) néu-a gàir
เนื้อแกะ

lamp kohm fai fáh
โคมไฟฟ้า

lane (motorway) chôrng
ช่อง
(small road) soy
ซอย

language pah-săh
ภาษา

language course bàirp ree-un

pah-săh
แบบเรียนภาษา

Laos bpra-tâyt lao
ประเทศลาว

large yài
ใหญ่

last sÒOt tái
สุดท้าย

last week mêu-a ah-tít gòrn
เมื่ออาทิตย์ก่อน

last Friday mêu-a wun sÒOk gòrn
เมื่อวันศุกร์ก่อน

last night mêu-a keun née
เมื่อคืนนี้

what time is the last train to Ubon? rót fai bpai OO-bon têe-o sÒOt tái òrk gèe mohng?
รถไฟไปอุบลเที่ยวสุดท้ายออกกี่โมง

late cháh
ช้า

sorry I'm late kŏr-tôht têe mah cháh
ขอโทษที่มาช้า

the train was late rót fai mah tĕung cháh
รถไฟมาถึงช้า

we must go – we'll be late rao dtôrng bpai dĕe-o ja mâi tun
เราต้องไป เดี๋ยวจะไม่ทัน

it's getting late dèuk láir-o
ดึกแล้ว

later tee lŭng
ทีหลัง

I'll come back later dĕe-o ja glùp mah
เดี๋ยวจะกลับมา

see you later dĕe-o jer gun èek
เดี๋ยวเจอกันอีก

later on tee lŭng
ทีหลัง

latest yàhng cháh têe sÒOt
อย่างช้าที่สุด

by Wednesday at the latest wun pÓOt yàhng cháh têe sÒOt
วันพุธอย่างช้าที่สุด

laugh (verb) hŏo-a rór
หัวเราะ

laundry (clothes) sêu-a pâh
เสื้อผ้า

(place) ráhn súk pâh
ร้านซักผ้า

lavatory hôrng náhm
ห้องน้ำ

law gòt-măi
กฎหมาย

lawn sa-năhm yâh
สนามหญ้า

118

lawyer ta-nai kwahm
ทนายความ

laxative yah tài
ยาถ่าย

lazy kêe gèe-ut
ขี้เกียจ

lead (electrical) săi fai fáh
สายไฟฟ้า

(verb) num
นำ

where does this lead to? nêe
bpai těung năi?
นี่ไปถึงไหน

leaf bai mái
ใบไม้

leaflet bai bplew
ใบปลิว

leak rôo-a
รั่ว

the roof leaks lăng-kah rôo-a
หลังคารั่ว

learn ree-un
เรียน

least: not in the least mâi ler-
ee
ไม่เลย

at least yàhng nóy têe sÒOt
อย่างน้อยที่สุด

leather nǔng
หนัง

leave (verb: behind) tíng wái
ทิ้งไว้

(go away) jàhk bpai
จากไป

I am leaving tomorrow
pǒm (chún) **bpai** prÔOng
née
ผม(ฉัน)ไปพรุ่งนี้

he left yesterday káo **bpai**
mêu-a wahn née
เขาไปเมื่อวานนี้

may I leave this here? kŏr
fâhk wái têe nêe dâi mái?
ขอฝากไว้ที่นี่ได้ไหม

I left my coat in the bar pǒm
(chún) **tíng** sêu-a wái têe
bah
ผม(ฉัน)ทิ้งเสื้อไว้ที่บาร์

when does the bus for
Bangsaen leave? rót bpai
bahng-săirn **òrk** gèe
mohng?
รถไปบางแสนออกกี่โมง

left sái
ซ้าย

on the left tahng sái
ทางซ้าย

to the left tahng sái
ทางซ้าย

turn left lée-o sái
เลี้ยวซ้าย

there's none left mâi mee
lěu-a yòo
ไม่มีเหลืออยู่

left-handed ta-nùt meu sái
ถนัดมือซ้าย

left luggage (office) têe fâhk gra-bpăo
ที่ฝากกระเป๋า

leg kăh
ขา

lemon ma-nao
มะนาว

lemonade núm ma-nao
น้ำมะนาว

lemon tea núm chah sài ma-nao
น้ำชาใส่มะนาว

lend: will you lend me your ... ? kŏr yeum ... nòy, dâi mái?
ขอยืม ... หน่อยได้ไหม

lens (of camera) layn
เลนส์

lesbian 'lesbian'
เล็สเบียน

less nóy gwàh
น้อยกว่า

less than ... nóy gwàh ...
น้อยกว่า ...

less expensive tòok gwàh
ถูกกว่า

lesson bòt ree-un
บทเรียน

let (allow) hâi
ให้

will you let me know? chôo-ay bòrk hâi pŏm (chún) sâhp dôo-ay
ช่วยบอกให้ผม(ฉัน)ทราบด้วย

I'll let you know pŏm (chún) ja bòrk hâi sâhp
ผม(ฉัน)จะบอกให้ทราบ

let's go for something to eat bpai tahn kâo mái?
ไปทานข้าวไหม

let off: will you let me off at ...? kŏr long têe ... dâi mái?
ขอลงที่ ... ได้ไหม

letter jòt-măi
จดหมาย

do you have any letters for me? mee jòt-măi mah tĕung pŏm (chún) mái?
มีจดหมายมาถึงผม(ฉัน)ไหม

letterbox dtôo jòt-măi
ตู้จดหมาย

lettuce pùk-gàht
ผักกาด

lever (noun) kun yók
คันยก

library hŏr sa-mÒOt
หอสมุด

licence bai un-nÓO-yâht
ใบอนุญาต

lid făh
ฝา

lie (verb: tell untruth) goh-hòk
โกหก

lie down norn
นอน

life chee-wít
ชีวิต

lifebelt choo chêep
ชูชีพ

life jacket sêu-a choo chêep
เสื้อชูชีพ

lift (in building) líf
ลิฟท์

could you give me a lift? chôo-ay bpai sòng nòy, dâi mái?
ช่วยไปส่งหน่อยได้ไหม

would you like a lift? bpai sòng hâi ao mái?
ไปส่งให้เอาไหม

light (noun) fai
ไฟ

(not heavy) bao
เบา

do you have a light? (for cigarette) mee fai mái?
มีไฟไหม

light green sěe kěe-o òrn
สีเขียวอ่อน

light bulb lòrt fai fáh
หลอดไฟฟ้า

I need a new light bulb pǒm

(chún) dtôrng-gahn lòrt fai fáh
ผม(ฉัน)ต้องการหลอดไฟฟ้า

lighter (cigarette) fai cháirk
ไฟแช็ก

lightning fáh lâirp
ฟ้าแลบ

like (verb) chôrp
ชอบ

I like it pǒm (chún) chôrp
ผม(ฉัน)ชอบ

I like going for walks pǒm (chún) chôrp bpai dern lên
ผม(ฉัน)ชอบไปเดินเล่น

I like you pǒm (chún) chôrp kOOn
ผม(ฉัน)ชอบคุณ

I don't like it pǒm (chún) mâi chôrp
ผม(ฉัน)ไม่ชอบ

do you like ...? kOOn chôrp ... mái?
คุณชอบ ...ไหม

I'd like a beer pǒm (chún) **ao** bee-a kòo-ut nèung
ผม(ฉัน)เอาเบียร์ขวดหนึ่ง

I'd like to go swimming pǒm (chún) **yàhk** bpai wâi náhm
ผม(ฉัน)อยากไปว่ายน้ำ

would you like a drink? kOOn dèum a-rai mái?
คุณดื่มอะไรไหม

would you like to go for a walk? kOOn **yàhk** bpai dern lên mái?
คุณอยากไปเดินเล่นไหม

what's it like? bpen **yung ngai**?
เป็นอย่างไร

I want one like this ao **bàirp née**
เอาแบบนี้

lime ma-nao
มะนาว

line (on paper) sên
เส้น

(phone) săi
สาย

could you give me an outside line? chôo-ay dtòr săi kâhng nôrk hâi nòy, dâi mái?
ช่วยต่อสายข้างนอกให้หน่อยได้ไหม

lips rim fĕe bpàhk
ริมฝีปาก

lip salve kêe pêung tah rim fĕe bpàhk
ขี้ผึ้งทาริมฝีปาก

lipstick líp sa-dtík
ลิปสติก

listen fung
ฟัง

litre* lít
ลิตร

little lék
เล็ก

just a little, thanks nít dee-o
nít dee-o tâo-nún
นิดเดียวเท่านั้น

a little milk nom nít nòy
นมนิดหน่อย

a little bit more èek nít nèung
อีกนิดหนึ่ง

live (verb) mee chee-wít yòo
มีชีวิตอยู่

we live together rao yòo dôo-ay gun
เราอยู่ด้วยกัน

dialogue

where do you live? kOOn yòo têe năi?
I live in London pŏm (chún) yòo têe lorn-dorn

lively (person, town) mee chee-wít chee-wah
มีชีวิตชีวา

liver (in body, food) dtùp
ตับ

loaf bporn
ปอนด์

lobby (in hotel) pa-nàirk dtôrn
rúp
แผนกต้อนรับ

lobster gôOng yài
กุ้งใหญ่

local tăir-o née
แถวนี้

**can you recommend a local
restaurant?** chôo-ay náir-
num ráhn ah-hăhn tăir-o
née hâi nòy dâi mái?
ช่วยแนะนำร้านอาหารแถวนี้
ให้หน่อยได้ไหม

lock (noun) gOOn-jair
กุญแจ

(verb) sài gOOn-jair
ใส่กุญแจ

it's locked sài gOOn-jair
láir-o
ใส่กุญแจแล้ว

**lock out: I've locked myself
out** bpìt gOOn-jair láir-o
kâo hôrng mâi dâi
ปิดกุญแจแล้วเข้าห้องไม่ได้

locker (for luggage etc) dtôo
ตู้

lollipop om-yím
อมยิ้ม

London lorn-dorn
ลอนดอน

long yao
ยาว

how long will it take to fix it?
chái way-lah sôrm **nahn**
tâo-rài?
ใช้เวลาซ่อมนานเท่าไร

how long does it take? chái
way-lah **nahn** tâo-rài?
ใช้เวลานานเท่าไร

a long time nahn
นาน

one day/two days longer èek
wun sŏrng wun
อีกวันสองวัน

long-distance call toh tahng
glai
โทรทางไกล

long-tailed boat reu-a hăhng
yao
เรือหางยาว

look: I'm just looking, thanks
pŏm (chún) chom doo tâo-
nún
ผม(ฉัน)ชมดูเท่านั้น

you don't look well kOOn
tâh tahng mâi sa-bai
คุณท่าทางไม่สบาย

look out! ra-wung ná!
ระวังนะ

can I have a look? kŏr doo
nòy, dâi mái?
ขอดูหน่อยได้ไหม

look after doo lair
ดูแล

look at doo
ดู

look for hăh
หา

I'm looking for ... pŏm
(chún) gum-lung hăh ...
ผม(ฉัน)กำลังหา ...

loose (handle etc) lòOt
หลุด

lorry rót bun-tóOk
รถบรรทุก

lose hăi
หาย

I've lost my way pŏm (chún)
lŏng tahng
ผม(ฉัน)หลงทาง

I'm lost, I want to get to ...
pŏm (chún) lŏng tahng,
dtôrng-gahn bpai ...
ผม(ฉัน)หลงทาง ต้องการไป ...

I've lost my bag gra-bpăo
pŏm (chún) hăi
กระเป๋าผม(ฉัน)หาย

lost property (office) têe jâirng
kŏrng hăi
ที่แจ้งของหาย

lot: a lot, lots mâhk
มาก

not a lot mâi mâhk
ไม่มาก

a lot of people kon mâhk
คนมาก

a lot bigger yài mâhk gwàh
ใหญ่มากกว่า

I like it a lot pŏm (chún)
chôrp mâhk
ผม(ฉัน)ชอบมาก

lotion yah tah
ยาทา

loud dung
ดัง

lounge (in house, hotel) hôrng
nûng lên
ห้องนั่งเล่น
(in airport) hôrng púk pôo
doy-ee săhn
ห้องพักผู้โดยสาร

love (noun) kwahm rúk
ความรัก
(verb) rúk
รัก

I love Thailand pŏm (chún)
rúk meu-ung tai
ผม(ฉัน)รักเมืองไทย

lovely sŏo-ay
สวย

low (prices, bridge) dtùm
ต่ำ

luck chôhk
โชค

good luck! chôhk dee!
โชคดี

luggage gra-bpăo
กระเป๋า

Lo

luggage trolley rót kĕn
รถเข็น

lump (on body) néu-a ngôrk
เนื้องอก

lunch ah-hăhn glahng wun
อาหารกลางวัน

lungs bpòrt
ปอด

luxurious (hotel, furnishings) rŏo-răh
หรูหรา

luxury kŏrng fÔOm feu-ay
ของฟุ่มเฟือย

M

machine krêu-ung
เครื่อง

mad (insane) bâh
บ้า

(angry) gròht
โกรธ

magazine nít-ta-ya-săhn
นิตยสาร

maid (in hotel) yĭng rúp chái
หญิงรับใช้

maiden name nahm sa-gOOn derm
นามสกุลเดิม

mail (noun) jòt-măi
จดหมาย

(verb) sòng jòt-măi
ส่งจดหมาย

is there any mail for me? mee jòt-măi sŭm-rùp pŏm (chún) mái?
มีจดหมายสำหรับผม(ฉัน)ไหม
see **post office**

mailbox dtôo jòt-măi
ตู้จดหมาย

main sŭm-kun
สำคัญ

main post office bprai-sa-nee glahng
ไปรษณีย์กลาง

main road ta-nŏn yài
ถนนใหญ่

mains switch (for electricity) sa-wít săi fai yài
สวิชสายไฟใหญ่

make (brand name) yêe hôr
ยี่ห้อ

(verb) tum
ทำ

I make it 500 baht pŏm (chún) kít wâh hâh róy bàht
ผม(ฉัน)คิดว่าห้าร้อยบาท

what is it made of? tum dôo-ay a-rai?
ทำด้วยอะไร

make-up krêu-ung sŭm-ahng
เครื่องสำอาง

malaria kâi jùp sùn,

mah-lay-ree-a
ไข้จับสั่น, มาเลเรีย

malaria tablets yah gâir mah-lay-ree-a
ยาแก้มาเลเรีย

Malay (adj) ma-lah-yoo
มลายู

Malaysia bpra-tâyt mah-lay-see-a
ประเทศมาเลเซีย

man pôo-chai
ผู้ชาย

manager pôo-jùt-gahn
ผู้จัดการ

can I see the manager? kŏr póp pôo-jùt-gahn nòy
ขอพบผู้จัดการหน่อย

mango ma-môo-ung
มะม่วง

manners
According to ancient Hindu belief the head is the most sacred part of the body and the feet the most unclean. This belief, imported into Thailand, means that it's very rude to touch another person's head or to point your feet either at a human being or at a sacred image. When sitting on a temple floor for example, you should tuck your legs beneath you rather than stretch

them out towards the Buddha. These beliefs also forbid people from wearing shoes (which are even more unclean than feet) inside temples and most private homes. By extension, Thais take offence when they see someone sitting on the 'head', or prow, of a boat.

The left hand is used for washing after defecating, so Thais never use it to put food in their mouth, pass things or shake hands – as a foreigner though, you'll be assumed to have different customs, so left-handers shouldn't worry unduly.

many mâhk
มาก

not many mâi mâhk
ไม่มาก

map păirn-têe
แผนที่

Bangkok bookshops are the best source of maps.

March mee-nah-kom
มีนาคม

margarine ner-ee tee-um
เนยเทียม

market dta-làht
ตลาด

 Smaller markets selling only foodstuffs, cheap household goods and toiletries can still be found even in the centre of Bangkok. They are usually at their busiest at about 7 a.m. as housewives and maids do the day's shopping. Bangkok's biggest market is at Chatuchak Park near the Northern Bus Station; held on Saturday and Sunday, it sells virtually everything, including tapes, books, furniture, 'antiques', plants, pets, electrical goods, as well as every conceivable kind of foodstuff.

marmalade yairm
แยม

married: I'm married pǒm
(chún) dtàirng ngahn
láir-o
ผม(ฉัน)แต่งงานแล้ว
are you married? kOOn
dtàirng ngahn láir-o rěu
yung?
คุณแต่งงานแล้วหรือยัง

mascara mair-sa-kah-rah
แมสคารา

massage nôo-ut
นวด

match (football etc) gahn kàirng
kǔn
การแข่งขัน

matches mái kèet
ไม้ขีด

material (fabric) pâh
ผ้า

matter: it doesn't matter mâi
bpen rai
ไม่เป็นไร

what's the matter? bpen
a-rai?
เป็นอะไร

mattress têe norn
ที่นอน

May préut-sa-pah-kom
พฤษภาคม

may: may I have another one?
kǒr èek un nèung **dâi
mái?**
ขออีกอันหนึ่งได้ไหม
may I come in? kâo mah **dâi
mái?**
เข้ามาได้ไหม
may I see it? kǒr doo nòy
dâi mái?
ขอดูหน่อยได้ไหม
may I sit here? nûng têe nêe
dâi mái?
นั่งที่นี่ได้ไหม

127

maybe bahng tee
บางที

mayonnaise núm sa-lùt
น้ำสลัด

me* (male) pǒm
ผม

(female) dee-chún, chún
ดิฉัน, ฉัน

that's for me nûn sǔm-rùp
pǒm (chún)
นั่นสำหรับผม(ฉัน)

send it to me sòng mah hâi
pǒm (chún)
ส่งมาให้ผม(ฉัน)

me too pǒm (chún) gôr
měu-un gun
ผม(ฉัน)ก็เหมือนกัน

meal ah-hǎhn
อาหาร

dialogue

did you enjoy your meal?
ah-hǎhn a-ròy mái?
it was excellent, thank you
a-ròy mâhk

mean (verb) mǎi kwahm
หมายความ

what do you mean? kOOn
mǎi kwahm wâh a-rai?
คุณหมายความว่าอะไร

dialogue

what does this word
mean? kum née bplàir
wâh a-rai?
it means ... in English
pah-sǎh ung-grìt bplair
wâh ...

measles rôhk hùt
โรคหัด

meat néu-a
เนื้อ

mechanic châhng krêu-ung
ช่างเครื่อง

medicine yah
ยา

medium (adj: size) glahng
กลาง

medium-rare (steak) sÒOk
sÒOk dìp dìp
สุกๆดิบๆ

medium-sized ka-nàht glahng
ขนาดกลาง

meet (verb) póp
พบ

nice to meet you yin dee têe
dâi róo-jùk gun
ยินดีที่ได้รู้จักกัน

where shall I meet you? póp
gun têe nǎi?
พบกันที่ไหน

meeting bpra-chOOm
ประชุม

meeting place têe nút póp
ที่นัดพบ

melon dtairng tai
แตงไทย

men pôo-chai
ผู้ชาย

mend sôrm
ซ่อม

could you mend this for me?
kOOn sôrm hâi dâi mái?
คุณซ่อมให้ได้ไหม

men's room bOO-rÒOt
บุรุษ

menswear krêu-ung dtàirng
gai bOO-rÒOt
เครื่องแต่งกายบุรุษ

mention (verb) glào tĕung
กล่าวถึง

don't mention it mâi bpen rai
ไม่เป็นไร

menu may-noo
เมนู

may I see the menu, please?
kŏr doo may-noo nòy krúp
(kâ)
ขอดูเมนูหน่อยครับ(ค่ะ)
see **Menu Reader** page 271

message kào
ข่าว

are there any messages for

me? mee krai sùng a-rai wái
rĕu bplào?
มีใครสั่งอะไรไว้หรือเปล่า

I want to leave a message
for ... pŏm (chún) yàhk ja
fàhk bòrk a-rai hâi ...
ผม(ฉัน)อยากจะฝากบอก
อะไรให้ ...

metal (noun) loh-hà
โลหะ

metre* mét
เมตร

midday têe-ung wun
เที่ยงวัน

at midday têe-ung wun
เที่ยงวัน

middle: in the middle yòo
dtrong glahng
อยู่ตรงกลาง

in the middle of the night
dtorn glahng keun
ตอนกลางคืน

the middle one un glahng
อันกลาง

midnight têe-ung keun
เที่ยงคืน

at midnight têe-ung keun
เที่ยงคืน

might: I might ... bahng tee
pŏm (chún) àht ja ...
บางทีผม(ฉัน)อาจจะ ...

I might not ... bahng tee pŏm

Mi

129

(chún) àht ja mâi …
บางทีผม(ฉัน)อาจจะไม่ …

I might want to stay another
day bahng tee pŏm (chún)
àht ja yòo èek wun nèung
บางทีผม(ฉัน)อาจจะอยู่อีกวัน
หนึ่ง

migraine bpòo-ut hŏo-a
kâhng dee-o
ปวดหัวข้างเดียว

mild (taste) mâi pèt
ไม่เผ็ด

mile* mai
ไมล์

milk nom
นม

millimetre* min-li-mét
มิลลิเมตร

minced meat néu-a sùp
เนื้อสับ

mind: never mind mâi bpen rai
ไม่เป็นไร

I've changed my mind pŏm
(chún) bplèe-un jai láir-o
ผม(ฉัน)เปลี่ยนใจแล้ว

dialogue

do you mind if I open the
window? kŏr bpèrt nâh-
dtàhng nòy, dâi mái?
no, I don't mind dâi

mine*: it's mine kŏrng pŏm
(chún)
ของผม(ฉัน)

mineral water núm râir
น้ำแร่

minute nah-tee
นาที

in a minute èek bpra-dĕe-o
อีกประเดี๋ยว

just a minute dĕe-o, dĕe-o
เดี๋ยว ๆ

mirror gra-jòk ngao
กระจกเงา

Miss nahng-săo
นางสาว

miss: I missed the bus pŏm
(chún) dtòk rót may
ผม(ฉัน)ตกรถเมล์

missing hăi bpai
หายไป

one of my … is missing kŏng
pŏm (chún) hăi bpai …
ของผม(ฉัน)หายไป …

there's a suitcase
missing mee gra-bpăo hăi
bpai
มีกระเป๋าหายไป

mist mòrk
หมอก

mistake (noun) kwahm pìt
ความผิด

I think there's a mistake pŏm

(chún) kít wâh mee kŏr pìt
lék nóy

ผม(ฉัน)คิดว่ามีข้อผิด
เล็กน้อย

sorry, I've made a mistake
kŏr-tôht, pŏm (chún) tum
pìt

ขอโทษผม(ฉัน)ทำผิด

misunderstanding kwahm
kâo jai pìt

ความเข้าใจผิด

**mix-up: sorry, there's been a
mix-up** kŏr-tôht, mee
kwahm kâo jai pìt

ขอโทษ มีความเข้าใจผิด

mobile phone toh-ra-sùp rái
săi

โทรศัพท์ไร้สาย

modern tun sa-măi

ทันสมัย

moisturizer kreem
bum-rOOng pĕw

ครีมบำรุงผิว

moment: I won't be a moment
ror dĕe-o

รอเดี๋ยว

monastery wút

วัด

Monday wun jun

วันจันทร์

money ngern

เงิน

monk prá

พระ

 Monks come only just
beneath the monarchy in
the social hierarchy, and
they too are addressed and
discussed in a special respectful
language. If there's a monk around,
he'll always get a seat on the bus,
usually the back one. Theoretically,
monks are forbidden to have any
close contact with women which
means that females shouldn't sit or
stand next to a monk, or even brush
against his robes. If a woman has to
pass something to a monk, she has
to put the object down so that he
can then pick it up – rather than
hand it over directly.

monsoon mor-ra-sŎOm

มรสุม

month deu-un

เดือน

monument a-nÓO-săh-wa-
ree

อนุสาวรีย์

moon prá-jun

พระจันทร์

moped rót mor-dter-sai

รถมอร์เตอร์ไซค์

most: I like this one most of all
pǒm (chún) chôrp un née
mâhk têe sòOt
ผม(ฉัน)ชอบอันนี้มากที่สุด

most of the time sòo-un
mâhk
ส่วนมาก

most tourists núk tôrng
têe-o sòo-un mâhk
นักท่องเที่ยวส่วนมาก

mostly sòo-un mâhk
ส่วนมาก

mother mâir
แม่

mother-in-law (of a man) mâir
yai
แม่ยาย

(of a woman) mâir pǒo-a
แม่ผัว

motorbike rót mor-dter-sai
รถมอร์เตอร์ไซค์

motorboat reu-a yon
เรือยนต์

motorway tahng dòo-un
ทางด่วน

mountain poo-kǎo
ภูเขา

in the mountains nai poo-
kǎo
ในภูเขา

mouse nǒo
หนู

moustache nòo-ut
หนวด

mouth bpàhk
ปาก

mouth ulcer plǎir nai
bpàhk
แผลในปาก

move: he's moved to another
room káo yái bpai yòo èek
hôrng nèung
เขาย้ายไปอยู่อีกห้องหนึ่ง

could you move your car?
chôo-ay lêu-un rót kǒrng
kOOn, dâi mái?
ช่วยเลื่อนรถของคุณได้ไหม

could you move up a little?
chít nai nòy dâi mái?
ชิดในหน่อยได้ไหม

where has it moved to? (shop,
restaurant etc) yái bpai yòo têe
nǎi?
ย้ายไปอยู่ที่ไหน

movie nǔng
หนัง

movie theater rohng nǔng
โรงหนัง

Mr nai
นาย

Mrs nahng
นาง

much mâhk
มาก

more* èek
อีก

can I have some more water,
please? kŏr náhm èek nòy
krúp (kâ)
ขอน้ำอีกหน่อยครับ(ค่ะ)

more expensive/interesting
pairng/nâh sŏn jai gwàh
แพง/น่าสนใจกว่า

more than 50 hâh sìp gwàh
ห้าสิบกว่า

more than that mâhk gwàh
nún
มากกว่านั้น

a lot more èek mâhk
อีกมาก

dialogue

> would you like some
> more? ao èek mái?
> no, no more for me, thanks
> por láir-o, kòrp-kOOn
> krúp (kâ)
> how about you? láir-o
> kOOn lâ?
> I don't want any more,
> thanks por láir-o krúp
> (kâ)

morning dtorn cháo
ตอนเช้า

this morning cháo née
เช้านี้

in the morning dtorn cháo
ตอนเช้า

mosquito yOOng
ยุง

Malarial mosquitoes are active from dusk until dawn and during this time you should smother yourself and your clothes in mosquito repellent: this is stocked in shops, guesthouses and department stores all over Thailand. At night you should either sleep under a mosquito net or in a room with screens across the windows. Many hotels in tourist areas provide screens or a net – and the latter can be bought very cheaply in Bangkok. The first signs of malaria are remarkably similar to flu: if you suspect anything go to a hospital or clinic immediately. Mosquito coils – widely available in Thailand – also help keep the insects at bay.

mosquito net mÓOng
มุ้ง
mosquito repellent yah gun
yOOng
ยากันยุง

much better/worse dee/yâir mâhk gwàh
ดี/แย่มากกว่า

much hotter rórn mâhk gwàh
ร้อนมากกว่า

not much mâi mâhk
ไม่มาก

not very much mâi kôy mâhk
ไม่ค่อยมาก

I don't want very much pŏm (chún) mâi ao mâhk
ผม(ฉัน)ไม่เอามาก

mud klohn
โคลน

mug: I've been mugged pŏm (chún) tòok jêe
ผม(ฉัน)ถูกจี้

mum mâir
แม่

mumps kahng toom
คางทูม

museum pí-pít-ta-pun
พิพิธภัณฑ์

National museums tend to stick to government office hours and are open Monday to Friday from 8.30 a.m. to noon and from 1 to 4.30 p.m.; some close on Mondays and Tuesdays rather than at weekends.

mushrooms hèt
เห็ด

music don-dtree
ดนตรี

musician núk don-dtree
นักดนตรี

Muslim (adj) ì-sa-lahm
อิสลาม

mussels hŏy mairng pôo
หอยแมงภู่

must*: I must pŏm (chún) dtôrng
ผม(ฉัน)ต้อง

I mustn't drink alcohol pŏm (chún) dtôrng mâi gin lâo
ผม(ฉัน)ต้องไม่กินเหล้า

mustard núm jim mut-sa-dtàht
น้ำจิ้มมัสตาด

my* kŏrng pŏm (chún)
ของผม(ฉัน)

myself: I'll do it myself pŏm (chún) ja tum ayng
ผม(ฉัน)จะทำเอง

by myself dôo-ay dton ayng
ด้วยตนเอง

N

nail (finger) lép meu
เล็บมือ

(metal) dta-bpoo
ตะปู

nailbrush bprairng kùt lép
แปรงขัดเล็บ

nail varnish yah tah lép
ยาทาเล็บ

name chêu
ชื่อ

my name's ... pǒm chêu ...
ผมชื่อจอห์น ...

what's your name? kOOn
chêu a-rai?
คุณชื่ออะไร

**what is the name of this
street?** nêe ta-nǒn a-rai?
นี่ถนนอะไร

First names are more
important in Thailand than
family names. Do not
mistake this use of first names for
informality. When addressing people of
similar age or older, regardless of their
sex, you should use the polite term
'**kOOn**' in front of their first name.

napkin pâh chét bpàhk
ผ้าเช็ดปาก

nappy pâh òrm
ผ้าอ้อม

narrow (street) kâirp
แคบ

nasty nâh tOO-râyt
น่าทุเรศ

national hàirng châht
แห่งชาติ

national anthem
You should be prepared to
stand when the national
anthem is played at the beginning of
every cinema programme, and to
stop in your tracks if you hear the
national anthem being played over a
town's public address system –
many small towns do this twice a
day at 8 a.m. and 6 p.m.

nationality sǔn-châht
สัญชาติ

natural tum-ma-châht
ธรรมชาติ

nausea ah-gahn klêun
hěe-un
อาการคลื่นเหียน

navy (blue) sěe fáh gàir
สีฟ้าแก่

near glâi
ใกล้

is it near the city centre? yòo
glâi meu-ung mái?
อยู่ใกล้เมืองไหม

do you go near the museum?
kOOn pàhn bpai glâi glâi

pí-pít-ta-pun mái?

คุณผ่านไปใกล้ๆ
พิพิธภัณฑ์ไหม

where is the nearest ...?
... glâi têe sÒOt yòo têe
năi?
... ใกล้ที่สุดอยู่ที่ไหน

nearby yòo glâi
อยู่ใกล้

nearly gèu-up
เกือบ

necessary jum-bpen
จำเป็น

neck kor
คอ

necklace sôy kor
สร้อยคอ

necktie nék-tai
เน็คไท

need: I need ... pŏm (chún)
dtôrng-gahn ...
ผม(ฉัน)ต้องการ ...

do I need to pay? dtôrng jài
rĕu bplào?
ต้องจ่ายหรือเปล่า

needle kĕm
เข็ม

negative (film) feem
nay-gah-dteef
ฟิล์มเนกาตีฟ

nephew lăhn chai
หลานชาย

net (in sport) dtah-kài
ตาข่าย

never mâi ker-ee
ไม่เคย

dialogue

**have you ever been to Hua
Hin?** kOOn ker-ee bpai
hŏo-a hĭn mái?
**no, never, I've never
been there** mâi ker-ee,
pŏm (chún) mâi ker-ee
bpai

new mài
ใหม่

news (radio, TV etc) kào
ข่าว

newsagent's ráhn kăi núng-
sĕu pim
ร้านขายหนังสือพิมพ์

newspaper núng-sĕu pim
หนังสือพิมพ์

newspaper kiosk dtôo núng-
sĕu pim
ตู้หนังสือพิมพ์

New Year bpee mài
ปีใหม่

Happy New Year! sa-wùt dee
bpee mài!
สวัสดีปีใหม่

The traditional Thai New Year festival is called Songkran and occurs in the middle of April. January 1st is, however, recognized as the beginning of the calendar year in Thailand, although the year is calculated according to Buddhist Era, which is 543 years ahead of the AD year.

New Year's Eve wun sîn bpee
วันสิ้นปี

New Zealand bpra-tâyt new see-láirn
ประเทศนิวซีแลนด์

New Zealander: I'm a New Zealander pŏm (chún) bpen kon new see-láirn
ผม(ฉัน)เป็นคนนิวซีแลนด์

next nâh
หน้า

the next turning on the left lée-o sái têe tahng yâirk kâhng nâh
เลี้ยวซ้ายที่ทางแยกข้างหน้า

at the next stop bpâi nâh
ป้ายหน้า

next week ah-tít nâh
อาทิตย์หน้า

next to dtìt gùp
ติดกับ

nice (food) a-ròy
อร่อย

(looks, view etc) sŏo-ay
สวย

(person) dee
ดี

niece lăhn săo
หลานสาว

night glahng keun
กลางคืน

at night dtorn glahng keun
ตอนกลางคืน

good night sa-wùt dee
สวัสดี

dialogue

do you have a single room for one night? mee hôrng sŭm-rùp keun dee-o mái?
yes, madam mee krúp
how much is it per night? keun la tâo-rài?
it's 1,000 baht for one night keun la pun bàht
thank you, I'll take it kòrp-kOOn ao hôrng née

nightclub náit klúp
ไนทคลับ

nightdress chÓOt norn
ชุดนอน

no* mâi
ไม่

I've no change mâi mee sàyt
sa-dtahng
ไม่มีเศษสตางค์

there's no ... left mâi mee ...
lĕu-a yòo
ไม่มี ... เหลืออยู่

no way! mâi mee tahng!
ไม่มีทาง

oh no! (upset) dtai jing!
ตายจริง

nobody mâi mee krai
ไม่มีใคร

there's nobody there mâi
mee krai yòo
ไม่มีใครอยู่

noise sĕe-ung
เสียง

noisy: it's too noisy nòo-uk
hŏo
หนวกหู

non-alcoholic mâi mee un-
gor-horl
ไม่มีอัลกอฮอล

nonsmoking hâhm sòop
bOO-rèe
ห้ามสูบบุหรี่

noodles gŏo-ay dtĕe-o
ก๋วยเตี๋ยว

noodle shop ráhn gŏo-ay
dtĕe-o
ร้านก๋วยเตี๋ยว

noon têe-ung wun
เที่ยงวัน

at noon têe-ung wun
เที่ยงวัน

no-one mâi mee krai
ไม่มีใคร

nor: nor do I pŏm (chún) gôr
mâi mĕu-un gun
ผม(ฉัน)ก็ไม่เหมือนกัน

normal tum-ma-dah
ธรรมดา

north nĕu-a
เหนือ

in the north nai pâhk nĕu-a
ในภาคเหนือ

to the north tahng nĕu-a
ทางเหนือ

north of Bangkok tahng
nĕu-a kŏrng grOOng-tâyp
ทางเหนือของกรุงเทพฯ

northeast dta-wun òrk chĕe-
ung nĕu-a
ตะวันออกเฉียงเหนือ

Northern Ireland ai-lairn
nĕu-a
ไอร์แลนด์เหนือ

northwest dta-wun dtòk
chĕe-ung nĕu-a
ตะวันตกเฉียงเหนือ

Norway bpra-tâyt nor-way
ประเทศนอรเว

nose ja-mòok
จมูก

nosebleed lêu-ut gum-dao
ŏrk
เลือดกำเดาออก

not* mâi
ไม่

no thanks, I'm not hungry
mâi krúp (kâ) pŏm (chún)
mâi hěw
ไม่ครับ (ค่ะ) ผม(ฉัน)ไม่หิว

I don't want any, thank you
pŏm (chún) mâi ao kòrp-
kOOn
ผม(ฉัน)ไม่เอาขอบคุณ

it's not necessary mâi jum-
bpen
ไม่จำเป็น

I didn't know that pŏm
(chún) mâi sâhp rêu-ung
nún
ผม(ฉัน)ไม่ทราบเรื่องนั้น

not that one – this one mâi
châi un nún – un nêe
ไม่ใช่อันนั้นอันนี้

note (banknote) bai báirng
ใบแบ๊งค์

notebook sa-mÒOt
สมุด

notepaper (for letters) gra-dàht

kěe-un jòt-mǎi
กระดาษเขียนจดหมาย

nothing mâi mee a-rai
ไม่มีอะไร

nothing for me, thanks mâi
ao a-rai krúp (kâ) kòrp-
kOOn
ไม่เอาอะไรครับ(ค่ะ)ขอบคุณ

nothing else mâi mee a-rai
èek
ไม่มีอะไรอีก

novel na-wa-ni-yai
นวนิยาย

November préut-sa-ji-gah-yon
พฤศจิกายน

now děe-o née
เดี๋ยวนี้

number mǎi-lâyk
หมายเลข

I've got the wrong number
toh pìt **ber**
โทรผิดเบอร์

what is your phone number?
ber toh-ra-sùp kŏrng
kOOn lâyk a-rai?
เบอร์โทรศัพท์ของคุณเลขอะไร

number plate bpâi ta-bee-un
rót
ป้ายทะเบียนรถ

nurse (woman) nahng pa-yah-
bahn
นางพยาบาล

nut (for bolt) glee-o
เกลียว
nuts tòo-a
ถั่ว

O

occupied (line etc) mâi wâhng
ไม่ว่าง
o'clock* mohng
โมง
October dtOO-lah-kom
ตุลาคม
odd (strange) bplàirk
แปลก
of* kŏrng
ของ
off (lights) bpìt
ปิด
it's just off Sukhumwit Road
yòo tăir-o ta-nŏn sOO-
kŎOm-wít
อยู่แถวถนนสุขุมวิท
we're off tomorrow (leaving)
rao bpai prÔOng née
เราไปพรุ่งนี้
offensive nâh rung-gèe-ut
น่ารังเกียจ
office (place of work) sǔm-núk
ngahn
สำนักงาน

140

officer (said to policeman) nai
dtum-ròo-ut
นายตำรวจ
often bòy bòy
บ่อย ๆ
not often mâi bòy
ไม่บ่อย
how often are the buses? rót
mah bòy kâir nǎi?
รถมาบ่อยแค่ไหน
oil núm mun
น้ำมัน
(motor) núm mun
krêu-ung
น้ำมันเครื่อง
ointment yah tah
ยาทา
OK oh-kay
โอเค
are you OK? kOOn oh-kay
mái?
คุณโอเคไหม
is that OK with you? kOOn
oh-kay mái?
คุณโอเคไหม
is it OK to ...? ... dâi mái?
... ได้ไหม
that's OK thanks (it doesn't
matter) mâi bpen rai
ไม่เป็นไร
I'm OK (nothing for me, I've got
enough) pŏm (chún) por

láir-o
ผม(ฉัน)พอแล้ว
(I feel OK) pǒm (chún) oh kay
ผม(ฉัน)โอเค

is this train OK for ...? rót fai
née bpai ... châi mái?
รถไฟนี้ไป ... ใช่ไหม

old (person) gàir
แก่
(thing) gào
เก่า

dialogue

how old are you? kOOn
ah-yÓO tâo-rài?
I'm 25 pǒm (chún) ah-
yÓO yêe-sìp hâh bpee
and you? láir-o kOOn lâ?

old-fashioned láh sa-mǎi
ล้าสมัย
old town (old part of town) meu-
ung gào
เมืองเก่า
olive oil núm mun
ma-gòrk
น้ำมันมะกอก
olives ma-gòrk
มะกอก
omelette kài jee-o
ไข่เจียว

on* bon
บน
on the beach têe chai hàht
ที่ชายหาด
on the street bon ta-nǒn
บนถนน
is it on this road? yòo ta-nǒn
née rěu bplào?
อยู่ถนนนี้หรือเปล่า
on the plane bon krêu-ung
bin
บนเครื่องบิน
on Saturday wun sǎo
วันเสาร์
on television nai tee wee
ในทีวี
I haven't got it on me pǒm
(chún) mâi dâi ao maḥ
dôo-ay
ผม(ฉัน)ไม่ได้เอามาด้วย
this one's on me (drink) pǒm
(chún) lée-ung
ผม(ฉัน)เลี้ยง
the light wasn't on fai mâi
bpèrt yòo
ไฟไม่เปิดอยู่
what's on tonight? keun née
mee a-rai?
คืนนี้มีอะไร
once (one time) krúng
nèung
ครั้งหนึ่ง

at once (immediately) tun-tee
ทันที

one* nèung
หนึ่ง

the white one un sěe kǎo
อันสีขาว

one-way ticket dtǒo-a bpai
ตั๋วไป

onion hǒo-a hǒrm
หัวหอม

only tâo-nún
เท่านั้น

only one un dee-o tâo-nún
อันเดียวเท่านั้น

it's only 6 o'clock pee-ung
hòk mohng tâo-nún
เพียงหกโมงเท่านั้น

I've only just got here pǒm
(chún) pêung mah děe-o
née ayng
ผม(ฉัน)เพิ่งมาเดี๋ยวนี้เอง

on/off switch sa-wít bpèrt/
bpìt
สวิชเปิด/ปิด

open (adj, verb) bpèrt
เปิด

when do you open? bpèrt
gèe mohng?
เปิดกี่โมง

I can't get it open bpèrt mâi
dâi
เปิดไม่ได้

in the open air glahng
jâirng
กลางแจ้ง

opening times way-lah bpìt-
bpèrt
เวลาปิดเปิด

open ticket dtǒo-a mâi jum-
gùt way-lah
ตั๋วไม่จำกัดเวลา

operation (medical) gahn pàh
dtùt
การผ่าตัด

operator (telephone) pa-núk
ngahn toh-ra-sùp
พนักงานโทรศัพท์

opposite: the opposite
direction tahng dtrong
kâhm
ทางตรงข้าม

the bar opposite bah dtrong
kâhm
บาร์ตรงข้าม

opposite my hotel
dtrong kâhm rohng
rairm
ตรงข้ามโรงแรม

optician jùk-sǒo pâirt
จักษุแพทย์

or rěu
หรือ

orange (fruit) sôm
ส้ม

142

(colour) sěe sôm
สีส้ม

orange juice núm sôm
น้ำส้ม

orchestra wong don-dtree
วงดนตรี

order: can we order now? (in restaurant) kŏr sùng děe-o née dâi mái?
ขอสั่งเดี๋ยวนี้ได้ไหม

I've already ordered, thanks pŏm (chún) sùng láir-o
ผม(ฉัน)สั่งแล้ว

I didn't order this pŏm (chún) mâi dâi sùng
ผม(ฉัน)ไม่ได้สั่ง

out of order sěe-a
เสีย

ordinary tum-ma-dah
ธรรมดา

other èun
อื่น

the other one (person) èek kon nèung
อีกคนหนึ่ง

(thing) èek un nèung
อีกอันหนึ่ง

the other day (recently) mêu-a mái gèe wun
เมื่อไม่กี่วัน

I'm waiting for the others (other people) pŏm (chún) ror

kon èun
ผม(ฉัน)รอคนอื่น

do you have any others? mee yàhng èun mái?
มีอย่างอื่นไหม

otherwise mí-cha-nún
มิฉะนั้น

our* kŏrng rao
ของเรา

ours* kŏrng rao
ของเรา

out: he's out (not at home) káo mâi yòo
เขาไม่อยู่

three kilometres out of town nôrk meu-ung bpai săhm gi-loh
นอกเมืองไปสามกิโล

outdoors glahng jâirng
กลางแจ้ง

outside kâhng nôrk
ข้างนอก

can we sit outside? nûng kâhng nôrk dâi mái?
นั่งข้างนอกได้ไหม

oven dtao
เตา

over: over here têe nêe
ที่นี่

over there têe nôhn
ที่โน่น

over 500 hâh róy gwàh
ห้าร้อยกว่า

it's over (finished) jòp
láir-o
จบแล้ว

**overcharge: you've
overcharged me** kOOn kít
ngern mâhk bpai
คุณคิดเงินมากไป

overcoat sêu-a nôrk
เสื้อนอก

overnight (travel) dern tahng
glahng keun
เดินทางกลางคืน

overtake sairng
แซง

owe: how much do I owe you?
pǒm (chún) bpen nêe
kOOn tâo-rài?
ผม(ฉัน)เป็นหนี้คุณเท่าไร

own: my own ... kǒrng pǒm
(chún) ayng ...
ของผม(ฉัน)เอง ...

are you on your own?
kOOn mah **kon dee-o** rěu
bplào?
คุณมาคนเดียวหรือเปล่า

I'm on my own pǒm (chún)
mah **kon dee-o**
ผม(ฉัน)มาคนเดียว

owner jâo-kǒrng
เจ้าของ

oyster hǒy nahng rom
หอยนางรม

P

pack (verb) jùt gra-bpǎo
จัดกระเป๋า

a pack of ... hòr ...
ห่อ ...

package (parcel) hòr
ห่อ

packed lunch ah-hǎhn glahng
wun glòrng
อาหารกลางวันกล่อง

packet: a packet of cigarettes
sorng bOO-rèe
ซองบุหรี่

paddy field nah
นา

page (of book) nâh
หน้า

could you page Mr ...? chôo-
ay hǎh ber toh-ra-sùp kOOn
... hâi dôo-ay
ช่วยหาเบอร์โทรศัพท์คุณ ...
ให้ด้วย

pagoda jay-dee
เจดีย์

pain kwahm jèp bpòo-ut
ความเจ็บปวด

I have a pain here jèp

dtrong née
เจ็บตรงนี้

painful jèp bpòo-ut
เจ็บปวด

painkillers yah ra-ngúp
bpòo-ut
ยาระงับปวด

paint (noun) sĕe
สี

painting (picture) pâhp kĕe-un
ภาพเขียน

pair: a pair of ... ... kôo
nèung
... คู่หนึ่ง

Pakistani (adj) kon bpah-gee-
sa-tăhn
คนปากีสถาน

palace wung
วัง

pale sĕe òrn
สีอ่อน

pale blue sĕe fáh òrn
สีฟ้าอ่อน

pan (frying pan) gra-tá
กระทะ

panties gahng gayng nai sa-
dtree
กางเกงในสตรี

pants (underwear: men's) gahng
gayng nai
กางเกงใน

(women's) gahng gayng nai

sa-dtree
กางเกงในสตรี

(US: trousers) gahng-gayng
กางเกง

pantyhose tŏOng yai boo-a
ถุงใยบัว

paper gra-dàht
กระดาษ

(newspaper) núng-sĕu-pim
หนังสือพิมพ์

a piece of paper gra-dàht
pàirn nèung
กระดาษแผ่นหนึ่ง

paper handkerchiefs gra-dàht
chét nâh
กระดาษเช็ดหน้า

parcel hòr
ห่อ

pardon (me)? (didn't understand,
hear) a-rai ná krúp (ká)?
อะไรนะครับ(คะ)

parents pôr mâir
พ่อแม่

parents-in-law (wife's parents)
pôr dtah mâir yai
พ่อตาแม่ยาย

(husband's parents) pôr pŏo-a
mâir pŏo-a
พ่อผัวแม่ผัว

park (noun) sŏo-un săh-tah-
ra-ná
สวนสาธารณะ

(verb) jòrt
จอด

can I park here? jòrt têe nêe
dâi mái?
จอดที่นี่ได้ไหม

parking lot têe jòrt rót
ที่จอดรถ

part (noun) sòo-un
ส่วน

partner (boyfriend, girlfriend etc)
fairn
แฟน

party (group) glÒOm kon
กลุ่มคน
(celebration) ngahn lée-ung
งานเลี้ยง

pass (in mountains) chôrng kǎo
ช่องเขา

passenger pôo doy-ee sǎhn
ผู้โดยสาร

passport núng-sěu dern
tahng
หนังสือเดินทาง

past*: in the past mêu-a
gòrn
เมื่อก่อน

just past the post office
ler-ee bprai-sa-nee bpai èek
nít nèung
เลยไปรษณีย์ไปอีกนิดหนึ่ง

path tahng
ทาง

pattern bàirp
แบบ

pavement bàht wít-těe
บาทวิถี

on the pavement bon bàht
wít-těe
บนบาทวิถี

pay (verb) jài
จ่าย

can I pay, please? kǒr bin
nòy
ขอบิลหน่อย

it's already paid for jài láir-o
จ่ายแล้ว

dialogue

who's paying? krai bpen
kon jài ngern?
I'll pay pǒm (chún) ayng
no, you paid last time, I'll
pay kOOn jài dtorn
krúng gòrn láir-o ná pǒm
(chún) jài ayng

pay phone toh-ra-sùp sǎh-
tah-ra-ná
โทรศัพท์สาธารณะ

peaceful (quiet) ngêe-up
เงียบ

peach lôok pêech
ลูกพีช

peanuts tòo-a
ถั่ว

pear lôok pair
ลูกแพร์

peculiar (taste, custom) bplàirk
แปลก

pedestrian crossing tahng
máh-lai
ทางม้าลาย

pedestrian precinct têe hâhm
rót kâo
ที่ห้ามรถเข้า

peg (for washing) mái nèep pâh
ไม้หนีบผ้า

pen bpàhk-gah
ปากกา

pencil din-sŏr
ดินสอ

penfriend pêu-un tahng
jòt-măi
เพื่อนทางจดหมาย

penicillin yah pen-ni-seen-lin
ยาเพนนิซีลลิน

penknife mêet púp
มีดพับ

people kon
คน

the other people in the
hotel kon èun nai rohng
rairm
คนอื่นในโรงแรม

too many people kon mâhk
bpai
คนมากไป

pepper (spice) prík tai
พริกไทย

(vegetable) prík yòo-uk
พริกหยวก

per: per night keun la ...
คืนละ ...

how much per day? wun la
tâo-rài?
วันละเท่าไร

per cent bper-sen
เปอร์เซ็นต์

perfect yôrt yêe-um
ยอดเยี่ยม

perfume núm hŏrm
น้ำหอม

perhaps bahng tee
บางที

perhaps not bahng tee
mâi
บางทีไม่

period (of time) chôo-a rá-yá
ชั่วระยะ

(menstruation) bpra-jum
deu-un
ประจำเดือน

perm dùt pŏm
ดัดผม

permit (noun) bai un-nÓO-
yâht
ใบอนุญาต

person kon
คน

personal stereo work–mairn
วอล์กแมน

petrol núm mun
น้ำมัน

Núm mun is the general word for oil but it is also the colloquial word for petrol. If you ask for núm mun in a petrol station you'll get petrol; if you want oil, you should ask for **núm mun krêu-ung**. Petrol is cheapest at the big petrol stations found in every town; most small villages have roadside huts where the fuel is pumped out of a large barrel. In most petrol stations, star symbols on the pumps are sufficient to indicate the grade of petrol; four-star/premium is sometimes called **pi-sàyt** (literally: special) while three-star/regular is **tum-ma-dah** (ordinary). Thais use the English word 'diesel' although it is normally pronounced **dee-sen**. Unleaded petrol is **núm mun rái sǎhn dta-gòo-a**.

petrol can gra-bpǒrng núm mun
กระบ๋องน้ำมัน

petrol station bpúm núm mun
ปั๊มน้ำมัน

pharmacy hâhng kǎi yah
ห้างขายยา

There's no need to bring huge supplies of non-prescription medicines with you as Thai pharmacies (open daily from 8.30 a.m. to 8 p.m.) are well-stocked with local and international brands of medicines, and are much cheaper than in the West. All pharmacies, whatever size the town, are run by highly-trained English-speaking pharmacists and they are usually the best people to talk to if your symptoms aren't bad enough to warrant seeing a doctor.

phone toh-ra-sùp
โทรศัพท์

Every so often phone lines get jammed and a whole town becomes incommunicado for a few hours, but usually the phone system works well. Payphones generally come in two colours: red for local calls and blue for long-distance calls within

Thailand. Red phones take the medium-sized one-baht coins and will give you three minutes per B1. The blue ones aren't very common outside Bangkok, so in smaller towns you usually have to go to a private long-distance telephone office, generally located near the post office, which will make the connection for you.

The cheapest way of making an international call is to use the government telephone centre. Nearly always located within or adjacent to the town's main post office, and open daily from about 7 a.m. to 11 p.m. (open 24 hours in Bangkok), the government phone centres allot you a booth and leave you to do the dialling (in Bangkok) or call via the operator for you (in other towns). If you can't get to one of the official places, try the slightly more expensive private international call offices in tourist areas, or the even pricier services offered by the posher hotels.

phone book sa-mòot măi-lâyk toh-ra-sùp
สมุดหมายเลขโทรศัพท์

phone box dtôo toh-ra-sùp
ตู้โทรศัพท์

phonecard bùt toh-ra-sùp
บัตรโทรศัพท์

phone number ber toh-ra-sùp
เบอร์โทรศัพท์

photo rôop tài
รูปถ่าย

excuse me, could you take a photo of us? kŏr-tôht krúp (kà), chôo-ay tài rôop rao hâi nòy dâi mái?
ขอโทษครับ(ค่ะ)ช่วยถ่ายรูปเราให้หน่อยได้ไหม

phrasebook kôo meu sŏn-ta-nah
คู่มือสนทนา

Phuket poo-gèt
ภูเก็ต

piano bpee-a-noh
เปียโน

pickpocket ka-moy-ee lóo-ung gra-bpǎo
ขโมยล้วงกระเป๋า

pick up: will you be there to pick me up? ja bpai rúp pŏm (chún) mái?
จะไปรับผม(ฉัน)ไหม

picnic (noun) bpìk-ník
ปิคนิค

picture (painting, photo) rôop
รูป

pie pai
ไพ

piece chín
ชิ้น

a piece of ... ... chín nèung
... ชิ้นหนึ่ง

pill (contraceptive pill) yah
kOOm gum-nèrt
ยาคุมกำเนิด

I'm on the pill chún chái yah
kOOm gum-nèrt
ฉันใช้ยาคุมกำเนิด

pillow mŏrn
หมอน

pillow case bplòrk mŏrn
ปลอกหมอน

pin (noun) kĕm mÒOt
เข็มหมุด

pineapple sùp-bpa-rót
สับปะรด

pineapple juice núm sùp-
bpa-rót
น้ำสับปะรด

pink sĕe chom-poo
สีชมพู

pipe (for smoking) glôrng yah
sên
กล้องยาเส้น
(for water) tôr
ท่อ

pipe cleaners mái tum
kwahm sà-aht glôrng yah
sên
ไม้ทำความสะอาดกล้องยาเส้น

150

pity: it's a pity nâh sŏng-săhn
น่าสงสาร

pizza pee-sâh
พีซซ่า

place (noun) sa-tăhn-têe
สถานที่

at your place têe bâhn
kOOn
ที่บ้านคุณ

at his place têe bâhn káo
ที่บ้านเขา

plain (not patterned) mâi mee
lôo-ut lai
ไม่มีลวดลาย

plane krêu-ung bin
เครื่องบิน

by plane doy-ee krêu-ung
bin
โดยเครื่องบิน

plant dtôn mái
ต้นไม้

plaster cast fèu-uk
เฝือก

plasters plah-sa-dter
พลาสเตอร์

plastic bplah-sa-dtìk
ปลาสติค
(credit cards) bùt kray-dìt
บัตรเครดิต

plastic bag tŎOng bplah-sa-
dtìk
ถุงปลาสติค

plate jahn
จาน

platform chahn chah-lah
ชานชาลา

which platform is it for Chiangmai? bpai chee-ung-mài chahn chah-lah a-rai?
ไปเชียงใหม่ชานชาลาอะไร

play (verb) lên
เล่น

(noun: in theatre) la-korn
ละคร

playground (for children) sa-nǎhm dèk lên
สนามเด็กเล่น

pleasant sa-nÒOk
สนุก

please (requesting something) kǒr ...
ขอ ...

(offering) chern krúp (kâ)
เชิญครับ(ค่ะ)

yes please ao krúp (kâ)
เอาครับ(ค่ะ)

could you please ...? chôo-ay ... nòy dâi mái?
ช่วยหน่อย ... ได้ไหม

please don't yàh ler-ee krúp (kâ)
อย่าเลยครับ(ค่ะ)

pleased: pleased to meet you yin dee têe dâi róo-jùk gun
ยินดีที่ได้รู้จักกัน

pleasure: my pleasure (response to thanks) mâi bpen rai
ไม่เป็นไร

plenty: plenty of ... ... mâhk
... มาก

there's plenty of time mee way-lah mâhk
มีเวลามาก

that's plenty, thanks por láir-o kòrp-kOOn
พอแล้วขอบคุณ

pliers keem bpàhk kêep
คีมปากคีบ

plug (electrical) bplúk
ปลั๊ก

(for car) hǒo-a tee-un
หัวเทียน

(in sink) jÒOk ÒOt
จุกอุด

plumber châhng bpra-bpah
ช่างประปา

p.m.*

pocket gra-bpǎo
กระเป๋า

point: two point five sǒrng jÒOt hâh
สองจุดห้า

there's no point mâi mee
bpra-yòht
ไม่มีประโยชน์

points (in car) torng kǎo
ทองขาว

poisonous bpen pít
เป็นพิษ

police dtum-ròo-ut
ตำรวจ

call the police! rêe-uk dtum-
ròo-ut mah!
เรียกตำรวจมา

There is a special
department for tourist-
related crimes and
complaints called the Tourist
Assistance Centre (TAC), set up to
mediate between tourists, police
and accused persons (particularly
shopkeepers and tour agents). In
emergencies, always contact the
English-speaking tourist police who
have offices within or adjacent to
many regional TAT (Tourist Authority
of Thailand) offices – this is
invariably more efficient than
directly contacting the local police,
ambulance or fire service.

policeman dtum-ròo-ut
ตำรวจ

police station sa-tǎh-nee
dtum-ròo-ut
สถานีตำรวจ

policewoman dtum-ròo-ut
yǐng
ตำรวจหญิง

polish (noun) yah kùt
ยาขัด

polite sOO-pâhp
สุภาพ

polluted bpen pít
เป็นพิษ

pony máh glàirp
ม้าแกลบ

pool (for swimming) sà wâi
náhm
สระว่ายน้ำ

poor (not rich) jon
จน

(quality) mâi ao nǎi
ไม่เอาไหน

pop music don-dtree pórp
ดนตรีพ๊อพ

pop singer núk rórng
นักร้อง

popular bpen têe nee-yom
เป็นที่นิยม

population
bpra-chah-gorn
ประชากร

pork néu-a mǒo
เนื้อหมู

port (for boats) tâh reu-a

ท่าเรือ

porter (in hotel) kon fâo bpra-dtoo

คนเฝ้าประตู

portrait pâhp kĕe-un dtoo-a jing

ภาพเขียนตัวจริง

posh (restaurant, people) rŏo-răh

หรูหรา

possible bpen bpai dâi

เป็นไปได้

is it possible to ...? ... bpen bpai dâi mái?

... เป็นไปได้ไหม

as ... as possible yàhng ... têe sÒOt têe ja ... dâi

อย่าง ... ที่สุดที่จะ ... ได้

post (noun: mail) jòt-măi

จดหมาย

(verb) sòng jòt-măi

ส่งจดหมาย

could you post this for me? chôo-ay sòng jòt-măi née hâi nòy dâi mái?

ช่วยส่งจดหมายนี้ให้หน่อยได้ไหม

postbox dtôo bprai-sa-nee

ตู้ไปรษณีย์

postcard bpóht-gáht

โปสการ์ด

postcode ra-hùt bprai-sa-nee

รหัสไปรษณีย์

poster bpoh-sa-dter

โปสเตอร์

poste restante 'poste restante'

post office bprai-sa-nee

ไปรษณีย์

 Post offices are open Monday to Friday from 8 a.m. to 4 p.m. and on Saturday from 8 a.m. to noon. On weekdays some are closed from noon to 1 p.m. and some may stay open until 6 p.m.

Mail takes about seven days to get between Bangkok and Europe or North America, and a little longer in isolated areas. Almost all main post offices across the country operate a poste restante service and will hold letters for two to three months. Mail should be addressed: Name (family name underlined or capitalized), Poste Restante, GPO, Town or City, Thailand. It will be filed by surname, though it's always wise to check under your initial as well. The poste restante at Bangkok GPO is open from Monday to Friday from 8 a.m.

to 8 p.m. and until 1 p.m. on
Saturdays; others follow regular
post office hours.
see **stamp**

potato mun fa-rùng
มันฝรั่ง

potato chips (US) mun fa-
rùng tôrt
มันฝรั่งทอด

pots and pans môr kâo môr
gairng
หม้อข้าวหม้อแกง

pottery krêu-ung bpûn din
pǎo
เครื่องปั้นดินเผา

pound* (money) bporn
ปอนด์

power cut dtùt fai
ตัดไฟ

power point bplúk fai
ปลั๊กไฟ

**practise: I want to practise my
Thai** pǒrm (chún) yàhk ja
fèuk pôot pah-sǎh tai
ผม(ฉัน)อยากจะฝึกพูด
ภาษาไทย

prawns gÔOng
กุ้ง

prefer: I prefer ... pǒrm
(chún) chôrp ... mâhk gwàh
ผม(ฉัน)ชอบ ... มากกว่า

pregnant mee tórng
มีท้อง

prescription (for medicine) bai
sùng yah
ใบสั่งยา

present (gift) kǒrng kwǔn
ของขวัญ

president (of country) bpra-tah-
nah-tí-bor-dee
ประธานาธิบดี

pretty sǒo-ay
สวย

it's pretty expensive pairng
měu-un gun ná
แพงเหมือนกันนะ

price rah-kah
ราคา

priest prá
พระ

prime minister nah-yók rút-
ta-mon-dtree
นายกรัฐมนตรี

printed matter sìng dtee
pim
สิ่งตีพิมพ์

priority (in driving) sìt pàhn bpai
gòrn
สิทธิผ่านไปก่อน

prison kÓOk
คุก

private sòo-un dtoo-a
ส่วนตัว

private bathroom hôrng náhm sòo-un dtoo-a
ห้องน้ำส่วนตัว

probably kong-ja
คงจะ

problem bpun-hǎh
ปัญหา

no problem! mâi mee bpun-hǎh!
ไม่มีปัญหา

program(me) (noun) bprohgrairm
โปรแกรม

promise: I promise pǒm (chún) sǔn-yah
ผม(ฉัน)สัญญา

pronounce: how is this pronounced? nêe òrk sěe-ung yung-ngai?
นี่ออกเสียงอย่างไร

properly (repaired, locked etc) tòok dtôrng
ถูกต้อง

Protestant krít
คริสต์

public convenience sôo-um sǎh-tah-ra-ná
ส้วมสาธารณะ

public holiday wun yÒOt râht-cha-gahn
วันหยุดราชการ

pudding (dessert) kǒrng wǎhn
ของหวาน

pull deung
ดึง

pullover sêu-a sa-wét-dtêr
เสื้อสเวตเตอร์

puncture (noun) yahng dtàirk
ยางแตก

purple sěe môo-ung
สีม่วง

purse (for money) gra-bpǎo sa-dtahng
กระเป๋าสตางค์

(US) gra-bpǎo těu
กระเป๋าถือ

push plùk
ผลัก

pushchair rót kěn
รถเข็น

put sài
ใส่

where can I put ...? ... sài dâi têe nǎi?
... ใส่ได้ที่ไหน

could you put us up for the night? kǒr káhng keun têe nêe nòy dâi mái?
ขอค้างคืนที่นี่หน่อยได้ไหม

pyjamas sêu-a gahng-gayng

norn
เสื้อกางเกงนอน

Q

quality kOOn-na-pâhp
คุณภาพ

quarantine (place) dâhn gùk
rôhk
ด่านกักโรค

(period) ra-yá way-lah têe
gùk rôhk wái
ระยะเวลาที่กักโรคไว้

quarter nèung nai sèe
หนึ่งในสี่

quayside: on the quayside têe
tâh reu-a
ที่ท่าเรือ

question kum tăhm
คำถาม

queue (noun) kew
คิว

quick ray-o
เร็ว

that was quick ray-o jing
เร็วจริง

what's the quickest way
there? bpai tahng năi ray-o
têe sÒOt?
ไปทางไหนเร็วที่สุด

fancy a quick drink? yàhk

bpai dèum a-rai mái?
อยากไปดื่มอะไรไหม

quickly ray-o
เร็ว

quiet (place, hotel) ngêe-up
เงียบ

quiet! ngêe-up ngêe-up nòy!
เงียบ ๆ หน่อย

quite (fairly) por sŏm-koo-un
พอสมควร

(very) tee dee-o
ทีเดียว

that's quite right tòok láir-o
ถูกแล้ว

quite a lot mâhk por sŏm-
koo-un
มากพอสมควร

R

rabbit (meat) gra-dtài
กระต่าย

race (for runners, cars) gahn
kàirng kŭn
การแข่งขัน

racket (tennis, squash) mái dtee
ไม้ตี

radiator môr náhm
หม้อน้ำ

radio wít-ta-yÓO
วิทยุ

on the radio tahng wít-ta-yÓO
ทางวิทยุ

rail: by rail doy-ee rót fai
โดยรถไฟ

railway tahng rót fai
ทางรถไฟ

rain (noun) fǒn
ฝน

in the rain dtàhk fǒn
ตากฝน

it's raining fǒn dtòk
ฝนตก

raincoat sêu-a fǒn
เสื้อฝน

rape (noun) kòm kěun
ข่มขืน

rare (uncommon) hǎh yâhk
หายาก

(steak) sòok sòok dìp dìp
สุก ๆ ดิบ ๆ

rash (on skin) pèun
ผื่น

rat nǒo
หนู

rate (for changing money) ùt-dtrah
อัตรา

rather: it's rather good kôrn kâhng dee
ค่อนข้างดี

I'd rather ... pǒm (chún)

yàhk ja ... dee gwàh
ผม(ฉัน)อยากจะ ... ดีกว่า

razor (dry, electric) mêet gohn
มีดโกน

razor blades bai mêet gohn
ใบมีดโกน

read àhn
อ่าน

ready prórm, sèt
พร้อม, เสร็จ

are you ready? sèt láir-o rěu yung?
เสร็จแล้วหรือยัง

I'm not ready yet pǒm (chún) yung mâi sèt
ผม(ฉัน)ยังไม่เสร็จ

dialogue

when will it be ready? sèt mêu-a rài?
it should be ready in a couple of days èek sǒrng sǎhm wun koo-un ja sèt

real jing
จริง

really jing jing
จริง ๆ

I'm really sorry pǒm (chún) sěe-a jai jing jing
ผม(ฉัน)เสียใจจริง ๆ

157

that's really great dee jung
ler-ee

ดีจังเลย

really? (doubt) jing lěr?

จริงหรือ

(polite interest) lěr?

หรือ

rear lights fai lǔng rót

ไฟหลังรถ

rearview mirror gra-jòk lǔng

กระจกหลัง

reasonable (price) rah-kah
yao

ราคาเยา

receipt bai sèt rúp ngern

ใบเสร็จรับเงิน

recently mêu-a ray-o ray-o
née

เมื่อเร็ว ๆ นี้

reception (in hotel) pa-nàirk
dtôrn rúp

แผนกต้อนรับ

(for guests) ngahn lée-ung
dtôrn rúp

งานเลี้ยงต้อนรับ

at reception têe pa-nàirk
dtôrn rúp

ที่แผนกต้อนรับ

reception desk pa-nàirk
dtôrn rúp

แผนกต้อนรับ

receptionist pa-núk ngahn

dtôrn rúp

พนักงานต้อนรับ

recognize jum dâi

จำได้

recommend: could you
recommend ...? kOOn náir-
num ... dâi mái?

คุณแนะนำ ... ได้ไหม

record (music) pàirn sěe-ung

แผ่นเสียง

red sěe dairng

สีแดง

red wine lâo wai dairng

เหล้าไวน์แดง

refund (noun) keun ngern

คืนเงิน

can I have a refund? keun
ngern hâi dâi mái?

คืนเงินให้ได้ไหม

region pâhk

ภาค

registered: by registered mail
jòt-mǎi long ta-bee-un

จดหมายลงทะเบียน

registration number ta-bee-un
rót

ทะเบียนรถ

relative (noun) yâht

ญาติ

religion sàh-sa-nǎh

ศาสนา

see Buddhism and monk

remember: I don't remember
pŏm (chún) jum mâi dâi
ผม(ฉัน)จำไม่ได้

I remember pŏm (chún) jum dâi
ผม(ฉัน)จำได้

do you remember? jum dâi mái?
จำได้ไหม

rent (noun: for apartment etc) kâh châo
ค่าเช่า

(verb: car etc) châo
เช่า

dialogue

I'd like to rent a car pŏm (chún) yàhk ja châo rót

for how long? châo gèe wun?

two days sŏng wun

this is our range nêe rót kŏrng rao

I'll take the ... ao ...

is that with unlimited mileage? lâirn dâi doy-ee mâi jum-gùt ra-yá tahng châi mái?

it is krúp

can I see your licence, please? kŏr doo bai kùp

kèe

and your passport láir-o núng-sěu dern tahng

is insurance included? roo-um kâh bpra-gun dôo-ay rěu bplào?

yes, but you pay the first 2,000 baht krúp dtàir kOOn jài sŏrng pun bàht râirk ná krúp

can you leave a deposit of 3,000 baht? chôo-ay wahng kâh mút-jum sǎhm pun bàht dâi mái?

rented car rót châo
รถเช่า

repair (verb) sôrm
ซ่อม

can you repair it? sôrm dâi mái?
ซ่อมได้ไหม

repeat pôot èek tee
พูดอีกที

could you repeat that? pôot èek tee dâi mái?
พูดอีกทีได้ไหม

reservation jorng
จอง

I'd like to make a reservation kŏr jorng
ขอจอง

dialogue

I have a reservation pǒm
(chún) dâi jorng wái láir-o
yes sir, what name please?
krúp kOOn chêu a-rai?

reserve (verb) jorng
จอง

dialogue

can I reserve a table for
tonight? chún kǒr jorng
dtór sǔm-rùp keun née
dâi mái?
yes madam, for how many
people? dâi krúp mee gèe
kon?
for two sǒrng kon
and for what time? láir-o
gèe mohng?
for eight o'clock sǒrng
tôOm
and could I have your
name, please? láir-o
kOOn chêu a-rai krúp?

rest: I need a rest pǒm (chún)
dtôrng púk pòrn
ผม(ฉัน)ต้องพักผ่อน
the rest of the group pôo-uk

kon èun
พวกคนอื่น
restaurant ráhn ah-hǎhn
ร้านอาหาร

 Throughout the country
most cheap Thai
restaurants and cafés
specialize in one general food type
or preparation method – a 'noodle
shop' for example will do fried
noodles and noodle soups, plus a
basic fried rice, but they won't have
curries, meat or fish dishes.
Similarly, a restaurant displaying
whole roast chickens and ducks in
its window will offer these sliced or
with chillis and sauces and served
over rice, but their menu probably
won't extend to noodles or fish,
while in 'curry shops' your options
are limited to the vats of curries
stewing away in the hot cabinet.
To get a choice of low-cost food, it's
sometimes best to head for the local
night market, a term for the
gatherings of open-air night-time
kitchens found in every town.
Operating from about 6 p.m. to 6
a.m., they are to be found close to
the fruit and vegetable market or
bus station. Having decided what

you want, you order from the cook and sit down at the nearest table; there's no territorialism about night markets, so it's normal to eat several dishes from separate stalls and rely on the nearest cook to sort out the bill.

For a more relaxing ambience, Bangkok and Chiangmai both have a range of gourmet restaurants specializing in 'royal' Thai cuisine, which differs from standard fare mainly in the quality of the ingredients and the way the food is presented.

restaurant car rót sa-bee-ung
รถเสบียง

rest room hôrng náhm
ห้องน้ำ

retired: I'm retired pŏm
(chún) ga-see-un
ผม(ฉัน)เกษียน

return: a return to ... dtŏo-a
bpai glùp ...
ตั๋วไปกลับ ...

return ticket dtŏo-a bpai glùp
ตั๋วไปกลับ
see ticket

reverse charge call toh-ra-sùp
gèp ngern bplai tahng
โทรศัพท์เก็บเงินปลายทาง

reverse gear gee-a tŏy lŭng
เกียร์ถอยหลัง

revolting nâh rung-gèe-ut
น่ารังเกียจ

rib sêe krohng
ซี่โครง

rice kâo
ข้าว

rich (person) roo-ay
รวย
(food) mun
มัน

ridiculous nâh hŏo-a rór
น่าหัวเราะ

right (correct) tòok
ถูก
(not left) kwăh
ขวา

you were right kOOn tòok
láir-o
คุณถูกแล้ว

that's right tòok láir-o
ถูกแล้ว

this can't be right mâi tòok
nâir nâir
ไม่ถูกแน่ๆ

right! ao lá!
เอาละ

is this the right road for ...?
bpai ... tahng ta-nŏn née
tòok mái?
ไป ... ทางถนนนี้ถูกไหม

on the right tahng **kwăh**
ทางขวา

turn right lée-o **kwăh**
เลี้ยวขวา

right-hand drive poo-ung
ma-lai kwăh
พวงมาลัยขวา

ring (on finger) wăirn
แหวน

I'll ring you pŏm (chún) ja
toh bpai tĕung
ผม(ฉัน)จะโทรไปถึง

ring back toh glùp mah
โทรกลับมา

ripe (fruit) sÒOk
สุก

rip-off: it's a rip-off lòrk
dtôm
หลอกต้ม

rip-off prices rah-kah lòrk
dtôm
ราคาหลอกต้ม

risky sèe-ung
เสี่ยง

river mâir náhm
แม่น้ำ

road (in town, country) ta-nŏn
ถนน

is this the road for ...?
nêe ta-nŏn bpai ... châi
mái?
นี่ถนนไป ... ใช่ไหม

down the road yòo glâi glâi
kâir née
อยู่ใกล้ๆแค่นี้

road accident rót chon gun
รถชนกัน

road map păirn-têe ta-nŏn
แผนที่ถนน

roadsign krêu-ung măi ja-rah
jorn
เครื่องหมายจราจร

rob: I've been robbed pŏm
(chún) tòok ka-moy-ee
ผม(ฉัน)ถูกขโมย

rock hĭn
หิน

(music) rórk
ร็อค

on the rocks (with ice) sài núm
kăirng
ใส่น้ำแข็ง

roll (bread) ka-nŏm-bpung
ขนมปัง

roof lŭng-kah
หลังคา

roof rack gròrp dtìt lŭng-kah
rót
กรอบติดหลังคารถ

room hôrng
ห้อง

in my room nai hôrng pŏm
(chún)
ในห้องผม(ฉัน)

dialogue

do you have any rooms?
mee hôrng wâhng mái?

for how many people?
sŭm-rùp gèe kon?

for one/for two kon dee-o/sŏrng kon

yes, we have rooms free
mee, mee hôrng wâhng

for how many nights will it be? yòo gèe keun?

just for one night keun dee-o tâo-nún

how much is it? keun la tâo-rài?

can I see it? kŏr doo nòy dâi mái?

OK, I'll take it oh-kay, ao

room service bor-ri-gahn rúp chái nai hôrng púk
บริการรับใช้ในห้องพัก

rope chêu-uk
เชือก

roughly (approximately) bpra-mahn
ประมาณ

round: it's my round bpen tee kŏrng pŏm
เป็นที่ของผม

roundabout (for traffic) wong wee-un
วงเวียน

round trip ticket dtŏo-a bpai glùp
ตั๋วไปกลับ

route tahng
ทาง

what's the best route?
bpai tahng năi dee têe sòOt?
ไปทางไหนดีที่สุด

royal family
The royal family is universally esteemed in Thailand, where almost every household displays a picture of King Bhumibol and Queen Sirikit in a prominent position. When addressing or speaking about royalty, Thais use a special language full of deferentials, called **râht-cha-sùp** (literally: royal language). Even a hint of disrespect will cause deep offence – as the monarch's head features on all Thai currency, you should never step on a coin or banknote because this would be tantamount to kicking the king in the face.

rubber (material) yahng
ยาง
(eraser) yahng lóp
ยางลบ

rubber band yahng rút
ยางรัด

rubbish (waste) ka-yà
ขยะ
(poor quality goods) mâi ao
nǎi
ไม่เอาไหน

rubbish! (nonsense) mâi bpen
rêu-ung!
ไม่เป็นเรื่อง

rucksack bpây lǔng
เป้หลัง

rude mâi sOO-pâhp
ไม่สุภาพ

ruins sâhk sa-lùk hùk
pung
ซากสลักหักพัง

rum lâo rum
เหล้ารัม

rum and Coke® rum airn
kóhk
รัมแอนด์โค้ก

run (verb: person) wîng
วิ่ง

how often do the buses run?
rót may wîng tèe mái?
รถเมล์วิ่งถี่ไหม

I've run out of money pǒm

(chún) mót ngern
ผม(ฉัน)หมดเงิน

S

sad sâo
เศร้า

saddle (for bike) ahn jùk-gra-
yahn
อานจักรยาน
(for horse) ahn máh
อานม้า

safe (not in danger) bplòrt-pai
ปลอดภัย
(not dangerous) mâi
un-dta-rai
ไม่อันตราย

safety pin kěm glùt
เข็มกลัด

sail (noun) bai reu-a
ใบเรือ

sailboard (noun) gra-dahn
dtôh lom
กระดานโต้ลม

sailboarding gahn lên gra-
dahn dtôh lom
การเล่นกระดานโต้ลม

salad sa-lùt
สลัด

salad dressing náhm sa-lùt
น้ำสลัด

sale: for sale kăi
ขาย

salt gleu-a
เกลือ

same: the same měu-un gun
เหมือนกัน

the same as this měu-un
yàhng née
เหมือนอย่างนี้

the same again, please kŏr
yàhng derm
ขออย่างเดิม

it's all the same to me a-rai
gôr dâi
อะไรก็ได้

sand sai
ทราย

sandals rorng táo dtàir
รองเท้าแตะ

sandwich sairn-wít
แซนด์วิช

sanitary napkins, sanitary
towels pâh un-nah-mai
ผ้าอนามัย

Saturday wun săo
วันเสาร์

sauce núm jîm
น้ำจิ้ม

saucepan môr
หม้อ

saucer jahn rorng tôo-ay
จานรองถ้วย

sauna sao-nah
เซานา

sausage sâi gròrk
ไส้กรอก

say (verb) bòrk, pôot
บอก, พูด

how do you say ... in Thai?
pah-săh tai ... pôot wâh
yung-ngai?
ภาษาไทย ... พูดว่าอย่างไร

what did he say? káo pôot
wâh yung-ngai?
เขาพูดว่าอย่างไร

she said ... káo bòrk wâh ...
เขาบอกว่า ...

could you say that again?
pôot èek tee dâi mái?
พูดอีกทีได้ไหม

scarf (for neck) pâh pun
kor
ผ้าพันคอ

(for head) pâh pôhk sĕe-sà
ผ้าโพกศีรษะ

scenery poo-mi-bpra-tâyt
ภูมิประเทศ

schedule (US) dtah-rahng
way-lah
ตารางเวลา

scheduled flight dtah-rahng
têe-o bin

school rohng ree-un
โรงเรียน

scissors: a pair of scissors
dta-grai
ตะไกร

scooter rót sa-góot-dter
รถสกู๊ตเตอร์

scotch lâo wít-sa-gêe
เหล้าวิสกี้

Scotch tape® sa-górt táyp
สก๊อตเทป

Scotland sa-górt-lairn
สกอตแลนด์

Scottish kon sa-górt
คนสกอต

I'm Scottish pǒm (chún)
bpen kon sa-górt
ผม(ฉัน)เป็นคนสกอต

scrambled eggs kài kon
ไข่ขน

scratch (noun) roy kòo-un
รอยขว่วน

screw (noun) dta-bpoo koo-
ung
ตะปูควง

screwdriver kǎi koo-ung
ไขควง

sea ta-lay
ทะเล

by the sea chai ta-lay
ชายทะเล

seafood ah-hǎhn ta-lay
อาหารทะเล

seafood restaurant pút-ta-
kahn ah-hǎhn ta-lay
ภัตตาคารอาหารทะเล

seafront chai ta-lay
ชายทะเล

seagull nók nahng noo-un
นกนางนวล

search (verb) hǎh
หา

seashell bplèu-uk hǒy
เปลือกหอย

seasick: I feel seasick pǒm
(chún) róo-sèuk mao klêun
ผม(ฉัน)รู้สึกเมาคลื่น

I get seasick pǒm (chún)
mao klêun ngâi
ผม(ฉัน)เมาคลื่นง่าย

seaside: by the seaside chai
ta-lay
ชายทะเล

seat têe nûng
ที่นั่ง

is this seat taken? têe nêe
wâhng mái?
ที่นี่ว่างไหม

seat belt kěm kùt ni-ra-pai
เข็มขัดนิรภัย

sea urchin bpling ta-lay
ปลิงทะเล

seaweed sǎh-rài-ta-lay
สาหร่ายทะเล

secluded dòht dèe-o
โดดเดี่ยว

second (adj) têe sŏrng
ที่สอง
(of time) wí-nah-tee
วินาที
just a second! děe-o gòrn!
เดี๋ยวก่อน
second class (travel etc) chún
sŏrng
ชั้นสอง
second floor (UK) chún nèung
ชั้นหนึ่ง
(US) chún sŏrng
ชั้นสอง
see hĕn
เห็น
can I see? kŏr doo nòy, dâi
mái?
ขอดูหน่อยได้ไหม
have you seen ...? hĕn ... rĕu
bplào?
เห็น ... หรือเปล่า
I saw him this morning hĕn
mêu-a cháo née
เห็นเมื่อเช้านี้
see you! jer gun mài ná!
เจอกันใหม่นะ
I see (I understand) kâo jai
láir-o
เข้าใจแล้ว
self-service bor-ri-gahn
chôo-ay dtoo-a ayng
บริการช่วยตัวเอง

sell kăi
ขาย
do you sell ...? mee ... kăi
mái?
มี ... ขายไหม
Sellotape® sa-górt táyp
สก๊อตเทป
send sòng
ส่ง
I want to send this to England
pŏm (chún) yàhk ja sòng
nêe bpai ung-grìt
ผม(ฉัน)อยากจะส่งนี้ไปอังกฤษ
senior citizen kon cha-rah
คนชรา
separate dtàhng hàhk
ต่างหาก
separated: I'm separated
(man) pŏm yâirk gun gùp
pun-ra-yah
ผมแยกกันกับภรรยา
(woman) chún yâirk gun gùp
săh-mee
ฉันแยกกันกับสามี
separately (pay, travel) yâirk
gun
แยกกัน
September gun-yah-yon
กันยายน
septic mee chéu-a
มีเชื้อ
serious (person) ao jing ao

jung
เอาจริงเอาจัง

(situation) dtreung krêe-ut
ตรึงเครียด

(problem, illness) nùk
หนัก

service charge (in restaurant)
kâh bor-ri-gahn
ค่าบริการ

service station bpúm núm
mun
ปั๊มน้ำมัน

serviette pâh chét bpàhk
ผ้าเช็ดปาก

set menu ah-hǎhn chóOt
อาหารชุด

several lǎi
หลาย

sew yép
เย็บ

could you sew this back on?
chôo-ay yép hâi nòy dâi
mái?
ช่วยเย็บให้หน่อยได้ไหม

sex gahn rôo-um bpra-way-
nee
การร่วมประเวณี

sexy sek-sêe
เซ็กซี่

shade: in the shade nai rôm
ในร่ม

shake: let's shake hands jùp

meu gun
จับมือกัน

shallow (water) dtêun
ตื้น

shame: what a shame! nâh
sěe-a dai!
น่าเสียดาย

shampoo (noun) chairm-poo
แชมพู

shampoo and set sà sét
สระเซ็ท

share (verb: room, table etc)
bàirng
แบ่ง

sharp (knife) kom
คม

(taste) bprêe-o
เปรี้ยว

(pain) sěe-o
เสียว

shattered (very tired) nèu-ay
mâhk
เหนื่อยมาก

shaver krêu-ung gohn nòo-
ut
เครื่องโกนหนวด

shaving foam kreem gohn
nòo-ut
ครีมโกนหนวด

shaving point bplúk krêu-ung
gohn nòo-ut
ปลั๊กเครื่องโกนหนวด

she* káo
เขา

is she here? káo yòo têe nêe
mái?
เขาอยู่ที่นี่ไหม

sheet (for bed) pâh bpoo têe
norn
ผ้าปูที่นอน

shelf hîng
หิ้ง

shellfish hŏy
หอย

ship reu-a
เรือ

by ship tahng reu-a
ทางเรือ

shirt sêu-a chért
เสื้อเชิ้ต

shit! âi hàh!
ไอ้ห่า

shock: I got an electric shock
from the ... pŏm (chún) tòok
fai chórk têe ...
ผม(ฉัน)ถูกไฟช็อคที่ ...

shock-absorber chórk
ช็อค

shocked dtòk jai
ตกใจ

shocking lĕu-a gern jing jing
เหลือเกินจริงๆ

shoe rorng táo
รองเท้า

a pair of shoes rorng táo
kôo nèung
รองเท้าคู่หนึ่ง

shoelaces chêu-uk pòok
rorng táo
เชือกผูกรองเท้า

shoe polish yah kùt rorng táo
ยาขัดรองเท้า

shoe repairer kon sôrm rorng
táo
คนซ่อมรองเท้า

shop ráhn
ร้าน

Most shops open at least
Monday to Saturday from
about 8 a.m. to 8 p.m.,
while department stores are open
daily from around 9.30 a.m. to 9
p.m.

shopping: I'm going shopping
pŏm (chún) bpai séu kŏrng
ผม(ฉัน)ไปซื้อของ

shopping centre sŏon gahn
káh
ศูนย์การค้า

shop window nâh gra-jòk
ráhn
หน้ากระจกร้าน

shore chai fûng
ชายฝั่ง

short (person) dtêe-a
เตี้ย

(time) sûn
สั้น

shortcut tahng lút
ทางลัด

shorts gahng-gayng kǎh sûn
กางเกงขาสั้น

(US: underwear) gahng gayng
nai
กางเกงใน

should: what should I do?
pǒm (chún) koo-un ja tum
yung-ngai?
ผม(ฉัน)ควรจะทำอย่างไร

you should ... kOOn
koo-un ja ...
คุณควรจะ ...

you shouldn't ... kOOn mâi
koo-un ja ...
คุณไม่ควรจะ ...

he should be back soon děe-
o káo kong glùp mah
เดี๋ยวเขาคงกลับมา

shoulder lài
ไหล่

shout (verb) dta-gohn
ตะโกน

show (in theatre) gahn sa-
dairng
การแสดง

could you show me? kǒr doo

nòy
ขอดูหน่อย

shower (rain) fǒn bproy bproy
ฝนปรอยๆ

(in bathroom) fùk boo-a
ฝักบัว

with shower mee fùk boo-a
มีฝักบัว

shower gel kreem àhp náhm
ครีมอาบน้ำ

shut (verb) bpìt
ปิด

when do you shut? kOOn
bpìt gèe mohng?
คุณปิดกี่โมง

when does it shut? bpìt gèe
mohng?
ปิดกี่โมง

they're shut káo bpìt láir-o
เขาปิดแล้ว

I've shut myself out leum ao
gOOn-jair òrk mah
ลืมเอากุญแจออกมา

shut up! yÒOt pôot ná!
หยุดพูดนะ

shutter (on camera) chút-dter
ชัตเตอร์

(on window) bahn glèt nâh-
dtàhng
บานเกล็ดหน้าต่าง

shy ai
อาย

sick (ill) mâi sa-bai
ไม่สบาย

I'm going to be sick (vomit)
róo-sèuk wâh klêun sâi
รู้สึกว่าคลื่นไส้

side kâhng
ข้าง

the other side of the street
èek fàhk nèung kŏrng ta-
nŏn
อีกฟากหนึ่งของถนน

sidelights fai kâhng
ไฟข้าง

side salad sa-lùt
สลัด

side street soy
ซอย

sidewalk bàht wít-tĕe
บาทวิถี

sight: the sights of ... sa-tăhn-
têe nâh têe-o nai ...
สถานที่น่าเที่ยวใน ...

sightseeing: we're going
sightseeing rao ja bpai têe-o
เราจะไปเที่ยว

sightseeing tour rai gahn
num têe-o
รายการนำเที่ยว

sign (roadsign etc) bpâi sŭn-
yahn ja-rah-jorn
ป้ายสัญญาณจราจร

signal: he didn't give a signal

(driver, cyclist) káo mâi dâi hâi
sŭn-yahn
เขาไม่ได้ให้สัญญาณ

signature lai sen
ลายเซ็น

signpost dtìt bpâi ja-rah-jorn
ติดป้ายจราจร

silence kwahm ngêe-up
ความเงียบ

silk măi
ไหม

silly ngôh
โง่

silver (noun) ngern
เงิน

silver foil gra-dàht dta-gòo-a
กระดาษตะกั่ว

similar mĕu-un
เหมือน

simple (easy) ngâi
ง่าย

since: since last week dtûng
dtàir ah-tít gòrn
ตั้งแต่อาทิตย์ก่อน

since I got here dtûng dtàir
pŏm (chún) mah tĕung
ตั้งแต่ผม(ฉัน)มาถึง

sing rórng playng
ร้องเพลง

singer núk rórng
นักร้อง

single: a single to ... dtŏo-a

Si

bpai ...
ตั๋วไป ...
I'm single pǒm (chún) bpen sòht
ผม(ฉัน)เป็นโสด
single bed dtee-ung dèe-o
เตียงเดี่ยว
single room hôrng dèe-o
ห้องเดี่ยว
single ticket dtŏo-a bpai
ตั๋วไป
sink (in kitchen) àhng
อ่าง
sister (older) pêe sǎo
พี่สาว
(younger) nórng sǎo
น้องสาว
sister-in-law (older) pêe sa-pái kǒrng
พี่สะใภ้ของ
(younger) nórng sa-pái kǒrng
น้องสะใภ้ของ
sit: can I sit here? kŏr nûng têe nêe, dâi mái?
ขอนั่งที่นี่ได้ไหม
is anyone sitting here? mee kon nûng têe nêe rěu bplào?
มีคนนั่งที่นี่หรือเปล่า
sit down nûng
นั่ง
do sit down chern nûng see
เชิญนั่งซิ

size ka-nàht
ขนาด
skin pěw
ผิว
skin-diving gahn dum náhm léuk
การดำน้ำลึก
skinny pǒrm
ผอม
skirt gra-bprohng
กระโปรง
sky fáh
ฟ้า
sleep (verb) norn lùp
นอนหลับ
did you sleep well? lùp dee mái?
หลับดีไหม
sleeper (on train) rót norn
รถนอน
sleeping bag tǒong norn
ถุงนอน
sleeping car rót norn
รถนอน
sleeping pill yah norn lùp
ยานอนหลับ
sleepy: I'm feeling sleepy pǒm (chún) ngôo-ung norn
ผม(ฉัน)ง่วงนอน
sleeve kǎirn sêu-a
แขนเสื้อ

slide (photographic) sa-lai
สไลด์

slip (garment) gra-bprohng
chún nai
กระโปรงชั้นใน

slippery lêun
ลื่น

slow cháh
ช้า

slow down! (driving) kùp cháh
cháh nòy!
ขับช้า ๆ หน่อย
(speaking) pôot cháh cháh
nòy!
พูดช้า ๆ หน่อย

slowly cháh
ช้า

very slowly cháh mâhk
ช้ามาก

small lék
เล็ก

smell: it smells (smells bad)
měn
เหม็น

smile (verb) yím
ยิ้ม

smoke (noun) kwun
ควัน

do you mind if I smoke?
kŏr sòop bOO-rèe dâi
mái?
ขอสูบบุหรี่ได้ไหม

I don't smoke pŏm (chún)
mâi sòop bOO-rèe
ผม(ฉัน)ไม่สูบบุหรี่

do you smoke? kOOn sòop
bOO-rèe mái?
คุณสูบบุหรี่ไหม

snake ngoo
งู

sneeze (verb) jahm
จาม

snorkel tôr hǎi jai
ท่อหายใจ

snow (noun) hí-má
หิมะ

so: it's so good dee jung ler-
ee
ดีจังเลย

it's so expensive pairng jung
ler-ee
แพงจังเลย

not so much mâi kôy mâhk
ไม่ค่อยมาก

not so bad mâi kôy lay-o
ไม่ค่อยเลว

so am I pŏm (chún) gôr
měu-un gun
ผม(ฉัน)ก็เหมือนกัน

so do I pŏm (chún) gôr
měu-un gun
ผม(ฉัน)ก็เหมือนกัน

so-so rêu-ay rêu-ay
เรื่อย ๆ

soap sa-bòo
สบู่

soap powder pǒng súk
fòrk
ผงซักฟอก

sober mâi mao
ไม่เมา

sock tǒOng táo
ถุงเท้า

socket (electrical) bplúk fai
ปลั๊กไฟ

soda (water) núm soh-dah
น้ำโซดา

sofa têe nûng rúp kàirk
ที่นั่งรับแขก

soft (material etc) nîm
นิ่ม

soft drink náhm kòo-ut
น้ำขวด

sole (of shoe, of foot) péun
rorng táo
พื้นรองเท้า

could you put new soles on
these? sài péun rórng táo
mài hâi nòy, dâi mái?
ใส่พื้นรองเท้าใหม่ให้หน่อย
ได้ไหม

some bahng
บาง

some people bahng kon
บางคน

can I have some? kǒr nòy,

dâi mái?
ขอหน่อยได้ไหม

somebody, someone krai
ใคร

something a-rai
อะไร

something to eat kǒrng gin
ของกิน

sometimes bahng tee
บางที

somewhere têe nǎi
ที่ไหน

son lôok chai
ลูกชาย

song playng
เพลง

son-in-law lôok kěr-ee
ลูกเขย

soon děe-o
เดี๋ยว

I'll be back soon děe-o glùp
ná
เดี๋ยวกลับนะ

as soon as possible yàhng
ray-o tée sÒOt tée ja ray-o
dâi
อย่างเร็วที่สุดที่จะเร็วได้

sore: it's sore jèp
เจ็บ

sore throat jèp kor
เจ็บคอ

sorry: (I'm) sorry pǒm (chún)

sĕe-a jai
ผม(ฉัน)เสียใจ

sorry? (didn't understand) a-rai na?
อะไรนะ

sort: what sort of ...? ... bàirp nǎi?
... แบบไหน

soup sÓOp
ซุป

sour (taste) bprêe-o
เปรี้ยว

south dtâi
ใต้

in the south nai pâhk dtâi
ในภาคใต้

South Africa ah-fri-gah dtâi
อาฟริกาใต้

South China Sea ta-lay jeen dtâi
ทะเลจีนใต้

southeast dta-wun òrk chêe-ung dtâi
ตะวันออกเฉียงใต้

southwest dta-wun dtòk chêe-ung dtâi
ตะวันตกเฉียงใต้

souvenir kŏrng têe ra-léuk
ของที่ระลึก

soy sauce núm see éw
น้ำซีอิ๊ว

Spain bpra-tâyt sa-bpayn
ประเทศสเปน

spanner gOOn-jair bpàhk dtai
กุญแจปากตาย

spare part a-lài
อะไหล่

spare tyre yahng a-lài
ยางอะไหล่

spark plug hǒo-a tee-un
หัวเทียน

speak: do you speak English? kOOn pôot pah-sǎh ung-grìt bpen mái?
คุณพูดภาษาอังกฤษเป็นไหม

I don't speak ... pǒm (chún) pôot ... mâi bpen
ผม(ฉัน)พูด ... ไม่เป็น

can I speak to ...? kŏr pôot gùp ... nòy, dâi mái?
ขอพูดกับ ... หน่อยได้ไหม

dialogue

can I speak to Tongchai? kŏr pôot gùp kOOn Tong-chai nòy, dâi mái kâ?
who's calling? krai pôot krúp?
it's Patricia chún Patricia pôot kâ
I'm sorry, he's not in, can I

take a message? káo mâi yòo krúp mee a-rai ja fàhk bòrk mái?

no thanks, I'll call back later mâi mee kâ ja toh glùp mah dtorn lǔng

please tell him I called chôo-ay bòrk káo wâh chún toh mah

spectacles wâirn dtah
แว่นตา

speed (noun) kwahm ray-o
ความเร็ว

speed limit ùt-dtrah kwahm ray-o
อัตราความเร็ว

speedometer krêu-ung wút kwahm ray-o
เครื่องวัดความเร็ว

spell: how do you spell it? sa-gòt yung-ngai?
สะกดอย่างไร

spend chái ngern
ใช้เงิน

spider mairng mOOm
แมงมุม

spin-dryer krêu-ung bpùn pâh hâi hâirng
เครื่องปั่นผ้าให้แห้ง

splinter sa-gèt mái
สะเก็ดไม้

spoke (in wheel) sêe lór rót
ซี่ล้อรถ

spoon chórn
ช้อน

sport gee-lah
กีฬา

sprain: I've sprained my ... pŏm (chún) tum ... klét
ผม(ฉัน)ทำเคล็ด ...

spring (season) réu-doo bai mái plì
ฤดูใบไม้ผลิ

in the spring dtorn réu-doo bai mái plì
ตอนฤดูใบไม้ผลิ

squid bplah-mèuk
ปลาหมึก

stairs bun-dai
บันได

stale mâi sòt
ไม่สด

stall: the engine keeps stalling krêu-ung dùp bòy
เครื่องดับบ่อย

stamp (noun) sa-dtairm
แสตมป์

dialogue

a stamp for England, please kŏr sa-dtairm sòng bpai ung-grìt

what are you sending?
kOOn ja sòng a-rai bpai?

this postcard bpóht-káht
nêe

Post offices are the best places to buy stamps, though hotels and guesthouses often sell them too, charging an extra baht per stamp. All parcels must be officially boxed and sealed at special counters within main post offices or in a private outlet just outside – you can't just turn up with a package and buy stamps for it.

standby 'standby'

star dao
ดาว
(in film) dah-rah nǔng
ดาราหนัง

start (verb) rêrm
เริ่ม

when does it start? rêrm
mêu-rai?
เริ่มเมื่อไร

the car won't start rót sa-
dtàht mâi dtìt
รถสตาร์ทไม่ติด

starter (of car) bpÒOm sa-
dtàht
ปุ่มสตาร์ท

starving: I'm starving pǒm
(chún) hěw jung ler-ee
ผม(ฉัน)หิวจังเลย

state (country) rút
รัฐ

the States (USA) sa-hǎh-rút
สหรัฐ

station sa-tǎh-nee rót fai
สถานีรถไฟ

statue rôop bpûn
รูปปั้น

**stay: where are you
staying?** kOOn púk yòo têe
nǎi?
คุณพักอยู่ที่ไหน

I'm staying at ... pǒm (chún)
púk yòo têe ...
ผม(ฉัน)พักอยู่ที่ ...

**I'd like to stay another two
nights** pǒm (chún) yàhk ja
púk yòo èek sǒrng keun
ผม(ฉัน)อยากจะพักอยู่
อีกสองคืน

steak néu-a sa-dték
เนื้อเสต๊ก

steal ka-moy-ee
ขโมย

my bag has been stolen gra-
bpǎo tòok ka-moy-ee
กระเป๋าถูกขโมย

steep (hill) chun
ชัน

177

steering mǒOn poo-ung mah-lai
หมุนพวงมาลัย

step: on the steps têe kûn bun-dai
ที่ขึ้นบันได

stereo sa-dtay-ri-oh
สเตริโอ

sterling ngern bporn
เงินปอนด์

steward (on plane) pa-núk ngahn krêu-ung bin
พนักงานเครื่องบิน

stewardess pa-núk ngahn dtôrn rúp bon krêu-ung bin
พนักงานต้อนรับบนเครื่องบิน

sticking plaster plah-sa-dter
พลาสเตอร์

sticky rice kâo něe-o
ข้าวเหนียว

still: I'm still here pǒm (chún) yung yòo têe nêe
ผม(ฉัน)ยังอยู่ที่นี่

is he still there? káo yung yòo têe nûn mái?
เขายังอยู่ที่นั่นไหม

keep still! yòo nîng nîng!
อยู่นิ่ง ๆ

sting: I've been stung pǒm (chún) tòok ma-lairng dtòy
ผม(ฉัน)ถูกแมลงต่อย

stockings tǒOng nôrng
ถุงน่อง

stomach tórng
ท้อง

stomach ache bpòo-ut tórng
ปวดท้อง

stone (rock) hǐn
หิน

stop (verb) yòOt
หยุด

please stop here (to taxi driver etc) yòOt dtrong née krúp (kâ)
หยุดตรงนี้ครับ(ค่ะ)

do you stop near ...? kOOn yòOt glâi glâi ... mái?
คุณหยุดใกล้ ๆ ... ไหม

stop it! yòOt na!
หยุดนะ

stopover wáir
แวะ

storm pah-yÓO
พายุ

straight: it's straight ahead yòo dtrong nâh
อยู่ตรงหน้า

a straight whisky wít-sa-gêe pee-o
วิสกี้เพียว

straightaway tun-tee
ทันที

strange (odd) bplàirk
แปลก

stranger kon bplàirk nâh
คนแปลกหน้า

I'm a stranger here pǒm
(chún) mâi châi kon têe
nêe
ผม(ฉัน)ไม่ใช่คนที่นี่

strap sǎi
สาย

strawberry sa-dtor-ber-rêe
สตรอเบอร์รี่

stream lum-tahn
ลำธาร

street ta-nǒn
ถนน

on the street bon ta-nǒn
บนถนน

streetmap pǎirn-têe ta-nǒn
แผนที่ถนน

string chêu-uk
เชือก

strong kǎirng rairng
แข็งแรง

stuck dtìt
ติด

it's stuck mun dtìt
มันติด

student núk-sèuk-sǎh
นักศึกษา

stupid ngôh
โง่

suburb bor-ri-wayn chahn
meu-ung
บริเวณชานเมือง

suddenly tun-tee
ทันที

suede nǔng glùp
หนังกลับ

sugar núm dtahn
น้ำตาล

suit (noun) chóOt
ชุด

it doesn't suit me (jacket etc)
mâi **mòr gùp** pǒm
(chún)
ไม่เหมาะกับผม(ฉัน)

it suits you **mòr gùp** kOOn
dâi dee
เหมาะกับคุณได้ดี

suitcase gra-bpǎo dern
tahng
กระเป๋าเดินทาง

summer nâh rórn
หน้าร้อน

in the summer dtorn nâh
rórn
ตอนหน้าร้อน

sun prá-ah-tít
พระอาทิตย์

in the sun dtàhk dàirt
ตากแดด

out of the sun nai rôm
ในร่ม

sunbathe àhp dàirt
อาบแดด

sunblock (cream) yah tah gun dàirt
ยาทากันแดด

sunburn tòok dàirt
ถูกแดด

sunburnt tòok dàirt mâi
ถูกแดดไหม้

Sunday wun ah-tít
วันอาทิตย์

sunglasses wâirn gun dàirt
แว่นกันแดด

sun lounger máh nûng àhp dàirt
ม้านั่งอาบแดด

sunny: it's sunny dàirt òrk
แดดออก

sunroof (in car) lŭng-kah gra-jòk
หลังคากระจก

sunset ah-tít dtòk
อาทิตย์ตก

sunshade ngao dàirt
เงาแดด

sunshine dàirt òrk
แดดออก

sunstroke rôhk páir dàirt
โรคแพ้แดด

suntan pĕw klúm dàirt
ผิวคล้ำแดด

suntan lotion kreem tah àhp dàirt
ครีมทาอาบแดด

suntanned mee pĕw klúm dàirt
มีผิวคล้ำแดด

suntan oil núm mun tah àhp dàirt
น้ำมันทาอาบแดด

super yôrt yêe-um
ยอดเยี่ยม

supermarket sOO-bper-mah-get
ซุปเปอร์มาร์เก็ต

supper ah-hăhn yen
อาหารเย็น

supplement (extra charge) kâh bor-ri-gahn pi-sàyt
ค่าบริการพิเศษ

sure: are you sure? kOOn nâir-jai rĕu?
คุณแน่ใจหรือ

sure! nâir-norn!
แน่นอน

surname nahm sa-gOOn
นามสกุล

swearword kum sa-bòt
คำสบถ

sweater sêu-a sa-wet-dter
สเวตเตอร์

Sweden bpra-tâyt sa-wee-den
ประเทศสวีเดน

sweet (taste) wǎhn
หวาน
(noun: dessert) kǒrng wǎhn
ของหวาน

sweets tórp-fêe
ท้อฟฟี่

swelling boo-um
บวม

swim (verb) wâi náhm
ว่ายน้ำ

I'm going for a swim pǒm
(chún) bpai wâi náhm
ผม(ฉัน)ไปว่ายน้ำ

let's go for a swim bpai wâi
náhm mái?
ไปว่ายน้ำไหม

swimming costume chÓOt
àhp náhm
ชุดอาบน้ำ

swimming pool sà wâi náhm
สระว่ายน้ำ

swimming trunks gahng-
gayng wâi náhm
กางเกงว่ายน้ำ

switch (noun) sa-wít
สวิช

switch off bpìt
ปิด

switch on bpèrt
เปิด

Switzerland bpra-tâyt sa-wít
ประเทศสวิส

swollen boo-um
บวม

T

table dtó
โต๊ะ

a table for two dtó sǔm-rùp
sǒrng kon
โต๊ะสำหรับสองคน

tablecloth pâh bpoo dtó
ผ้าปูโต๊ะ

table tennis bping bporng
ปิงปอง

tailback (of traffic) rót dtìt
รถติด

tailor châhng dtùt sêu-a
pâh
ช่างตัดเสื้อผ้า

take (lead: something somewhere)
ao ... bpai
เอา ... ไป
(someone somewhere) pah ...
bpai
พา ... ไป

take (accept) rúp
รับ

can you take me to the ...?
pah bpai ... dâi mái?
พาไป ... ได้ไหม

do you take credit cards? rúp

bùt kray-dìt rĕu bplào?
รับบัตรเครดิตหรือเปล่า

fine, I'll take it oh kay, pŏm
(chún) ao
โอเค ผม(ฉัน)เอา

can I take this? (leaflet etc) kŏr
un née dâi mái?
ขออันนี้ได้ไหม

how long does it take? chái
way-lah nahn tâo-rài?
ใช้เวลานานเท่าไร

it takes three hours chái
way-lah săhm chôo-a
mohng
ใช้เวลาสามชั่วโมง

is this seat taken? têe née
wâhng mái?
ที่นี่ว่างไหม

can you take a little off here?
(to hairdresser) dtùt dtrong née
òrk nít-nòy dâi mái?
ตัดตรงนี้ออกนิดหน่อยได้ไหม

talcum powder bpâirng
แป้ง

talk (verb) pôot
พูด

tall sŏong
สูง

tampons tairm-porn
แทมพอน

tan (noun) klúm
คล้ำ

to get a tan hâi pĕw klúm
ให้ผิวคล้ำ

tank (of car) tŭng núm mun
ถังน้ำมัน

tap górk náhm
ก๊อกน้ำ

tape (for cassette) táyp
เทป

tape measure săi wút
สายวัด

tape recorder krêu-ung bun-
téuk sĕe-ung
เครื่องบันทึกเสียง

taste (noun) rót
รส

can I taste it? kŏr **lorng
chim** nòy, dâi mái?
ขอลองชิมหน่อยได้ไหม

taxi táirk-sêe
แท็กซี่

will you get me a taxi? chôo-
ay rêe-uk táirk-sêe hâi nòy,
dâi mái?
ช่วยเรียกแท็กซี่ให้หน่อย
ได้ไหม

dialogue

to the airport/to the
Regent Hotel, please bpai
sa-năhm bin/rohng rairm
ree-yen

how much will it be? tâo-rài?

300 baht sǎhm róy bàht

that's fine right here, thanks jòrt dtrong née na

The three-wheeled open-sided **tuk-tuk** is the classic Thai vehicle and is very cheap to hire. Tuk-tuks are also sometimes known as **samlors** (literally: three wheels), but the real samlors are tricycle rickshaws propelled by pedal-power alone. Slower and a great deal more stately than tuk-tuks, samlors operate pretty much everywhere except in Bangkok. It is customary to negotiate the price before the journey begins.

Motorbike taxis feature in both big towns and out-of-the-way places. In remote spots, they are often the only alternative to hitching or walking and are especially useful for getting between bus stops on main roads and to national parks or ancient ruins. Within towns motorbike taxi fares are comparable to those for tuk-tuks, but for trips to the outskirts the cost rises steeply. Car taxis are generally available only in the biggest towns, and charge fares that begin at around B40; a few have air-conditioning.

see bargaining

taxi-driver kon kùp táirk-sêe
คนขับแท็กซี่

taxi rank têe jòrt rót táirk-sêe
ที่จอดรถแท็กซี่

tea (drink) núm chah
น้ำชา

tea for one/two, please kŏr núm chah têe nèung/sŏrng têe
ขอน้ำชาที่หนึ่ง/สองที่

teabags chah tŏOng
ชาถุง

teach: could you teach me? sŏrn hâi dâi mái?
สอนให้ได้ไหม

teacher kroo
ครู

team teem
ทีม

teaspoon chórn chah
ช้อนชา

tea towel pâh chét jahn
ผ้าเช็ดจาน

teenager dèk wai rôOn
เด็กวัยรุ่น

telegram toh-ra-lâyk
โทรเลข

telephone toh-ra-sùp
โทรศัพท์
see phone

television toh-ra-tút
โทรทัศน์

tell: could you tell him ...?
chôo-ay bòrk káo wâh ...
nòy, dâi mái?
ช่วยบอกเขาว่า ...
หน่อยได้ไหม

temperature (weather) OOn-
na-ha-poom
อุณหภูมิ
(fever) kâi
ไข้

temple wút
วัด

tennis tay-nit
เทนนิส

tennis ball lôok ten-nít
ลูกเทนนิส

tennis court sa-nǎhm ten-nít
สนามเทนนิส

tennis racket mái dtee
ten-nít
ไม้ตีเทนนิส

tent dten
เต็นท์

term term
เทอร์ม

terminus (rail) sa-tǎh-nee
สถานี

terrible yâir
แย่

terrific yôrt yêe-um
ยอดเยี่ยม

Thai (adj) tai
ไทย
(language) pah-sǎh tai
ภาษาไทย
a Thai, the Thais kon tai
คนไทย

Thai attitudes

There are three specifically Thai concepts you're bound to come across. The first is **sanuk**, the wide-reaching philosophy of 'fun', which, crass as it sounds, Thais do their best to inject into any situation, even work. Hence the crowds of inebriated Thais who congregate at waterfalls and other beauty spots on public holidays, and the national waterfight which takes place every April on streets right across Thailand.

The Thais sometimes have a laissez-faire attitude to delayed buses and other inconveniences which can be explained by the concept of **jai yen** (literally: cool heart) and this is something everyone tries to maintain – most Thais hate raised voices, visible irritation and confrontations of any kind. Related to this is the oft-quoted response to a difficulty, **mâi bpen rai** (never mind, no problem, or it can't be helped), the verbal equivalent of an open-handed shoulder shrug which has its base in the Buddhist notion of karma.

Thailand (formal) bpra-tâyt tai
ประเทศไทย
(informal) meu-ung tai
เมืองไทย
than* gwàh
กว่า
smaller than lék gwàh
เล็กกว่า
thanks, thank you
kòrp-kOOn
ขอบคุณ
thank you very much kòrp-kOOn mâhk
ขอบคุณมาก
thanks for the lift korp-kOOn tee mah song
ขอบคุณที่มาส่ง
no thanks mâi ao kòrp-kOOn
ไม่เอาขอบคุณ

dialogue

thanks kòrp-kOOn
that's OK, don't mention it
mâi bpen rai

that: that boy pôo-chai kon nún
ผู้ชายคนนั้น
that girl pôo-yĭng kon nún
ผู้หญิงคนนั้น
that one un nún
อันนั้น
I hope that ... pŏm (chún) wŭng wâh ...
ผม(ฉัน)หวังว่า ...
that's nice sŏo-ay
สวย
is that ...? ... châi mái?
... ใช่ไหม
that's it (that's right) châi láir-o
ใช่แล้ว
the*
theatre rohng la-korn
โรงละคร
their kŏrng káo
ของเขา
theirs kŏrng káo
ของเขา
them káo
เขา

185

for them sŭm-rùp káo
สำหรับเขา

with them gùp káo
กับเขา

to them gàir káo
แก่เขา

who? – them krai? – pôo-uk káo
ใคร - พวกเขา

then (at that time) dtorn nún
ตอนนั้น

(after that) lŭng jàhk nún
หลังจากนั้น

there têe nûn
ที่นั่น

over there têe-nôhn
ที่โน่น

up there kâhng bon nún
ข้างบนนั้น

is/are there ...? mee ... mái?
มี ... ไหม

there is/are ... mee ...
มี ...

there you are (giving something) nêe krúp (kâ)
นี่ครับ(คะ)

thermometer bpròrt
ปรอท

Thermos flask® gra-dtìk náhm
กระติกน้ำ

these*: these men pôo-chai pôo-uk lào née
ผู้ชายพวกเหล่านี้

these women pôo-yǐng pôo-uk lào née
ผู้หญิงพวกเหล่านี้

I'd like these ao pôo-uk lào née
เอาพวกเหล่านี้

they káo
เขา

thick nǎh
หนา

(stupid) ngôh
โง่

thief ka-moy-ee
ขโมย

thigh nôrng
น่อง

thin pǒrm
ผอม

thing kǒrng
ของ

my things kǒrng pǒrm (chún)
ของผม(ฉัน)

think kít
คิด

I think so pǒm (chún) kít wâh yung-ngún
ผม(ฉัน)คิดว่าอย่างนั้น

I don't think so pǒm (chún)

kít wâh kong mâi
ผม(ฉัน)คิดว่าคงไม่

I'll think about it pŏm
(chún) ja lorng kít doo
gòrn
ผม(ฉัน)จะลองคิดดูก่อน

thirsty: I'm thirsty pŏm (chún)
hěw náhm
ผม(ฉัน)หิวน้ำ

this: this boy pôo-chai kon
née
ผู้ชายคนนี้

this girl pôo-yǐng kon née
ผู้หญิงคนนี้

this one un née
อันนี้

this is my wife née pun-ra-
yah kòrng pŏm
นี่ภรรยาของผม

is this ...? ... châi mái?
... ใช่ไหม

those: those men pôo chai
pôo-uk lào nún
ผู้ชายพวกเหล่านั้น

those women pôo yǐng pôo-
uk lào nún
ผู้หญิงพวกเหล่านั้น

which ones? – those un nâi?
– un nún
อันไหน – อันนั้น

thread (noun) sên dâi
เส้นด้าย

throat kor hǒy
คอหอย

throat pastilles yah om gâir
kor jèp
ยาอมแก้คอเจ็บ

through pàhn
ผ่าน

does it go through ...? (train,
bus) pàhn ... rěu bplào?
ผ่าน ... หรือเปล่า

throw (verb) kwâhng
ขว้าง

throw away (verb) tíng
ทิ้ง

thumb néw hǒo-a mâir meu
นิ้วหัวแม่มือ

thunderstorm pah-yÓO fǒn
พายุฝน

Thursday wun pá-réu-hùt
วันพฤหัส

ticket dtǒo-a
ตั๋ว

Ti

dialogue

a return to Chiangmai
dtǒo-a bpai glùp chee-
ung-mài

coming back when? glùp
mêu-rai?

today/next Tuesday wun
née/wun ung-kahn nâh

that will be 200 baht sŏrng róy bàht

ticket office (bus, rail) têe jum-nài dtŏo-a
ที่จำหน่ายตั๋ว

tie (necktie) nék-tai
เน็คไท

tight (clothes etc) kúp
คับ

it's too tight kúp gern bpai
คับเกินไป

tights tŎOng yai boo-a
ถุงใยบัว

till (cash desk) têe gèp ngern
ที่เก็บเงิน

time* way-lah
เวลา

what's the time? gèe mohng láir-o?
กี่โมงแล้ว

this time krúng née
ครั้งนี้

last time krúng têe láir-o
ครั้งที่แล้ว

next time krúng nâh
ครั้งหน้า

three times sǎhm krúng
สามครั้ง

timetable dtah-rahng way-lah
ตารางเวลา

tin (can) gra-bpŏrng
กระป๋อง

tinfoil gra-dàht a-loo-mi-nee-um
กระดาษอลูมิเนียม

tin-opener têe bpèrt gra-bpŏrng
ที่เปิดกระป๋อง

tiny lék
เล็ก

tip (to waiter etc) ngern típ
เงินทิป

In restaurants and coffee shops it is usual to leave a small tip. It is unnecessary to tip in 'noodle shops', 'curry shops' and other cheap eating places; tipping is not usual either in taxis or tuk-tuks.

tired nèu-ay
เหนื่อย

I'm tired pŏm (chún) nèu-ay
ผม(ฉัน)เหนื่อย

tissues pâh chét meu
ผ้าเช็ดมือ

to: to Bangkok bpai grOOng-tâyp
ไปกรุงเทพฯ

to Thailand bpai meu-ung tai
ไปเมืองไทย

to the post office bpai bprai-sa-nee
ไปไปรษณีย์

toast (bread) ka-nǒm bpung bpîng
ขนมปังปิ้ง

today wun née
วันนี้

toe néw táo
นิ้วเท้า

together dôo-ay gun
ด้วยกัน

we're together (in shop etc) rao mah dôo-ay gun
เรามาด้วยกัน

toilet hôrng náhm
ห้องน้ำ

where is the toilet? hôrng náhm yòo têe nǎi?
ห้องน้ำอยู่ที่ไหน

I have to go to the toilet pǒm (chún) dtôrng bpai hôrng náhm
ผม(ฉัน)ต้องไปห้องน้ำ

 Public toilets are few and far between in Thailand. Take advantage of the facilities before you leave a restaurant!

toilet paper gra-dàht chum-rá
กระดาษชำระ

tomato ma-kěu-a tâyt
มะเขือเทศ

tomato juice núm ma-kěu-a tâyt
น้ำมะเขือเทศ

tomato ketchup sórt ma-kěu-a tâyt
ซอสมะเขือเทศ

tomorrow prôOng née
พรุ่งนี้

tomorrow morning cháo prôOng née
เช้าพรุ่งนี้

the day after tomorrow wun ma-reun née
วันมะรืนนี้

toner (cosmetic) toner

tongue lín
ลิ้น

tonic (water) núm toh-ník
น้ำโทนิค

tonight keun née
คืนนี้

tonsillitis dtòrm torn-sin ùk-sàyp
ต่อมทอนซิลอักเสป

too (excessively) ... gern bpai
... เกินไป

(also) dôo-ay
ด้วย

too hot rórn gern bpai
ร้อนเกินไป

too much mâhk gern bpai
มากเกินไป

me too pǒm (chún) gôr
měu-un gun
ผม(ฉัน)ก็เหมือนกัน

tooth fun
ฟัน

toothache bpòo-ut fun
ปวดฟัน

toothbrush bprairng sěe fun
แปรงสีฟัน

toothpaste yah sěe fun
ยาสีฟัน

top: on top of ... yòo bon ...
อยู่บน ...

at the top yòo kâhng bon
อยู่ข้างบน

top floor chún bon
ชั้นบน

topless bpleu-ay òk
เปลือยอก

torch fai chǎi
ไฟฉาย

total (noun) roo-um yôrt
รวมยอด

tour (noun) rai-gahn num
têe-o
รายการนำเที่ยว

is there a tour of ...? mee
rai-gahn num têe-o bpai ...
mái?
มีรายการนำเที่ยวไป ... ไหม

tour guide múk-kOO-tâyt
มัคคุเทศก์

tourist núk tôrng têe-o
นักท่องเที่ยว

tourist information office sǔm-
núk kào sǎhn núk tôrng
têe-o
สำนักงานข่าวสารนักท่องเที่ยว

tour operator pôo-jùt bor-ri-
gahn num têe-o
ผู้จัดการบริการนำเที่ยว

towards sòo
สู่

towel pâh chét dtoo-a
ผ้าเช็ดตัว

town meu-ung
เมือง

in town nai meu-ung
ในเมือง

just out of town nork meu-
ung bpai noy
นอกเมืองไปหน่อย

town centre jai glahng meu-
ung
ใจกลางเมือง

town hall tâyt-sa-bahn
เทศบาล

toy kǒrng lên
ของเล่น

track chahn chah-lah
ชานชาลา

which track is it for

Chiangmai? bpai chee-ung-mài chahn chah-lah a-rai?
ไปเชียงใหม่ชานชาลาอะไร

tracksuit chóot gee-lah
ชุดกีฬา

traditional bpen ka-nòp-tum nee-um
เป็นขนบธรรมเนียม

traffic ja-rah-jorn
จราจร

traffic jam rót dtìt
รถติด

traffic lights fai sǔn-yahn ja-rah-jorn
ไฟสัญญาณจราจร

trailer (for carrying tent etc) rót pôo-ung
รถพ่วง

train rót fai
รถไฟ

by train doy-ee rót fai
โดยรถไฟ

 Although usually slower than buses, trains are safer and offer the possibility of sleeping during overnight trips; moreover, if travelling by day you're likely to follow a more scenic route by rail than by road.
Managed by the State Railway of Thailand (SRT), the rail network consists of four main lines and a few branch lines. Fares depend on the class of seat, whether or not you want air-conditioning, and on the speed of the train. All long-distance trains have dining cars, and rail staff will also bring meals to your compartment. Tourist menus are written in English but have inflated prices – ask for the similar but cheaper 'ordinary' version, the menu 'tum-ma-dah'.
Advance booking of at least one day is essential for second-class and first-class seats on all lengthy journeys, and for sleepers needs to be done as far in advance as possible.

dialogue

is this the train for Korat?
rót fai née bpai koh-râht mái?

sure nâir-norn

no, you want that platform there mâi bpai kOOn dtôrng bpai chahn chah-lah un nún

trainers (shoes) rorng táo

191

gee-lah
รองเท้ากีฬา

train station sa-tǎhn-nee rót fai
สถานีรถไฟ

translate bplair
แปล

could you translate that? chôo-ay bplair hâi nòy, dâi mái?
ช่วยแปลให้หน่อยได้ไหม

translation gahn bplair
การแปล

translator pôo bplair
ผู้แปล

trash can tǔng ka-yà
ถังขยะ

travel gahn dern tahng
การเดินทาง

we're travelling around rao dern tahng bpai rêu-ay rêu-ay
เราเดินทางไปเรื่อย ๆ

travel agent's trah-wern ay-yen
ทราเวิลเอเยนต์

traveller's cheque chék dern tahng
เช็คเดินทาง

tray tàht
ถาด

tree dtôn mái
ต้นไม้

tremendous wí-sàyt
วิเศษ

trendy tun sa-mǎi
ทันสมัย

trim: just a trim, please (to hairdresser) chôo-ay dtùt òrk nít-nòy tâo-nún krúp (ká)
ช่วยตัดออกนิดหน่อยเท่านั้นครับ(คะ)

trip (excursion) têe-o
เที่ยว

I'd like to go on a trip to ... pǒm (chún) yàhk ja bpai têe-o ...
ผม(ฉัน)อยากจะไปเที่ยว ...

trolley rót kěn
รถเข็น

trouble (noun) bpun-hǎh
ปัญหา

I'm having trouble with ... pǒm (chún) mee bpun-hǎh gùp ...
ผม(ฉัน)มีปัญหากับ ...

trousers gahng-gayng
กางเกง

true jing
จริง

that's not true mâi jing
ไม่จริง

trunk (US: car) gra-bprohng tái rót
กระโปรงท้ายรถ

trunks (swimming) gahng-
  gayng wâi náhm
กางเกงว่ายน้ำ

try (verb) pa-yah-yahm
พยายาม

can I try it? kŏr lorng nòy,
  dâi mái?
ขอลองหน่อยได้ไหม

try on lorng sài doo
ลองใส่ดู

can I try it on? kŏr lorng sài
  doo nòy, dâi mái?
ขอลองใส่ดูหน่อยได้ไหม

T-shirt sêu-a yêut
เสื้อยืด

Tuesday wun ung-kahn
วันอังคาร

tuna bplah too-nah
ปลาทูนา

tunnel OO-mohng
อุโมงค์

turn: turn left/right lée-o
  sái/kwǎh
เลี้ยวซ้าย/ขวา

turn off: where do I turn off? ja
  lée-o têe nǎi?
จะเลี้ยวที่ไหน

can you turn the air-
  conditioning off? chôo-ay
  bpìt krêu-ung bprùp ah-
  gàht nòy, dâi mái?
ช่วยปิดเครื่องปรับอากาศ

หน่อยได้ไหม

turn on: can you turn the
  air-conditioning on?
  chôo-ay **bpèrt** krêu-ung
  bprùp ah-gàht nòy, dâi
  mái?
ช่วยเปิดเครื่องปรับอากาศ
หน่อยได้ไหม

turning (in road) tahng lée-o
ทางเลี้ยว

TV tee-wee
ทีวี

tweezers bpàhk kêep
ปากคีบ

twice sǒrng krúng
สองครั้ง

twice as much mâhk sǒrng
  tâo
มากสองเท่า

twin beds dtee-ung kôo
เตียงคู่

twin room hôrng kôo
ห้องคู่

twist: I've twisted my
  ankle kôr táo pǒm (chún)
  plík
ข้อเท้าผม(ฉัน)พลิก

type (noun) bàirp
แบบ

another type of ... ... èek
  bàirp nèung
... อีกแบบหนึ่ง

typical bàirp cha-bùp
แบบฉบับ

tyre yahng rót
ยางรถ

U

ugly nâh glèe-ut
น่าเกลียด

UK bpra-tâyt ung-grìt
ประเทศอังกฤษ

ulcer plăir gra-pór
แผลกระเพาะ

umbrella rôm
ร่ม

uncle (older brother of
mother/father) loong
ลุง
(younger brother of father) ah
อา
(younger brother of mother) náh
น้า

unconscious mòt sa-dtì
หมดสติ

under (in position) dtâi
ใต้
(less than) dtùm gwàh
ต่ำกว่า

underdone (meat) sÒOk-sÒOk
dìp-dìp
สุก ๆ ดิบ ๆ

underpants gahng-gayng
nai
กางเกงใน

understand: I understand
pŏm (chún) kâo jai
ผม(ฉัน)เข้าใจ

I don't understand pŏm
(chún) mâi kâo jai
ผม(ฉัน)ไม่เข้าใจ

do you understand? kâo jai
mái?
เข้าใจไหม

United States sa-hà-rút a-
may-ri-gah
สหรัฐอเมริกา

university ma-hăh-wít-ta-
yah-lai
มหาวิทยาลัย

unleaded petrol núm mun rái
săhn dta-gòo-a
น้ำมันไร้สารตะกั่ว

unlimited mileage mâi jum-
gùt ra-ya tahng
ไม่จำกัดระยะทาง

unlock kăi gOOn-jair
ไขกุญแจ

unpack gâir hòr
แก้ห่อ

until jon
จน

unusual pìt tum-ma-dah
ผิดธรรมดา

up kêun
ขึ้น

up there yòo bon nún
อยู่บนนั้น

he's not up yet (not out of bed) káo yung mâi dtèun
เขายังไม่ตื่น

what's up? (what's wrong?) bpen a-rai?
เป็นอะไร

upmarket rǒo-rǎh
หรูหรา

upset stomach tórng sěe-a
ท้องเสีย

upside down kwûm
คว่ำ

upstairs kâhng bon
ข้างบน

urgent dòo-un
ด่วน

us* rao
เรา

with us gùp rao
กับเรา

for us sǔm-rùp rao
สำหรับเรา

USA sa-hà-rút a-may-ri-gah
สหรัฐอเมริกา

use (verb) chái
ใช้

may I use ...? kǒr chái ... dâi mái?
ขอใช้ ... ได้ไหม

useful mee bpra-yòht
มีประโยชน์

usual tum-ma-dah
ธรรมดา

V

vacancy: do you have any vacancies? (hotel) mee hôrng wâhng mái?
มีห้องว่างไหม

see room

vacation wun yòOt
วันหยุด

on vacation yòOt púk pòrn
หยุดพักผ่อน

vaccination chèet wúk-seen
ฉีดวัคซีน

vacuum cleaner krêu-ung dòot fòOn
เครื่องดูดฝุ่น

valid (ticket etc) chái dâi
ใช้ได้

how long is it valid for? chái dâi těung mêu-a rài?
ใช้ได้ถึงเมื่อไร

valley hòOp kǎo
หุบเขา

valuable (adj) mee kâh
มีค่า

**can I leave my valuables
here?** ao kâo kŏrng
tíng wái têe nêe, dâi
mái?
เอาข้าวของทิ้งไว้ที่นี่ได้ไหม

value (noun) kâh
ค่า

van rót dtôo
รถตู้

vanilla wá-ní-lah
วานิลา

a vanilla ice cream ait kreem
wá-née-lah
ไอศกรีมวานิลา

vary: it varies láir-o dtàir
แล้วแต่

vase jair-gun
แจกัน

vegetables pùk
ผัก

vegetarian (noun) kon mâi gin
néu-a
คนไม่กินเนื้อ

vending machine dtôo
ตู้

very mâhk
มาก

very little for me kŏr nít dee-
o tâo-nún
ขอนิดเดียวเท่านั้น

I like it very much pŏm

(chún) chôrp mâhk
ผม(ฉัน)ชอบมาก

vest (under shirt) sêu-a glâhm
เสื้อกล้าม

via pàhn
ผ่าน

video (noun: film)
wee-dee-o
วีดีโอ

(recorder) krêu-ung
wee-dee-oh
เครื่องวีดีโอ

Vietnam bpra-tâyt
wêe-ut-nahm
ประเทศเวียดนาม

Vietnamese (adj) wêe-ut-
nahm
เวียดนาม

view wew
วิว

village mòo bâhn
หมู่บ้าน

vinegar núm sôm
น้ำส้ม

visa wee-sâh
วีซ่า

visit (verb: place) têe-o
เที่ยว

(person) yêe-um
เยี่ยม

I'd like to visit ... pŏm
(chún) yàhk ja bpai têe-

o/yêe-um ...
**ผม(ฉัน)อยากจะไปเที่ยว/
เยี่ยม ...**

vital: it's vital that ... **sŭm-
kun** mâhk têe ja dtôrng ...
สำคัญมากที่จะต้อง ...

vodka word-kâh
วอร์ดก้า

voice sĕe-ung
เสียง

voltage rairng fai fáh
แรงไฟฟ้า

Electricity is supplied at
220 volts and is available
at all but the most
remote villages and basic beach
huts.

vomit ah-jee-un
อาเจียน

W

waist ay-o
เอว

waistcoat sêu-a gúk
เสื้อกั๊ก

wait ror
รอ

wait for me ror pŏm (chún)

nòy ná
รอผม(ฉัน)หน่อยนะ

don't wait for me mâi dtôrng
ror pŏm (chún) ná
ไม่ต้องรอผม(ฉัน)นะ

can I wait until my
wife/partner gets here? ror
jon pun-ra-yah/fairn mah
dâi mái?
รอจนภรรยา/แฟนมาได้ไหม

can you do it while I wait?
pŏm (chún) ror ao dâi
mái?
ผม(ฉัน)รอเอาได้ไหม

could you wait here for me?
ror pŏm (chún) têe nêe dâi
mái?
รอผม(ฉัน)ที่นี่ได้ไหม

waiter kon sérp
คนเสริฟ

waiter! kOOn krúp (kâ)!
คุณครับ(ค่ะ)

waitress kon sérp
คนเสริฟ

waitress! kOOn krúp (kâ)!
คุณครับ(ค่ะ)

wake: can you wake me up at
5.30? chôo-ay **bplòok**
pŏm (chún) way-lah dtee
hâh krêung dâi mái?
**ช่วยปลุกผม(ฉัน)เวลาตีห้าครึ่ง
ได้ไหม**

Wales Wales
เวลส์

walk: is it a long walk? dern glai mái?
เดินไกลไหม

it's only a short walk dern mâi glai
เดินไม่ไกล

I'll walk pǒm (chún) dern bpai
ผม(ฉัน)เดินไป

I'm going for a walk pǒm (chún) bpai dern lên
ผม(ฉัน)ไปเดินเล่น

Walkman® walkman®
วอล์กแมน

wall (inside) fǎ
ฝา

(outside) gum-pairng
กำแพง

wallet gra-bpǎo sa-dtahng
กระเป๋าสตางค์

wander: I like just wandering around pǒm (chún) chôrp dern lên rêu-ay bpèu-ay bpai
ผม(ฉัน)ชอบเดินเล่นเรื่อยเปื่อยไป

want: I want a ... pǒm (chún) ao ...
ผม(ฉัน)เอา ...

I don't want any ... pǒm

(chún) mâi yàhk dâi ...
ผม(ฉัน)ไม่อยากได้ ...

I want to go home pǒm (chún) yàhk ja glùp bâhn
ผม(ฉัน)อยากจะกลับบ้าน

I don't want to ... pǒm (chún) mâi yàhk ...
ผม(ฉัน)ไม่อยาก ...

he wants to ... káo yàhk ja ...
เขาอยากจะ ...

what do you want? kOOn dtôrng-gahn a-rai?
คุณต้องการอะไร

ward (in hospital) hǒr pôo bpòo-ay
หอผู้ป่วย

warm rórn
ร้อน

I'm so warm pǒm (chún) rórn jung
ผม(ฉัน)ร้อนจัง

was*: he was káo bpen
เขาเป็น

she was káo bpen
เขาเป็น

it was (mun) bpen
มันเป็น

wash (verb) súk
ซัก

(oneself) láhng
ล้าง

can you wash these? súk un

née hâi nòy dâi mái?

ซักอันนี้ให้หน่อยได้ไหม

washer (for bolt etc) wong-wǎirn

วงแหวน

washhand basin àhng láhng nâh

อ่างล้างหน้า

washing machine krêu-ung súk pâh

เครื่องซักผ้า

washing powder pǒng súk fôrk

ผงซักฟอก

washing-up liquid núm yah láhng

น้ำยาล้าง

wasp dtairn

แตน

watch (wristwatch) nah-li-gah

นาฬิกา

will you watch my things for me? chôo-ay fâo kǒrng hâi nòy dâi mái?

ช่วยเฝ้าของให้หน่อยได้ไหม

watch out! ra-wung!

ระวัง

watch strap sǎi nah-li-gah

สายนาฬิกา

water náhm

น้ำ

may I have some water? kǒr

náhm nòy dâi mái?

ขอน้ำหน่อยได้ไหม

waterproof (adj) gun náhm

กันน้ำ

waterskiing sa-gee náhm

สกีน้ำ

wave (in sea) klêun

คลื่น

way: it's this way bpai tahng née

ไปทางนี้

it's that way bpai tahng nóhn

ไปทางโน้น

is it a long way to ...? bpai ... glai mái?

ไป ... ไกลไหม

no way! mâi mee tahng!

ไม่มีทาง

dialogue

could you tell me the way to ...? chôo-ay bòrk tahng bpai ... hâi nòy, dâi mái?

go straight on until you reach the traffic lights dern dtrong bpai jon těung fai sǔn-yahn

turn left lée-o sái

take the first on the right lée-o kwǎh têe tahng

yâirk un râirk
see **where**

we* rao
เรา

weak (person, drink) òrn-air
อ่อนแอ

weather ah-gàht
อากาศ

wedding pi-tee dtàirng ngahn
พิธีแต่งงาน

wedding ring wǎirn dtàirng
ngahn
แหวนแต่งงาน

Wednesday wun póOt
วันพุธ

week ah-tít
อาทิตย์

a week (from) today èek ah-
tít nèung jàhk wun née bpai
อีกอาทิตย์หนึ่งจากวันนี้ไป

a week (from) tomorrow èek
ah-tít nèung jàhk próOng
née bpai
อีกอาทิตย์หนึ่งจากพรุ่งนี้ไป

weekend wun sǎo wun ah-tít
วันเสาร์วันอาทิตย์

at the weekend wun sǎo ah-
tít
วันเสาร์อาทิตย์

weight núm-nùk
น้ำหนัก

weird bplàirk
แปลก

weirdo kon bplàirk
คนแปลก

welcome: welcome to ... kǒr
dtôrn rúp ...
ขอต้อนรับ ...

you're welcome (don't mention
it) mâi bpen rai
ไม่เป็นไร

well: I don't feel well pǒm
(chún) róo-sèuk mâi kôy sa-
bai
ผม(ฉัน)รู้สึกไม่ค่อยสบาย

she's not well káo mâi sa-bai
เขาไม่สบาย

you speak English very well
kOOn pôot pah-sǎh ung-
grìt dâi dee mâhk
คุณพูดภาษาอังกฤษได้ดีมาก

well done! dee mâhk!
ดีมาก

this one as well un née dôo-
ay
อันนี้ด้วย

well well! (surprise) mǎir!
แหม

dialogue

how are you? bpen yung-
ngai bâhng?

very well, thanks, and you?
sa-bai dee kòrp-kOOn,
láir-o kOOn lâ?

well-done (meat) sòOk sòOk
สุก ๆ

Welsh: I'm Welsh pǒm (chún)
bpen kon Wales
ผม(ฉัน)เป็นคนเวลส์

were*: we were rao bpen
เราเป็น

you were kOOn bpen
คุณเป็น

they were káo bpen
เขาเป็น

west dta-wun dtòk
ตะวันตก

in the west dta-wun dtòk
ตะวันตก

West Indian (adj) mah jàhk
mòo gòr in-dee-a dta-wun
dtòk
มาจากหมู่เกาะอินเดียตะวันตก

wet bpèe-uk
เปียก

what? a-rai?
อะไร

what's that? nûn a-rai?
นี่นอะไร

what should I do? ja tum
yung-ngai dee?
จะทำอย่างไรดี

what a view! wew sǒo-ay
jung ler-ee!
วิวสวยจังเลย

what bus do I take? kêun rót
may sǎi nǎi?
ขึ้นรถเมล์สายไหน

wheel lór
ล้อ

wheelchair rót kěn sǔm-rùp
kon bpòo-ay
รถเข็นสำหรับคนป่วย

when? mêu-rai?
เมื่อไร

when we get back mêu-a rao
glùp mah/bpai
เมื่อเรากลับมา/ไป

when's the train/ferry? rót
fai/reu-a òrk gèe mohng?
รถไฟ/เรือออกกี่โมง

where? têe-nǎi?
ที่ไหน

I don't know where it is pǒm
(chún) mâi sâhp wâh yòo
têe-nǎi
ผม(ฉัน)ไม่ทราบว่าอยู่ที่ไหน

dialogue

where is the temple? wút
yòo têe nǎi?
it's over there yòo têe-
nôhn

Wh

could you show me where it is on the map? chôo-ay chée hâi hĕn wâh yòo têe năi nai păirn-têe

it's just here yòo dtrong née

see way

which: which bus? rót may săi năi?
รถเมล์สายไหน

dialogue

which one? un năi?
that one? un nún
this one? un née, châi mái?
no, that one mâi châi un nún

while: while I'm here ka-nà têe pŏm (chún) yòo têe nêe
ขณะที่ผม(ฉัน)อยู่ที่นี่

whisky lâo wít-sa-gêe
เหล้าวิสกี้

white sĕe kăo
สีขาว

white wine lâo wai kăo
เหล้าไวน์ขาว

who? krai?
ใคร

who is it? nûn krai lâ?
นั่นใครล่ะ

the man who ... kon têe ...
คนที่ ...

whole: the whole week dta-lòrt ah-tít
ตลอดอาทิตย์

the whole lot túng mòt
ทั้งหมด

whose: whose is this? nêe kŏrng krai?
นี่ของใคร

why? tum-mai?
ทำไม

wide gwâhng
กว้าง

wife: my wife pun-ra-yah kŏrng pŏm
ภรรยาของผม

will*: will you do it for me? chôo-ay tum hâi nòy dâi mái?
ช่วยทำให้หน่อยได้ไหม

wind (noun) lom
ลม

window nâh-dtàhng
หน้าต่าง

near the window glâi nâh-dtàhng
ใกล้หน้าต่าง

in the window (of shop) têe nâh-dtàhng
ที่หน้าต่าง

window seat têe nûng dtìt nâh-dtàhng
ที่นั่งติดหน้าต่าง

windscreen gra-jòk nâh rót yon
กระจกหน้ารถยนต์

windscreen wiper têe bpùt núm fŏn
ที่ปัดน้ำฝน

windsurfing gahn lên gra-dahn dtôh lom
การเล่นกระดานโต้ลม

windy: it's so windy lom rairng jung
ลมแรงจัง

wine wai
ไวน์

can we have some more wine? kŏr wai èek dâi mái?
ขอไวน์อีกได้ไหม

Wine is not widely drunk in Thailand and many people feel it does not complement Thai food very well. A cheap local brand is produced but is not generally served in restaurants. Western wines will be available only in the more expensive restaurants.

wine list rai-gahn wai
รายการไวน์

winter nâh nǎo
หน้าหนาว

in the winter nai nâh nǎo
ในหน้าหนาว

wire lôo-ut
ลวด

(electric) sǎi fai fáh
สายไฟฟ้า

wish: best wishes dôo-ay kwahm bprah-ta-nǎh dee
ด้วยความปรารถนาดี

with gùp
กับ

I'm staying with ... pǒm (chún) púk yòo gùp ...
ผม(ฉัน)พักอยู่กับ ...

without doy-ee mâi
โดยไม่

witness pa-yahn
พยาน

will you be a witness for me? chôo-ay bpen pa-yahn hâi pǒm (chún) dâi mái?
ช่วยเป็นพยานให้ผม(ฉัน)ได้ไหม

woman pôo-yǐng
ผู้หญิง

women

On the whole, Thailand is a fairly hassle-free destination for women travellers. Though unpalatable and distressing, the high-profile sex industry is relatively unthreatening for Western women, with its energy focused exclusively on foreign men; it's also quite easily avoided, being contained within certain pockets of the capital and a couple of beach resorts. As for harassment from Thai men, it's hard to generalize, but most Western tourists find it less of a problem in Thailand than they do back home. Outside the main tourist spots, you're more likely to be an object of interest as a foreigner rather than as a woman and, if travelling alone, as an object of concern rather than of sexual aggression.

wonderful yôrt yêe-um
ยอดเยี่ยม

won't*: it won't start mâi
yorm dtìt
ไม่ยอมติด

wood (material) mái
ไม้

woods (forest) bpàh
ป่า

wool kŏn sùt
ขนสัตว์

word kum
คำ

work (noun) ngahn
งาน

it's not working mun sěe-a
มันเสีย

I work in ... pŏm (chún) tum
ngahn têe ...
ผม(ฉัน)ทำงานที่ ...

world lôhk
โลก

worry: I'm worried pŏm
(chún) bpen hòo-ung
ผม(ฉัน)เป็นห่วง

worse: it's worse yâir
gwàh
แย่กว่า

worst yâir têe sÒOt
แย่ที่สุด

worth: is it worth a visit? nâh
têe-o mái?
น่าเที่ยวไหม

**would: would you give this to
...?** chôo-ay ao nêe bpai hâi
... dâi mái?
ช่วยเอานี่ไปให้ ... ได้ไหม

wrap: could you wrap it up?
chôo-ay hòr hâi nòy, dâi
mái?
ช่วยห่อให้หน่อยได้ไหม

wrapping paper gra-dàht hòr
kŏrng kwǔn
กระดาษห่อของขวัญ

wrist kôr meu
ข้อมือ

write kĕe-un
เขียน

could you write it down?
chôo-ay kĕe-un long hâi
nòy, dâi mái?
ช่วยเขียนลงให้หน่อยได้ไหม

how do you write it? kĕe-un
yung-ngai?
เขียนอย่างไร

writing paper gra-dàht kĕe-
un jòt-mǎi
กระดาษเขียนจดหมาย

wrong: it's the wrong key
gOOn-jair pìt
กุญแจผิด

this is the wrong train rót fai
pìt ka-boo-un
รถไฟผิดขบวน

the bill's wrong kít bin pìt
คิดบิลผิด

sorry, wrong number kŏr-
tôht dtòr ber pìt
ขอโทษ ต่อเบอร์ผิด

sorry, wrong room kŏr-tôht,
pìt hôrng
ขอโทษ ผิดห้อง

there's something wrong

with ... ... mee a-rai pìt
... มีอะไรผิด

what's wrong? bpen a-rai?
เป็นอะไร

X

X-ray 'X-ray'
เอ็กซ์เรย์

Y

yacht reu-a yórt
เรือยอชท์

yard*

year bpee
ปี

yellow sěe lěu-ung
สีเหลือง

yes* krúp (kâ); châi
ครับ(ค่ะ); ใช่

yesterday mêu-a wahn
née
เมื่อวานนี้

yesterday morning cháo
wahn née
เช้าวานนี้

the day before yesterday
wun seun née
วันซืนนี้

yet yung
ยัง

dialogues

is it here yet? mah láir-o
rĕu yung?
no, not yet yung
you'll have to wait a little
longer yet kOOn dtôrng
koy èek sùk nòy

yoghurt yoh-gut
โยกัด

you* kOOn
คุณ

this is for you nêe sŭm-rùp
kOOn
นี่สำหรับคุณ

with you gùp kOOn
กับคุณ

young (man) nòOm
หนุ่ม

(woman) sǎo
สาว

young (child) dèk lék
เด็กเล็ก

your* kǒrng kOOn
ของคุณ

your camera glôrng tài rôop
kǒrng kOOn
กล้องถ่ายรูปของคุณ

yours kǒrng kOOn
ของคุณ

Z

zero sŏon
ศูนย์

zip sìp
ซิบ

could you put a new zip on?
chôo-ay sài sìp mài dâi mái?
ช่วยใส่ซิบใหม่ได้ไหม

zip code ra-hùt bprai-sa-nee
รหัสไปรษณีย์

zoo sŏo-un sùt
สวนสัตว์

Thai

→

English

Colloquialisms

You might well hear the following expressions but you shouldn't be tempted to use any of the stronger ones – local people will not be amused or impressed by your efforts.

âi hàh! shit!
bpai (hâi pón)! go away!
bpai năi! hi!
chìp-hăi! damn!
dtai hàh! oh hell!
dtai jing! oh no!
mâi chêu-a! come on!, I don't believe you!
mâi mee tahng! no chance!, no way!
măir! goodness!
òrk bpai hâi pón! get out!
tôh! good heavens!
yòot pôot ná! shut up!
yôrt! great!

Entries are listed alphabetically
according to the first complete
word, for example, entries beginning
with **bâhn** precede those beginning
with **bahng**.

A

ah uncle (younger brother of
father); aunt (younger sister of
father)
ah-fri-gah Africa; African
ah-gahn klêun hĕe-un
nausea
ah-gahn ùk-sàyp infection
ah-gàht air; weather
ah-hăhn meal; food; cuisine;
cooking
ah-hăhn bpen pít food
poisoning
ah-hăhn cháo breakfast
ah-hăhn glahng wun lunch
ah-hăhn kao savoury
ah-hăhn mâi yôy indigestion
ah-hăhn pí-sàyt speciality
ah-hăhn yen evening meal;
supper; dinner
ah-jahn teacher
ah-kahn building
àhn read
àhng sink, basin
àhng àhp náhm bath
àhng láhng nâh washbasin
àhp dàirt sunbathe
ah-tít week
ah-tít dtòk sunset
ah-tít kêun sunrise
ah-yóo age

kOOn ah-yóo tâo-rài? how
old are you?
ai cough; shy
âi hàh! shit!
ai-lairn Ireland
ai-lairn nĕu-a Northern
Ireland
air hóht-tet air stewardess
ai-rít Irish
airm amp
airt-pai-rin aspirin
a-lài spare part(s)
a-may-ri-gah America;
American (person)
a-may-ri-gun American (adj)
a-nah-kót future
a-nóo-săh-wa-ree
monument; statue
ao like; want
ào bay
ao ... bpai take; remove
ao jing ao jung serious
ao krúp (kâ) yes please
ao lá! right!, OK!
ao ... mah fetch; bring
ao ... mái? do you want ...?
ào tai Gulf of Siam
a-páht-mén flat, apartment
a-rai something
 a-rai? what?
a-rai èek something else
 a-rai èek? what else?
a-rai gôr dâi anything
a-rai ná? pardon (me)?,
sorry?; excuse me?
a-ròy nice, delicious
àyk-ga-săhn document;
leaflet
ay-o waist

AY

ay-see-a Asia
ay-see-a ah-ka-nay South
  East Asia

B
—

bâh mad, crazy
bâhn house; home
  têe bâhn at home
bâhn tùt bpai nextdoor
bahng thin; some
bâhng a few; some
bahng krúng bahng krao
  occasionally
bahng tee sometimes; maybe;
  perhaps
bàht baht (unit of currency)
bàht jèp injured
bàht plǎir wound
bàht wít-těe pavement,
  sidewalk
bài afternoon
  bài ... mohng ... p.m. (in the
    afternoon)
  bài née this afternoon
  bài prôong née tomorrow
    afternoon
  bài wahn née yesterday
    afternoon
bai bai ná cheerio, bye
bai báirng banknote, (US) bill
bai bplew leaflet
bai bpra-gàht kôht-sa-nah
  poster
bai kùp kèe driving licence
bai kùp kèe sǎh-gon
  international driving licence
bai mái leaf

bai mêet gohn razor blade(s)
bai reu-a sail
bai rúp bpra-gun guarantee
bai rúp-rorng guarantee;
  certificate
bai sèt rúp ngern receipt
bai sùng yah prescription
bai ùn-nóo-yâht licence,
  permit
bair-dta-rêe battery
bàirk carry
bairn flat (adj)
bàirng share; divide
bàirp sort, kind, type; pattern
bàirp cha-bùp typical
bàirp fa-rùng European-style
bàirp form form
bàirp ree-un pah-sǎh
  language course
bàirp yàhng pattern
bao light (not heavy)
ber toh-ra-sùp phone
  number
bèu-a bored
bin bill, (US) check; fly (verb)
bòhk rót hitchhike, hitch
boh-rahn ancient
boh-rahn wút-thóo antique
bon on; on top of
  bon péun din on the ground
bòn complain
bóop-fay buffet
bòo-rèe cigarette(s)
bòo-rèe gôn grorng tipped
  cigarettes
bòo-ròot gents' toilet, men's
  room
bòo-uk plus
boo-um swollen

bòrk say; tell
bòrk wâh say
bor-ri-gahn service
bor-ri-gahn ngern dòo-un cashpoint, ATM
bor-ri-gahn num têe-o excursion
bor-ri-gahn rót châo car rental
bor-ri-gahn rúp chái nai hôrng púk room service
bor-ri-gahn sòrp tăhm ber toh-ra-sùp directory enquiries
bor-ri-sòot innocent
bor-ri-sùt company, firm
bor-ri-wayn bâhn backyard
bor-ri-wayn chahn meu-ung suburb
bòt ree-un lesson
bòy bòy often
bpà-dti-tin calendar
bpâh aunt (elder sister of mother/father)
bpàh jungle; forest
bpàh cháh cemetery
bpàh dong dìp forest, jungle
bpàh mái sùk teak forest
bpah-gee-sa-tăhn Pakistan
bpàhk mouth
bpàhk-gah pen
bpàhk-gah lôok lêun ballpoint pen
bpai to; go; go away
bpai (hâi pón)! go away!
bpai tèr let's go
bpâi label
bpai glùp wun dee-o day trip
bpai gùp pŏm (chún) come with me
bpai năi! hi!

bpâi rót may bus stop
bpai séu kŏrng go shopping
bpâi ta-bee-un rót licence plates
bpâirng powder; face powder; talcum powder
bpàirt eight
bpa-rin-yah degree
bpây lŭng rucksack
bpee year
bpee têe láir-o last year; a year ago
bpee mài New Year
bpèek wing
bpèe-uk wet
bpen be; is; in; can; be capable of
bpen ... it is ...; it was ...
bpen a-rai? what's up?, what's wrong?
bpen bâi dumb (can't speak)
bpen bpai dâi possible
bpen bpai mâi dâi impossible
bpen bpra-yòht beneficial
bpen gun ayng informal
bpen hòo-ung worry
bpen ìt-sa-rá independent
bpen ka-nòp-tum nee-um traditional
bpen lom faint (verb); stroke; attack
bpen mun greasy
bpen nêe bOOn-kOOn grateful
bpen nern hilly
bpen pèun heat rash
bpen pêu-un friendly
bpen pít poisonous; polluted
bpen sai sandy
bpen sòht single, unmarried

bpen tahng gahn formal
bpen têe nâh por jai satisfactory
bpen têe nee-yom popular
bpen yung-ngai bâhng? how are you?
bper-sen per cent
bpèrt open (adj); on
bpèt duck
bpeun gun
bpeun pók pistol
bpeun yao rifle
bpìt close, shut; closed
bplah fish
bplah cha-lǎhm shark
bplah-sa-dter Elastoplast®, Bandaid®
bplah-sa-dtìk plastic
bplair interpret; translate
bplàirk strange, odd, funny, weird
bplàirk bpra-làht strange
bplay cot
bplèe-un change
  bplèe-un rót fai change trains
bpleu-ay naked
bplòrk condom
bplòrk mŏrn pillow case
bplòrt-pai safe
bplúk plug; adaptor
bplúk fai power point
bplúk krêu-ung gohn nòo-ut shaving point
bpoh-sa-dter poster
bpóht-gáht postcard
bpoo crab
bpòo grandfather (paternal)
bpÒOm dtìt krêu-ung ignition
bpÒOm sa-dtàht starter (of car)

bpòo-ut it aches
bpòo-ut fun toothache
bpòo-ut hŏo-a headache; hangover
bpòo-ut lǔng backache
bpòo-ut tórng stomach ache
bpòrt lungs; nervous
bpra-chah-chon public; population
bpra-chOOm meeting
bpra-chót sarcastic
bpra-dtoo door; gate; goal
bpra-gun insurance
bprah-sàht castle
bprairng brush
bprairng pǒm hairbrush
bprairng sěe fun toothbrush
bprairng tah kreem gohn nòo-ut shaving brush
bprairng tǒo lép nailbrush
bprai-sa-nee post office; mail
bprai-sa-nee dòo-un express mail
bprai-sa-nee glahng central post office
bpra-jum deu-un period (menstruation)
bpra-làht jai suprised
bpra-mahn roughly, about, approximately
bpra-pay-nee custom
bpra-tahn director, president (of company)
bpra-tah-nah-tí-bor-dee president (of country)
bpra-tâyt country
bpra-tâyt bayl-yee-um Belgium
bpra-tâyt fa-rùng-sàyt France

bpra-tâyt fi-líp-bpin Philippines
bpra-tâyt gao-lĕe Korea
bpra-tâyt gum-poo-chah Cambodia
bpra-tâyt hor-lairn Holland
bpra-tâyt ì-dtah-lee Italy
bpra-tâyt in-dee-a India
bpra-tâyt in-don-nee-see-a Indonesia
bpra-tâyt jeen China
bpra-tâyt kairn-nah-dah Canada
bpra-tâyt lao Laos
bpra-tâyt mah-lay-see-a Malaysia
bpra-tâyt new see-láirn New Zealand
bpra-tâyt pa-mâh Burma
bpra-tâyt sa-bpayn Spain
bpra-tâyt sa-górt-lairn Scotland
bpra-tâyt tai Thailand (formal)
bpra-tâyt ung-grìt England; Britain
bpra-tâyt wêe-ut-nahm Vietnam
bpra-tâyt yêe-bpòOn Japan
bpra-tâyt yer-ra-mun Germany
bpra-wùt-sàht history
bprêe-o sour; sharp (taste)
bprèe-up têe-up compare
bpròht favourite
bpròrt thermometer
bpúm núm mun petrol station, gas station
bpun-hǎh problem; trouble
bpùt-jOO-bun-née nowadays

brayk meu handbrake
bum-nahn pension
bun-dai ladder; stairs
bun-dai lêu-un escalator
bun-dai sǔm-rùp nĕe fai fire escape
bung-ern quite by chance
bun-yai describe
bùt bpra-jum dtoo-a identity card
bùt chern invitation
bùt kray-dìt credit card
bùt têe-nûng boarding pass

C

cháh late; slow; slowly
cháh cháh slowly
chahm dish, bowl
chahn chah-lah platform, (US) track
chahn meu-ung outskirts
cháhng elephant
châhng bpra-bpah plumber
châhng dtùt pŏm hairdresser; barber
châhng dtùt sêu-a pâh tailor
châhng fai fáh electrician
châhng ngern silversmith
châhng tài rôop photographer
châhng torng goldsmith
chai man; male
chái use
chái dâi valid
chai dairn border
chai hàht beach
châi láir-o that's it, that's right
châi láir-o! exactly!

châi mái? isn't it?
chái ngern spend
chái ... rôo-um gun share
chai ta-lay seaside; coast
châir kǎirng deep-freeze;
  frozen
cha-làht clever, intelligent
cha-ná win
châo rent, hire
cháo morning
  cháo née this morning
  cháo prôong née tomorrow
  morning
  cháo wahn née yesterday
  morning
chao bâhn villager
chao dtàhng bpra-tâyt
  foreigner
chao kǎo hill tribe
chao nah rice farmer
chao yóo-rôhp European
chèet yah injection
chee-wít life
chék cheque, (US) check
chék dern tahng traveller's
  cheque
chék doo check (verb)
chên for example
chern choo-un invite
chern gòrn after you
chern kâo mah! come in!
chern krúp (kâ) ... please ...
cherng kǎo hillside
chêu first name
  koon chêu a-rai? what's your
  name?
chêu lên nickname
chêu-a believe
chêu-a châht race (ethnic)

chéun humid; damp
chêu-uk rope; string
chêu-uk rorng táo shoelaces
chim taste
chín piece
  chín yài a big bit
chìp-hǎi! damn!
chôhk luck
chôhk dee fortunately; good
  luck!
chôhk rái unfortunately; hard
  luck!
chon glòom nói ethnic
  minority
chon-na-bòt countryside
choo chêep lifebelt
chôo-a krao temporary
chôo-a mohng hour
chôo-a rá-yá period (of time)
chôo-ay help
  chôo-ay ...? please ...?,
  would you please ...?
  chôo-ay dôo-ay! help!
chòok chěrn emergency
chôok-la-hòok hectic
chóot suit
chóot ah-hǎhn course (of meal)
chóot àhp náhm swimming
  costume
chóot bpa-thǒm pa-yah-bahn
  first-aid kit
chóot fun tee-um false teeth
chóot norn nightdress
chórk shock-absorber
chórn spoon
chórn sôrm cutlery
chôhng lane (on motorway)
chôhng kâo gate
chôhng kǎo mountain pass

chôrp like
chôrp ... mâhk gwàh prefer
chun steep
chún I; me; myself (said by a woman); floor, storey
chún nèung first class; ground floor, (US) first floor
chún săhm third class; second floor, (US) third floor
chún sŏrng second class; first floor, (US) second floor

D

dâhm handle
dâi get, obtain; may; might; be able
dâi glìn smell
... dâi mái? can I/you ... ?
dâi yin hear
dàirt òrk sunny; sunshine
dao star
dee good; fine; nice
dee! good!
dee gwàh better
dee jai happy; pleased
dee kêun mâhk much better
dee láir-o! good!; that'll do nicely!
dee mâhk! well done!; magnificent!
dee têe sòot (the) best
dee-chún I; me (said by a woman)
dee-o just, only
dĕe-o soon
dĕe-o, dĕe-o just a minute
dĕe-o gòrn! just a second!

dĕe-o née now; at present
dèk child; children
dèk chai boy
dèk òrn baby; young child
dèk wai rôOn teenager
dèk yĭng girl
dern walk
dern bpai on foot
dern tahng travel
dern tahng bpai tóO-rá gìt business trip
dèuk late
dèum drink (verb)
deung pull
deu-un in; month
din earth; land
din-sŏr pencil
dìp raw
dòht dĕe-o secluded
don-dtree music
don-dtree péun meu-ung folk music
don-dtree pórp pop music
don-dtree tai derm Thai classical music
doo look (at); watch
doo lair take care of
doo mĕu-un look, seem; look like
dôo-ay too, also
dôo-ay gun together
dôo-ay kwahm bprah-ta-nah dee with best wishes
dòo-un urgent
dòrk gOO-làhp rose
dòrk-mái flower
doy-ee by
doy-ee rót yon by car
doy-ee cha-pòr especially

doy-ee jay-dta-nah deliberately

doy-ee mâi without

dta-bai (fŏn) lép nailfile

dta-gèe-up chopsticks

dta-gla greedy

dta-gohn shout

dta-grâh basket

dta-grâh ka-yà wastepaper basket

dta-grai scissors

dtah eye; grandfather (maternal)

dtah bòrt blind

dtahm follow

dtahm tum-ma-dah as usual

dtàhng different

dtàhng bpra-tâyt abroad; foreign

dtàhng dtàhng various

dtàhng hàhk separate

dtàhng jung-wùt up-country (outside Bangkok)

dtah-rahng têe-o bin scheduled flight

dtah-rahng way-lah timetable, (US) schedule

dtai die; dead; kidneys (in body)

dtâi south; under, below

dtai hàh! oh hell!

dtai jing! oh no!

dtàir but

dtàir la kon each of them (people)

dtàir la krúng each time

dtàir la un each of them (things)

dtàirk break

dtàirk láir-o broken

dtàirk ngâi fragile

dtâirm score

dtàirng ngahn láir-o married

dta-làht market

dta-làht náhm floating market

dta-làht yen night market

dta-lòk funny, amusing; joke

dta-lòrt throughout; whole

dtao cooker

dtào turtle; tortoise

dtao òp oven

dtao rêet iron

dta-wun dtòk west

dta-wun dtòk chĕe-ung dtâi southwest

dta-wun dtòk chĕe-ung nĕu-a northwest

dta-wun òrk east

dta-wun òrk chĕe-ung dtâi southeast

dta-wun òrk chĕe-ung nĕu-a northeast

dtee hit

dtêe-a short

dteen bottom (of hill)

dtee-ung bed

dtee-ung dèe-o single bed

dtee-ung kôo twin beds

dtem, dtem láir-o full

dten tent

dtên rum dance

dterm fill

dtèuk block of flats, apartment block

dtêun shallow

dtèun awake; wake up; get up

dtèun-dtên excited; nervous

dtìt stuck

dtìt dtòr contact
dtìt gùp next to
dtó table
dtó jài ngern cash desk, cashier
dtòk miss (bus etc)
dtòk jai shock
dtôn bpahm palm tree
dtôn mái plant; tree
dtôo cupboard, closet; compartment; kiosk
dtôo bprai-sa-nee letterbox, mailbox
dtôo châir kăirng freezer
dtôo gèp gra-bpăo locker
dtôo jòt-măi letterbox, mailbox
dtôo norn sleeper, sleeping car
dtôo núng-sĕu pim newsstand
dtôo toh-ra-sùp phone box, phone booth
dtôo yen fridge; refrigerator
dtŏo-a ticket
dtŏo-a bpai single ticket, one-way ticket
dtŏo-a bpai glùp return ticket, round trip ticket
dtoo-a yàhng example
dtóOk-ga-dtah doll
dtoo-lah-kom October
dtôOm hŏo earring(s)
dtòr connection
dtòr rah-kah bargain (verb)
dtòr wâh complain
dtorn bài afternoon
dtorn cháo morning
dtorn glahng keun evening; night
dtorn yen late afternoon
dtôrng must; have to
dtôrng-gahn need
dtòy sting (verb)
dtrah brand
dtreung krêe-ut serious
dtrong direct
dtrong dtrong straight
dtrong kâhm opposite
dtrong nâh straight ahead
dtrong née right here, just here
dtrong way-lah on time
dtròOt jeen Chinese New Year
dtròo-ut examine
dtròo-ut chûng núm-nùk check-in
dtròrk lane (off a soi)
dtúk-dtúk tuk-tuk (motorized three-wheeled taxi)
dtùm low
dtùm gwàh under, less than
dtum-ròo-ut police; policeman
dtun blocked
dtûng-dtàir since (time)
dtùp liver
dtùp ùk-sàyp hepatitis
dtùt cut
dtùt fai power cut
dtùt pŏm haircut
dum dark (adj)
dum náhm dive
dung loud

E

èek more; again
èek bpra-děe-o in a minute
èek kon nèung the other one (person)
èek mâhk a lot more
èek ... nèung another ... ; the other ...
èek un nèung the other one (thing)
èun other; others; another

F

fáh sky
fǎh wall; lid
fáh lâirp lightning
fáh rórng thunder
fai fire; light
fâi cotton
fai chǎi torch, flashlight
fai cháirk cigarette lighter
fai fáh electric; electricity
fai kâhng sidelights
fai krêu-ung yon ignition
fai lée-o indicator
fai lǔng rót rear lights
fai mâi fire (blaze)
  fai mâi! fire!, it's on fire!
fai mòrk fog lights
fai nâh rót headlights
fairn boyfriend; girlfriend; partner
fàirt twins
fa-rùng European; Caucasian; Westerner; foreigner

fa-rùng-sàyt France; French
feem film (for camera); negative
feem sěe colour film
fláirt flat, apartment; flash
fók-chúm bruise
fǒn rain
  fǒn dtòk it's raining
fǒong kon crowd
fóot-born football
fùk boo-a shower
fun tooth
fung listen (to)
  fung sì! listen!
fùng shore; bank
... fùng dtrong kâhm across the ...

G

gah núm chah teapot
gahn bpa-tǒm pa-yah-bahn first aid
gahn bplair translation
gahn bpra-gun pai insurance
gahn chók dtòy fight
gahn dern tahng journey; travel
gahn dtai death
gahn dtôrn rúp kùp sôo hospitality
gahn dum náhm léuk skin-diving
gahn fórn rum péun meu-ung folk dancing
gahn jùp bplah fishing
gahn kàirng kǔn match; race
gahn lót rah-kah reduction
gahn meu-ung politics

gahn pàh dtùt operation

gahn rôo-um bpra-way-nee sex

gahn sa-dairng don-dtree concert

gahn sòrp exam

gahn sùng ngót cancellation

gahn ta-hăhn military

gahn wâi náhm swimming

gahng-gayng trousers, (US) pants

gahng-gayng kăh sûn shorts

gahng-gayng nai underpants, underwear

gahng-gayng nai sa-dtree pants, panties

gahng-gayng wâi náhm swimming trunks

gahng-gayng yeen jeans

gàir strong; dark; old

gâir hòr unpack

gâirm cheek (on face)

gâir-o glass

gáirt gas

gao glue; scratch

gào old

gâo nine

gâo êe chair

gâo êe pâh bai deckchair

gâo êe rúp kàirk sofa

gâo êe sŏong highchair

ga-rúk-ga-dah-kom July

ga-see-un retired

găy gài smart

gáyt háot guesthouse

gèe? how many?

 gèe mohng láir-o? what time is it?

gee-a tŏy lŭng reverse gear

gee-lah sport

gee-lah náhm water sports

gèng well

... gern bpai too ...

gèrt kêun happen

 gèrt a-rai kêun? what's happening?

gèu-up nearly, almost

gin dâi edible

gin (kâo) eat

gin yòo prórm full board

glâh hăhn brave

glahng medium; middle

glahng jâirng outdoors

glahng keun night; overnight

glahng meu-ung central

glai far (away)

 glai gwàh farther (than)

glâi near; near here

 ... têe glâi têe sòot the nearest ...

glèe-ut hate

gler pal, mate

glom round

gloo-a afraid; fear

glòom group

glòom jai depressed

glòom kon party, group

glòrng carton

glòrng gee-a gearbox

glôrng tài nŭng movie camera

glôrng tài pâhp-pa-yon camcorder

glôrng tài rôop camera

glôrng yah sên, glôrng yah sòop pipe (for smoking)

glùp get back

glùp bâhn go home

glùp bpai go back

glùp mah come back
  glùp mah nêe! come back!
goh-hòk lie (tell untruth)
gohn shave
goh-roh-goh-sǒh junk,
  rubbish
gôn bottom (of body)
gôn grorng filter-tipped
gOOm-pah-pun February
gOOn-jair key; lock
gôr then
gòr island
gòr ai-lairn Ireland
gôr měu-un gun too, also
gôr yàhng nún làir so-so
górk náhm tap, faucet
gòrn ago; before
  sǎhm wun gòrn three days
  ago
gorng dtum-ròo-ut dùp plerng
  fire brigade
górp golf
gòt-mǎi law
gra-bpǎo bag; briefcase;
  luggage, baggage; pocket
gra-bpǎo dern tahng suitcase;
  baggage
gra-bpǎo kwâi lǔng backpack
gra-bpǎo sa-dtahng purse;
  wallet, billfold
gra-bpǎo těu handbag, (US)
  purse; hand luggage, hand
  baggage
gra-bpǒrng can, tin
gra-bprohng skirt
gra-bprohng rót bonnet (of
  car), (US) hood
gra-bprohng tái (rót) boot (of
  car), (US) trunk

gra-dàht paper
gra-dàht chét meu, gra-dàht
  chét nâh paper
  handkerchiefs, Kleenex®
gra-dàht chum-rá toilet paper
gra-dàht hòr kǒrng kwǔn
  wrapping paper
gra-dàht kěe-un jòt-mǎi
  writing paper
gra-dìng bell
gra-dòok bone
gra-dòok hùk fracture
gra-dOOm button
gra-dtìk náhm vacuum flask
gra-jòk nâh rót yon
  windscreen
gra-jòk ngao mirror
gra-ter-ee gay, homosexual
grìng bell
gròht angry
grom dtròo-ut kon kâo meu-
  ung Immigration
  Department
grOOng-tâyp Bangkok
grum gramme
gum-lai meu bracelet
... gum-lung pôot speaking
gum-pairng wall
gun chon bumper, (US) fender
gun-chah marijuana
gun-grai scissors
gun-yah-yon September
gùp with
gùp kâo dish; meal
gùt insect bite
gwàh than; more; over, more
  than
gwâhng wide

H

hâh five
hăh look for
hăh yâhk rare
hâhm prohibited, forbidden; prohibit
hâhm sòop boO-rèe non-smoking
hâhng department store
hàhng glai remote
hâhng kăi yah pharmacy
hàht beach
hâi give; for
hăi lose
hăi bpai disappear
hâi châo for hire, to rent
hăir fishing net
hâirng dry
hàirng châht national
hăi-ya-ná disaster
hàyt cause
hèep box
hĕn see
hĕn dôo-ay agree
hĕw hungry
hêw carry
hĕw kâo hungry
hĕw náhm thirsty
hi-má snow
hĭn stone, rock
hîng shelf
hòk six
hŏo ear
hŏo nòo-uk deaf
hŏo-a head; corner
hŏo-a jai heart
hŏo-a jai wai heart attack

hŏo-a kào knee
hŏo-a láhn bald
hŏo-a mOOm corner
hŏo-a nom lòrk dummy
hŏo-a rór laugh
hŏo-a tee-un spark plug
hòop kăo valley
hòr package, parcel
hŏr sa-mòot library
hôrng room
hôrng ah-hăhn dining room
hôrng air air-conditioned room
hôrng bprùp ah-gàht air-conditioned room
hôrng dèe-o single room
hôrng kôo twin-bedded room
hôrng kórk-tayn cocktail bar
hôrng kroo-a kitchen
hôrng náhm bathroom; toilet, rest room
hôrng náhm pôo-chai gents' toilet, men's room
hôrng náhm pôo-yĭng ladies' toilet, ladies' room
hôrng náhm sòo-un dtoo-a private bathroom
hôrng norn bedroom
hôrng pôo doy-ee săhn kăh òrk departure lounge
hôrng púk waiting room
hôrng rúp kàirk living room
hôrng rúp-bpra-tahn ah-hăhn dining room
hôrng sa-mòot library
hôrng tŏhng lounge
hŏy shell
hùk break; deduct

Hu

hǔn bpai tahng ... facing
 the ...
hun-loh hello

I

ì-sa-rá free

J

jàhk from
 jàhk .... bpai ... from ... to ...
jàhk bpai leave, go away
jàhk meu-ung 'Wales' Welsh
jahn dish; plate
jahn rorng tôo-ay saucer
jahn sěe-ung record
jài pay
jai dee kind, generous
jai glahng meu-ung city
 centre
jair-gun vase
jàirm sǎi pleasant
ja-mòok nose
jâo-bào bridegroom
jâo-fáh chai prince
jâo-fáh yǐng princess
jâo-kǒrng owner
jâo kǒrng bâhn landlord
jâo nai boss
jâo-sǎo bride
ja-rah-jorn traffic
jay-dee pagoda
jeen China; Chinese
jèp sore; hurt
jèp bpòo-ut painful
jer find

jèt seven
jing true; real
jing jai sincere
jing jing lěr? honestly?
jîng-jòk lizard
jìt-dta-gum fǎh pa-nǔng
 murals
jon until; poor
jòop kiss
jòot-mǎi bplai tahng
 destination
jòp finish, end
jor-jair busy
jorng reservation; reserve
jor-ra-kây crocodile
jòrt park (verb)
jòt-mǎi letter; mail
jòt-mǎi ah-gàht aerogramme
jòt-mǎi long ta-bee-un
 registered letter
jùk-gra-yahn bicycle
jùk-sòo pâirt optician
jum dâi remember; recognize
jum-bpen necessary
jung ler-ee so
jung-wùt changwat, province
jùp catch; arrest
jùp bplah fishing
jùt arrange; bright; strong
jùt gahn organize

K

kǎh leg
kâh kill; value
kǎh kâo arrival
kâh bor-ri-gahn service
 charge

kâh bor-ri-gahn pi-sàyt
 supplement (extra charge)

kâh châo rent

kâh doy-ee sǎhn fare

kâh mút-jum deposit

kǎh òrk departure

kâh pàhn tahng toll

kǎh-gun-grai jaw

kâhm ta-lay crossing

kahng chin

kâhng beside; side

kâhng bon above, over;
 upstairs

kâhng lâhng downstairs

kâhng lǔng back; behind; rear

kâhng nâh in front (of); at the
 front

kâhng nai indoors; inside

kâhng nôrk outside

kahng toom mumps

kài egg

kâi temperature, fever;
 feverish

kǎi sell

kǎi gOOn-jair unlock

kâi jùp sùn malaria

kài móok pearl

kâi wùt flu

kàirk Indian; guest

kǎirn arm

kǎirn sêu-a sleeve

kair-nah-dah Canada;
 Canadian

kǎirng solid; hard

kǎirng rairng strong

kâirp narrow

ka-mǎyn Cambodian

ka-moy-ee steal; thief; burglar

ka-nà têe while

ka-nàht size; measurements

ka-nàht glahng medium-sized

ka-nòp-tum-nee-um tradition

káo he; him; she; her; they;
 them

kâo rice

kǎo hill; mountain

kào message; news

kâo bpai go in

kâo jai understand
 kâo jai láir-o I understand

kào-sǎhn information

ka-yà rubbish, litter, trash

kàyt district

kêe fòon dirt

kêe gèe-ut lazy

kèet sǒong sòot maximum

kǎe-un write

kem salty

kěm needle

kěm glùt sêu-a brooch

kěm kùt belt

kěm kùt ni-ra-pai seatbelt

kěm mòot pin

kěm-tít compass

ker-ee ever

kêrn embarrassed;
 embarrassing

keun night; give back
 keun la ... ... per night

kêun up

kêun bpai go up

keun née tonight; this
 evening

keun ngern refund

kêun rót may catch a bus

kew queue, line

kít think

klohn mud

klorng canal
kohm fai (fáh) lamp
koh-ték tampon
kŏhn classical masked drama
kòht hĭn rocky
kom sharp
kŏm bitter
kòm-kĕun rape
kon person; people
kŏn hair (on the body)
kon bâh idiot
kon bpah-gee-sa-tăhn a Pakistani; Pakistanis
kon bplàirk nâh stranger
kon châo tenant
kon cha-rah senior citizen
kon dee-o just, only; alone, by oneself
kon dern táo pedestrian
kon fâo bpra-dtoo doorman; porter
kon fâo dèk baby-sitter
kon fa-rùng-sàyt a French person; the French
kon hŏo-a sŏong snob
kon jai yen calm
kon jeen a Chinese person; the Chinese
kon jùp bplah fisherman
kon ka-măyn a Cambodian; the Cambodians
kon kùp (rót) driver
kon kùp táirk-sêe taxi-driver
kon lao a Lao; the Laos
kon lée-ung doo dèk child minder
kon mâi gin néu-a vegetarian
kon nâirn crowded
kon new see-láirn a New

Zealander; New Zealanders
kon ngôh fool
kon nún chap
kon pa-mâh a Burmese person; the Burmese
kon sa-górt a Scot; the Scots
kon sérp waiter; waitress
kon sèrp yĭng waitress
kon sŏrm rorng táo shoe repairer
kŏn sùt wool
kon tai a Thai person; the Thais
kon tèep jùk-ra-yahn cyclist
kon tum ka-nŏm-bpung baker
kon ung-grìt an English person; the English; a Briton; the British
kon yêe-bpòon a Japanese person; the Japanese
kon yer-ra-mun a German; the Germans
kong (ja) probably
kôo pair
kôo meu num têe-o guidebook
kôo meu sŏn-ta-nah phrasebook
kôo mûn fiancé; fiancée
koo-ee chat
kóok prison
koOn you
koOn krúp (kâ) excuse me
koOn-na-pâhp quality
koo-un ja should
kòo-ut bottle
kor neck; collar
kŏr please
pŏm (chún) kŏr I would like

kor bpòk sêu-a collar
kôr glào hăh complaint
kŏr hâi dern tahng doy-ee bplòrt-pai! have a safe journey!
kor hŏy throat
kôr meu wrist
kŏr ... nòy can I have ...?
kŏr rórng request
kŏr sa-dairng kwahm yin dee! congratulations!
kôr sòrk elbow
kôr táo ankle
kôr tét jing fact
kórn hammer
kórng gong
kŏrng thing; of
kŏrng bplorm fake
kŏrng bpròht favourite
kŏrng fôOm feu-ay luxury
kŏrng káo his; her; hers; their; theirs
kŏrng kOOn your; yours
kŏrng kwŭn present, gift
kŏrng lên toy
kŏrng pŏm (chún) my; mine
... kŏrng pŏm (chún) ayng my own ...
kŏrng rao our; ours
kŏrng têe ra-léuk souvenir
kôrn-kâhng ja ... rather ...
kòrp-kOOn thank; thanks, thank you
kòrp-kOOn mâhk thank you very much
kŏr-tôht excuse me; sorry; I beg your pardon?
krai somebody
krai? who?

krai gôr dâi anybody
krao beard
kreem bum-rOOng pěw moisturizer
kreem gohn nòo-ut shaving foam
kreem nôo-ut pŏm conditioner
kreem rorng péun foundation cream
kreem sa-măhn pěw cold cream
kreem tah àhp dàirt suntan lotion
kreem tah nŭng dtah eye shadow
krêung half
krêung chôo-a mohng half an hour
krêung lŏh half a dozen
krêu-ung air air-conditioning
krêu-ung bàirp uniform
krêu-ung bin plane, airplane
krêu-ung bpào pŏm hairdryer
krêu-ung bplairng fai fáh adaptor (for voltage)
krêu-ung bpra-dùp ornament
krêu-ung bprùp ah-gàht air-conditioning
krêu-ung bpûn din păo pottery, earthenware
krêu-ung bun-téuk sěe-ung tape recorder
krêu-ung chái sŏy equipment
krêu-ung chôo-ay fung hearing aid
krêu-ung dèum drink
krêu-ung dòot fòOn vacuum cleaner

krêu-ung dùp plerng fire extinguisher
krêu-ung gohn nòo-ut shaver
krêu-ung kít lâyk calculator
krêu-ung kOOm gum-nèrt contraceptive
krêu-ung lên pàirn sěe-ung record player
krêu-ung lên tâyp kah-set cassette player
krêu-ung reu-un furniture
krêu-ung súk pâh washing machine
krêu-ung sǔm-ahng make-up
krêu-ung wee-dee-oh videorecorder
krêu-ung wút OOn-na-ha-poom thermometer
krêu-ung yon motor; engine
krít Protestant
krít-dtung Roman Catholic
krít-sa-maht Christmas
kroo teacher
krôrp-kroo-a family
krúng time
krúng nèung once
krúp (kâ) yes

kum word
kûm dark
kum chern invitation
kum dtòrp answer
kum tǎhm question
kun itch
kûn bun-dai step
kun gee-a gear lever
kun rêng accelerator
kun yôhk lever
kúp tight
kùp drive

kwǎh right (not left)
kwahm bpra-préut behaviour
kwahm bun-terng entertainment
kwahm chéun humidity
kwahm chôo-ay lěu-a help
kwahm dtai death
kwahm dtàirk dtàhng difference
kwahm fǔn dream
kwahm jèp bpòo-ay illness
kwahm jèp bpòo-ut pain
kwahm jing truth
kwahm kâo jai pìt misunderstanding
kwahm kít idea
kwahm lúp secret
kwahm ngêe-up silence
kwahm pìt fault; mistake
kwahm ray-o speed
kwahm rórn heat
kwahm rúk love
kwahm sǒong height
kwǎhng throw
kwai water buffalo
kwûm upside down
kwun smoke

L

lah gòrn bye
láh sa-mǎi old-fashioned
lâhm interpreter
lǎhn chai grandson; nephew
lǎhn sǎo niece; granddaughter
láhng wash; develop (film)
lǎi several

lâi shoulder
lai sen signature
láir and
lâirk bplèe-un exchange (verb: money)
... láir-o already
láir-o dtàir it depends (on); it's up to you
la-korn play
lâo alcohol
lay-kăh-nóo-gahn secretary
layn glôrng lens (of camera)
lée-o kwăh turn right
lée-o sái turn left
lèe-um sŏong cheeky
lék small, little, tiny
lèk iron
lék nóy only a few
lên play
lép meu fingernail
ler-ee bpai further; beyond
ler-ee bpai èek further on
lěu-a gern jing jing shocking
léuk deep
leum forget
lêun slippery
lêu-ut blood
líf lift, elevator
likay popular folk theatre
lín tongue
lít litre
lŏh dozen
loh-hà metal
loh-hà sŭm-rít bronze
lôhk world; earth
lom wind
lom òrn òrn breeze
long bpai go down

long bpai! get down!
long mah! get down!
long ta-bee-un register
lôok child; children (one's own)
lôok born ball
lôok bpùt beads
lôok chai son
lôok gwàht sweets, candies
lôok kĕr-ee son-in-law
lôok ra-bèrt bomb
lôok săo daughter
lôok sa-pái daughter-in-law
loong uncle (older brother of father or mother)
lôo-ung nâh in advance
lóp minus
lòr good-looking
lór wheel
lorng try; try out, test
lòrt fai fáh lightbulb
lum-tahn stream
lŭng after; back (of body)
lŭng jàhk nún then, after that
lŭng-kah roof

M

mah come
măh dog
máh horse
mah gèp ... collect
máh glàirp pony
mah nêe come here
mah tĕung arrive
ma-hăh-wít-ta-yah-lai university
mah-dtra-tăhn standard

mâhk a lot, lots; many; much; very; very much
... **mâhk** plenty of ...
mâhk (gern) bpai too much; excessive
màhk fa-rùng chewing gum
mâhk lěu-a gern extremely
mâhk por sŏm-koo-un quite a lot
màhk róok chess
mâhn curtain
mai mile
măi silk
mái wood
mài new
mâi no; not
mâi ao ... no ...
mâi (ao) ... èek no more ...
mâi ao năi poor (quality); disgusting
mâi bòy seldom
mâi bpen rai don't mention it; it doesn't matter; never mind; that's all right
mâi bpen rêu-ung nonsense
mâi chêu-a! come on!, I don't believe you!
mâi dàirt sunburn
mâi dee bad
mái dtee racket (tennis)
mâi dtôrng sĕe-a pah-sĕe duty-free goods
mâi gin néu-a vegetarian
mái gwàht brush
mâi jing false
mâi jum-gùt ra-ya tahng unlimited mileage
mái kèet match
mâi ker-ee never

mâi kôy hardly
mâi lay-o it's not bad
mâi ler-ee not in the least
mâi mâhk not a lot, not much
 mâi mâhk gwàh ... no more than ...
 mâi mâhk tâo-rài not so much
mâi mao sober
mâi mee ... there isn't/ aren't ...; no ...
mâi mee a-rai nothing
mâi mee bpra-sìt-ti-pâhp inefficient
mâi mee krai nobody, no-one
mâi mee lôo-ut lai plain
mâi mee mah-ra-yâht rude
mâi mee tahng! no chance!, no way!
mâi nâh chêu-a amazing
mái nèep (pâh) clothes peg
mái pài bamboo
mâi pèt mild
mâi rêe-up bumpy
mâi ròrk! certainly not!
mâi sài without
mái sùk teak
mâi tĕung ... less than ...
mâi wâhng engaged, occupied
mái-lâyk number, figure
măir! well well!
máir dtàir ... even the ...
mâir (kŏrng) mother
mâir mái widow
mâir náhm river
máir wâh although
 máir wâh ... even if ...
mâir-náhm kŏhng Mekhong

River
mairng ga-prOOn jellyfish
mair-o cat
ma-lairng insect
ma-lairng gùt insect bite
ma-lairng sàhp cockroach
ma-lairng wun fly
mao drunk
ma-reun-née the day after tomorrow
mâyk kréum cloudy
may-săh-yon April
máyt metre
mee have
  mee ... there is/are ...
  mee ... mái? have you got ...?; is/are there ...?
mee bpra-sìt-ti-pâhp efficient
mee bpra-yòht useful
mee chee-wít chee-wah lively
mee chee-wít yòo alive
mee chêu sĕe-ung famous
mee fùk boo-a with shower
mee hàyt-pŏn sensible
mee kâh valuable
mee kwahm pìt guilty
mee lom òrn òrn breezy
mee-nah-kom March
mee pĕw klúm dàirt suntanned
mee sa-này charming
mee sòOk-ka-pâhp dee healthy
mee tórng pregnant
mêet knife
mêet gohn razor
mêet púp penknife
mĕn smell, stink
meu hand

mêu-a gòrn née once, formerly
mêu-a keun née last night
mêu-a rài? when?
mêu-a ray-o ray-o née lately, recently
mêu-a wahn née yesterday
mĕu-un similar, like
mĕu-un gun same
meu-ung city; town; country
meu-ung boh-rahn Ancient City
meu-ung gào old town
meu-ung lŏo-ung capital city
meu-ung tai Thailand (informal)
mí-cha-nún otherwise
mí-tOO-nah-yon June
mók-ga-rah-kom January
mŏo pig
moo-ay (săh-gon) boxing (international)
moo-ay tai Thai-style boxing
mòo-bâhn village
mòo-bâhn bon poo-kăo mountain village
mòo bâhn bpra-mong fishing village
mòo gòr in-dee-a dta-wun dtòk West Indies
môo-lêe blinds
móOng mosquito net
mòo-uk hat; cap
móo-un tâyp kah-set cassette
mŏr doctor
mòr ideal
mŏr saucepan
mŏr fun dentist
mòr sŏm suitable, appropriate
mòrk mist

mòrk long foggy
mŏrn pillow; cushion
mor-ra-sŏom monsoon
mor-sor scruffy
mòt láir-o empty
mòt sa-dtì unconscious
múk-koo-tâyt guide, courier
mun it; it is; they; fat (on meat);
rich
  mun bpen it's
mûn engaged (to be married)
mun fa-rùng tôrt chips,
  French fries; crisps, (US)
  chips
mùt flea

N

năh thick
nah paddy field
náh uncle (younger brother of
  mother); aunt (younger sister of
  mother)
nâh face; front (part); page;
  season; next
nâh bèu-a boring
nâh dtèun dtên exciting
nâh fŏn rainy season
nâh glèe-ut ugly; horrible;
  disgusting
nâh năo winter
nâh nèu-ay nài tiring
nâh òk chest; bust
nâh rórn summer
nâh rung-gèe-ut unpleasant;
  revolting
nâh sĕe-a dai! what a shame!
nâh sèet pale

nâh sŏn jai interesting
nâh sŏng-săhn! what a pity!
nâh têung impressive
nâh too-râyt nasty
nâh-dtàhng window
nah-li-gah clock; watch
nah-li-gah bplòòk alarm
  clock
nah-li-gah kôr meu watch
náhm water
nahm bùt business card
náhm dèum drinking water
nahm sa-goon surname, last
  name
nahm sa-goon derm maiden
  name
nahn a long time
nahng Mrs
nahng pa-yah-bahn nurse
nahng-săo Miss
nah-tee minute
nah-yók director, president
nah-yók rút-ta-mon-dtree
  prime minister
nai on; in; into; Mr
năi? which?
nai a-nah-kót in future
nai bpra-tâyt rao at home
nai lŏo-ung king
nai ra-wàhng during; among
nai têe sòot eventually, at last
nâir jai certain, sure
nâir norn of course, certainly,
  definitely
nâirn crowded, busy
năo cold; feel cold
née this; these
nêe ... this is ...
  nêe a-rai? what's this?

nêe kŏrng krai? whose is this?
nêe krúp (kâ) there you are
nêe ngai here you are
nĕe-o sticky; sultry
nék-tai tie, necktie
nĕu-a north
nèu-ay tired
nèung one
nèung nai sèe quarter
néw inch
néw hŏo-a mâir meu thumb
néw meu finger
néw táo toe
ngah cháhng tusk
ngahm sa-ngàh elegant
ngahn job; work; carnival; festival
ngahn lée-ung party
ngahn sa-dairng sĭn-káh trade fair
ngahn sòp funeral
ngâi easy; simple
ngao shadow
ngăo lonely
ngao dàirt sunshade
ngêe-up quiet; silent
ngêe-up ngêe-up nòy! be quiet!
ngern money; silver
ngern bporn sterling
ngern deu-un salary
ngern dorn-lâh dollar
ngern dtàhng bpra-tâyt foreign exchange
ngern rĕe-un coin
ngern sòt cash
ngern típ tip
ngèu-uk gum
ngêu-un kăi bpra-gun insurance policy
ngôh stupid, silly, dumb
ngoo snake
ngoo hào cobra
ngôo-ung norn sleepy
ngót cancel
nîm soft
nít dee-o tâo-nún just a little
ní-tahn story
ní-tá-sa-gahn exhibition
nít-nòy a little bit
nít-ta-ya-săhn magazine
nók bird
nom milk
nŏo mouse; rat
nòOm young; young man
nòOm nòOm săo săo young people
nòo-uk hŏo noisy
nôo-ut massage
nòo-ut moustache
nôrk jàhk apart from
norn lie down
norn lùp sleep
norn lùp yòo asleep
nôrng thigh
nŏrng swamp
nórng chai younger brother
nórng săo younger sister
nórng sa-pái younger sister-in-law
nòy some
nóy few
nóy gwàh ... less than ...
nóy têe sòOt minimum
nùk heavy; serious
núk don-dtree musician
núk moo-ay boxer
núk rórng singer

Nu

núk sa-dairng chai actor
núk sa-dairng yǐng actress
núk sèuk-sǎh student
núk tôrng têe-o tourist
núm dtòk waterfall
núm hǒrm toilet water; perfume
núm kǎirng ice
núm mun oil; petrol, (US) gas
núm mun gáht petrol, (US) gas
núm mun krêu-ung oil (motor oil)
núm mun rót dee-sen diesel (fuel)
núm mun tah àhp dàirt suntan oil
núm nùk weight
núm nùk gern excess baggage
núm póo fountain
núm tôo-um flood
núm yah àhp náhm bubble bath
núm yah láhng chahm washing-up liquid
nún that
nûn a-rai? what's that?
nûng sit
nǔng leather; film, movie
nǔng glùp suede
nûng sì! sit down!
núng-sěu book
núng-sěu dern tahng passport
núng-sěu num têe-o guidebook
núng-sěu pim newspaper
nút appointment

O

oh-gàht chance, opportunity
ong-sǎh degree
òo sôrm rót garage
oo-bùt-dti-hàyt accident
ôo-ee! ouch!
ôom carry
oo-mohng tunnel
oon-na-ha-poom temperature
òop-bpa-gorn equipment
òot fun filling
òot-sǎh-ha-gum industry
ôo-un fat
òrk bpai go out
  òrk bpai hâi pón! get out!
òrk sěe-ung pronounce
òrn weak (drink)
òrn-air weak (person)

P

pâh material, cloth
pah bpai take
pâh bpòo têe norn sheet; bed linen
pâh chét bpàhk napkin
pâh chét dtoo-a towel
pâh chét jahn tea towel
pâh chét meu napkin, serviette; tissues, Kleenex®
pâh chét nâh handkerchief; flannel
pâh hòm blanket
pâh kêe réw cloth, rag
pâh ôrm nappy, diaper

pâh pôhk sĕe-sà headscarf
pâh pun kor scarf (for neck)
pâh pun plăir bandage;
  dressing
pâh un-nah-mai sanitary
  towel, sanitary napkin
pâhk region
pâhk bung-kúp compulsory
pâhk dtâi southern region of
  Thailand
pâhk ee-sähn north-eastern
  region of Thailand
pâhk glahng central region of
  Thailand
pàhn through; via
pàhn bpai go through
pâhp kĕe-un painting; picture
pah-săh language
pah-săh tai Thai (language)
pah-săh tìn dialect
pah-săh ung-grìt English
  (language)
pah-sĕe duty; tax
pah-sĕe sa-năhm bin airport
  tax
pah-yóo storm
pah-yóo fŏn thunderstorm
pâi cards
páir goat; allergic to
páir dàirt heat stroke
pàirn slice
pàirn sĕe-ung record
pairng expensive
păirn-têe map
păirn-têe ta-nŏn road map,
  streetmap
pa-mâh Burma; Burmese
pa-nàirk dtôrn rúp reception;
  reception desk

pa-núk ngahn dtôrn rúp
  receptionist
pa-núk ngahn krêu-ung bin
  steward
pa-núk ngahn toh-ra-sùp
  operator
pa-nun gamble
pa-yah-yahm try; persevere
pay-dahn ceiling
pêe older brother/sister
pêe chai older brother
pêe săo older sister
pêe sa-pái older sister-in-law
pêrm increase
pèt hot, spicy
pét diamond
pét ploy jewellery
péun floor
  yòo bon péun on the floor
pèun rash (on skin)
péun din ground
péun rorng táo sole (of shoe)
pêu-un friend
pêu-un bâhn neighbour
pêu-un rôo-um ngahn partner
  (in business)
pêu-un tahng jòt-măi
  penfriend
pĕw skin
pĕw klúm dàirt suntan
pĕw nŭng skin
pí-gahn disabled
pí-pít-ta-pun museum
pí-pít-ta-pun hàirng châht
  National Museum
pi-sàyt special; de luxe
pìt wrong; faulty
pìt gòt-măi illegal
pìt tum-ma-dah unusual

pìt wǔng disappointed
pi-tee dtàirng ngahn wedding
plǎir bàht jèp injury
plǎir gra-pór ulcer
plǎir mâi burn
plǎir porng blister
plǎir wèr nasty
plǎirng eccentric
playng song
playng póp pop song
plùk push
pǒm I; me; myself (said by a man); hair
pǒng súk fôrk soap powder
pǒn-la-mái fruit
pôo bplair translator
pôo doy-ee sǎhn passenger
pôo-chai boy; man
poo-gèt Phuket
pôo-jùt-gahn manager
poo-kǎo mountain
poo-mi-bpra-tâyt scenery; landscape
pôot speak; talk
pôot èek tee repeat
pôot lên joke
pôo-uk group
pôo-uk née these
pôo-uk nún those
pôo-uk pôo-yǐng women
poo-ung mah-lai sái left-hand drive
poo-ung ma-lai kwǎh right-hand drive
pôo-yài adult
pôo-yài bâhn village headman
pôo-yǐng woman; lady; girl
pôo-yǐng bah hostess (in bar)
pôo-yǐng ung-grìt English

girl/woman
por enough
pôr father
pôr dtah father-in-law (of a man)
pôr dtah mâir yai parents-in-law (wife's parents)
por jai satisfied
por láir-q no more; that's enough
pôr mái widower
pôr mâir parents
pôr pǒo-a father-in-law (of a woman)
pôr pǒo-a mâir pǒo-a parents-in-law (husband's parents)
por sǒm-koo-un quite, fairly
pǒrm thin, skinny
pòt prickly heat
pót-ja-nah-nóo-grom dictionary
prá monk; priest
prá-ah-tít sun
prá-jâo God
prá-jun moon
prá-póot-ta-jâo Buddha
prá-póot-ta-rôop Buddha image
prá-rah-chi-nee queen
prá-râht-cha-wung palace
prá-tóo-dong mendicant monk
pree-o slim
préut-sa-jìk-gah-yon November
préut-sa-pah-kom May
prom carpet; rug
prôong née tomorrow
prór because

prórm ready
púk stay
pùk vegetables
púk krêung interval
púk pòrn rest
pun-ra-yah wife
pút fan (handheld)
pùt stir-fry
pút lom fan (mechanical)

R

ra-bee-ung patio; terrace; balcony
rah-kah cost; price
rah-kah tòok downmarket
ráhn shop, store
ráhn ah-hǎhn restaurant
ráhn ah-hǎhn jeen Chinese restaurant
ráhn gǒo-ay dtěe-o café; noodle shop
ráhn kǎi dòrk-mái florist
ráhn kǎi kǒrng chum food store
ráhn kǎi kǒrng gào antique shop
ráhn kǎi krêu-ung lèk hardware store
ráhn kǎi krêu-ung pét ploy jeweller's
ráhn kǎi lâo liquor store, shop selling wines and spirits
ráhn kǎi núng-sěu bookshop, bookstore
ráhn kǎi pâhp kěe-un art gallery

ráhn kǎi pùk greengrocer's
ráhn kǎi yah chemist's, pharmacy
ráhn kǎi yah sòop tobacconist's, tobacco store
ráhn néu-a butcher's
ráhn sěrm sǒo-ay beauty salon
ráhn súk hâirng dry-cleaner's
ráhn súk (sêu-a) pâh laundry
ráhn tum ka-nǒm-bpung bakery
râhng-gai body
rahng-wun prize
ra-hùt toh-ra-sùp dialling code
rai-gahn schedule
rai-gahn num têe-o tour
râirk first
rairng fai fáh voltage
ra-kung bell
rao we; us
ra-wàhng between
ra-wung! be careful!; look out!
ra-wung ná! look out!
ra-yá tahng distance
ray-o early; quick, fast; quickly
ray-o ray-o kâo! hurry up!
ray-o ray-o nòy! come on!
rêep rêep nòy! hurry up!
rêe-uk call; be called
ree-un learn
rêe-up smooth
rêe-up róy neat
rêrm begin, start
rěu or

... **rĕu** ... either ... or ...
reu-a ship; boat
reu-a bpra-mong fishing boat
reu-a choo chêep lifeboat
reu-a hǎhng yao long-tailed boat
reu-a kâhm fâhk ferry
reu-a pai rowing boat
reu-a ray-o speedboat
reu-a sǔm-bpûn sampan
reu-a sǔm-pao junk
reu-a yon motorboat
reu-a yórt yacht
rêu-ay rêu-ay so-so
reu-doo season
reu-doo bai mái plì spring
réu-doo bai-mái rôo-ung autumn, (US) fall
rêu-ung story
  rêu-ung a-rai gun? what's going on?
rim fěe bpàhk lip
rôhk disease
rôhk áyd Aids
rôhk bìt dysentery
rôhk bpòo-ut nai kôr rheumatism
rôhk gloo-a náhm rabies
rôhk hèut hay fever; asthma
rôhk hùt measles
rôhk hùt yer-ra-mun German measles
rôhk páir dàirt sunstroke
rôhk sâi dtìng appendicitis
rohng la-korn theatre
rohng ngahn factory
rohng nǔng cinema, movie theater
rohng pa-yah-bahn hospital

rohng rairm hotel
rohng ree-un school
rohng rót garage
rohng rúp jum-num pawnshop
rohng yim gym
rôm umbrella; parasol
  nai rôm in the shade
rôm gun dàirt beach umbrella
roo hole
róo know
róo-a fence
rôo-a leak
roo-ay rich
róo-jùk know
rôong dawn
  rôong cháo at dawn
rôop picture
rôop gàir sa-lùk carving
rôop lòr handsome
rôop-song figure
rôop tài photograph
rǒo-rǎh posh; luxurious; upmarket
róo-sèuk feel
róo-sèuk ja ah-jee-un feel sick
róo-sèuk kòrp-koOn feel grateful
róo-sèuk mâi sa-bai feel unwell
roo-um include
roo-um yòo dôo-ay included
roo-um yôrt total
róp-goo-un disturb
ror wait
rórn hot; warm
rórng hâi cry
rórng playng sing
rorng táo shoe(s); boot(s)
rorng táo dtàir sandal(s)

rorng táo gee-lah trainer(s)

rorng táo ma-nóot gòp flipper(s)

rót car; taste; flavour

rót air air-conditioned bus

rót bprùp ah-gàht air-conditioned bus

rót bun-tóok lorry, truck

rót châo rented car

rót dtôo van

rót fai train

rót fai dòo-un express train

rót kĕn pushchair

rót kĕn sŭm-rùp kon bpòo-ay wheelchair

rót may bus

rót may bprùp ah-gàht air-conditioned bus

rót mor-dter-sai motorbike; moped

rót norn sleeping car

rót num têe-o coach trip

rót pa-yah-bahn ambulance

rót sa-bee-ung dining car

rót sa-góot-dter scooter

rót săhm lór trishaw

rót sa-năhm bin airport bus

rót too-a tour bus

rót yon car

rúk love

rûm roo-ay wealthy

rum tai Thai classical dancing

rum-kahn annoying; annoy

rum-wong ramwong dance (popular Thai folk dance)

rúp accept; receive

rút state

rút-ta-bahn government

S

sà

sà pond; wash

sà pŏm wash one's hair

sà wâi náhm swimming pool

sa-àht clean

sa-bai well, in good health

  sa-bai dee OK, all right

sa-bòo soap

sa-bòo gohn nòo-ut shaving soap

sa-bpay chèet pŏm hairspray

sa-dòo-uk convenient; comfortable

sa-dtahng satang (unit of currency)

sa-dtairm stamp

sa-dtree ladies' toilet, ladies' room

sa-gee náhm waterskiing

sa-górt táyp Sellotape®, Scotch tape®

sa-hà-rút a-may-ri-gah United States

săh-gon international

sâhk sa-lùk hùk pung remains, ruins

săh-lah pavilion

săhm three

săhm lèe-um torng kum Golden Triangle

săh-mee husband

sâhp know

sàh-sa-năh religion

sàh-sa-năh póot Buddhism; Buddhist

săh-tah-ra-ná public

sai sand

sài put
sái left
săi late; telephone line; strap
săi fai fáh wire; lead
sài goon-jair lock
săi pahn fanbelt
săi rút fastener
săi yahng yêut elastic
sairng overtake
sa-lai slide
sa-lĕung salung (unit of currency)
sa-lùk nâh-dtàhng shutter
sa-mĕr always
sa-moh-sŏrn club, clubhouse
sa-moon prai herbs (medicinal)
sa-mòot notebook
sa-mòot bun-téuk bpra-jum wun diary
sa-mòot măi lâyk toh-ra-sùp phone book
sa-mòot yay-loh páyt yellow pages
sa-năhm playing field; pitch
sa-năhm bin airport
sa-năhm gee-lah hàirng châht National Stadium
sa-năhm górp golf course
sa-năhm ten-nít tennis court
sa-năhm yâh lawn
sa-ngòp calm
sa-nòok pleasant
sa-nòok dee enjoyable, fun
sâo sad
sǎo young (girl)
sa-pahn bridge
sa-tăhn bor-ri-gahn rót châo car rental company
sa-tăhn gong-sŏon consulate
sa-tăhn lée-ung dèk lék nursery
sa-tăhn sùk-gah-rá shrine
sa-tăhn tôot embassy
sa-tăhn-na-gahn situation
sa-tǎh-nee terminus; station
sa-tǎh-nee dtum-ròo-ut police station
sa-tǎh-nee rót fai railway station
sa-tǎh-nee rót may bus station
sa-tǎhn-têe place
sa-wàhng bright
sa-wít switch
sa-wít fai switch
sa-wùt dee hello
sa-wùt dee bpee mài! happy New Year!
sa-wùt dee kâ hello
sa-wùt dee krúp hello
sàyt sa-dtahng small change
sèe four
sĕe colour; paint
sĕe chom-poo pink
sĕe dairng red
sĕe dum black
sĕe kǎo white
sĕe kĕe-o green
sĕe krohng rib
sĕe lĕu-ung yellow
sĕe lêu-ut mŏo scarlet
sĕe môo-ung purple
sĕe néu-a beige
sĕe núm dtahn brown
sĕe núm ngern blue
sĕe òrn pale
sĕe sôm orange
sĕe tao grey
sĕe tao gairm lĕu-ung fawn
sèe yâirk crossroads,

intersection
sěe-a broken, faulty, out of order; polluted
sěe-a jai sorry
sěe-a láir-o damage; damaged
sěe-o sharp
sèe-ung risky
sèe-ung sound, noise; voice
sên line
sên dâi thread, cotton
sên lôo-ut wire
sèt ready; over, finished
séu buy
sêu dtrong honest
sêu-a chért shirt
sêu-a choo chêep lifejacket
sêu-a chóot dress
sêu-a fŏn raincoat
sêu-a gahng-gayng norn pyjamas
sêu-a glâhm vest (under shirt)
sêu-a gúk waistcoat
sêu-a klOOm coat, overcoat
sêu-a klOOm chóot norn dressing gown
sêu-a nôrk jacket
sêu-a pâh clothes
sêu-a pâh chún nai underwear
sêu-a pôo-yĭng blouse
sêu-a sa-wet-dter sweater; sweatshirt
sêu-a yêut T-shirt
sêu-a yók song bra
si-gah cigar
sîn sòot end
sǐng-hǎh-kom August
sǐn-la-bpà art
sǐn-la-bpà sa-mǎi mài modern art
sǐn-la-bpin artist
sìp ten; zip
sìp-hâh nah-tee quarter of an hour
sǒh-pay-nee prostitute
sòht single (unmarried)
sòk-ga-bpròk dirty
sôn rorng táo heel (of shoe)
sôn táo heel (of foot)
sòng send
sòng dtòr forward
sòng jòt-mǎi post, mail
sòng jòt-mǎi dtahm bâhn delivery
sòng tahng ah-gàht by airmail
sǒng-grahn Thai New Year
sǒng-krahm war
sòo towards
sǒo-ay beautiful
sòok ripe
sòok sòok well-done (steak)
sòok sòok dìp dìp rare (steak)
sòok-ka-pâhp health
sòok-ka-pâhp mâi dee unhealthy
sòok-ka-pâhp sǒm-boon fit, healthy
sôom sâhm clumsy
sǒon zero
sǒon glahng centre
sǒong tall; high
sOOn-la-gah-gorn Customs
sOO-pâhp polite
sOO-pâhp bOO-ròot gentleman
sOO-pâhp sa-dtree lady
sòop bOO-rèe smoke
sòot bottom (of road)

sòot tái last
sôo-um săh-tah-ra-ná public convenience
sòo-un part
sŏo-un garden
sòo-un dtoo-a private
sòo-un mâhk most (of)
sòo-un pa-sŏm mixture
sŏo-un săh-tah-ra-ná park
sŏo-un sùt zoo
sòo-ut mon pray
sôrm repair, mend; fork
sŏrn teach
sôrn hide
sorng pack, packet
sŏrng two
sŏrng ah-tít fortnight
sorng jòt-măi envelope
sŏrng krúng twice
sŏrng tâir-o van with two benches used as a bus
sòt fresh
sòt chêun refreshing
soy side street; lane; soi
sôy kor necklace, chain
súk wash
... sùk nít nèung a little ...
súk pâh wash clothes; laundry
sŭm-kun important; main
sŭm-lee cotton wool, absorbent cotton
sŭm-núk kào săhn núk tôrng têe-o tourist information office
sŭm-núk ngahn office
sŭm-núk ngahn kào săhn information office
sŭm-rùp for
  sŭm-rùp koon for you

240

sûn short
sŭn-châht nationality
sùng order
sŭn-yah promise
sŭn-yahn fay mâi fire alarm
sùp-sŏn complicated
sùt animal

T

ta-bee-un rót car registration number
tâh if
tâh reu-a docks; harbour, port; jetty; quay(side)
tâh yàhng nún then, in that case
tăhm ask
tahn (kâo) eat
tahng direction; path; route; way
tahng ah-gàht by air
tahng dern corridor
tahng dòo-un motorway, highway, freeway
tahng kâo entrance
tahng kóhng bend
tahng kwăh on the right
tahng lée-o turning
tahng lŏo-ung highway
tahng máh-lai pedestrian crossing
tahng òrk exit
tahng ôrm detour
tahng rót fai railway
tahng rót fai pàhn level crossing
tahng sái on the left

tahng yâirk junction; fork
tàht tray
tai Thai (adj)
tái tights, pantyhose
tài rôop photograph
táir genuine; original
tairm-porn tampon
tairn instead
  tairn têe ja ... instead of ...
tăir-o queue, line
ta-lay sea
ta-lay sàhp lake
ta-nah-kahn bank
ta-nai kwahm lawyer
ta-nŏn street; road
ta-nŏn yài main road
ta-nùt meu sái left-handed
táo foot
tâo-nún just; only
tâo-rài? how much?
tâyp něe-o Sellotape®, Scotch tape®
tee time
têe at
  têe bâhn at home
têe bpèrt gra-bpŏrng can-opener
têe bpèrt kòo-ut bottle-opener; corkscrew
têe bpùt núm fŏn windscreen wipers
têe èun somewhere else
têe fàhk gra-bpăo left luggage, baggage check
têe fàhk kŏrng cloakroom
têe hâhm rót kâo pedestrian precinct
têe jâirng kŏrng hăi lost property office

têe jòrt rót car park, parking lot
têe jòrt rót táirk-sêe taxi rank
têe jum-nài dtŏo-a ticket office
têe kèe-a boo-rèe ashtray
têe láir-o last, previous
tee la nóy gradually
têe lĕu-a rest
tee lŭng afterwards; later, later on
têe năi somewhere
têe năi? where?
têe nêe here; over here
têe nôhn there; over there
têe norn mattress; berth
têe nûn there
têe nûng seat
têe nûng dtìt nâh-dtàhng window seat
têe nûng kâhng lŭng back seat
têe nûng rúp kàirk couch
têe pìt error
têe púk accommodation(s)
têe râhp lôom plain
tee râirk at first
têe rúk darling
têe rút kĕm kùt seatbelt
têe sŏrng second (adj)
têe sòrp tăhm information desk
têe tum ngahn office
têe yòo address
têe-o visit; trip
têe-o bin flight
têe-o bin măo charter flight
têe-o hâi sa-nòok! enjoy yourself!

têe-o sa-nòok ná! have fun!; have a good journey!

tee-um imitation

tee-un candle

têe-ung keun at midnight

têe-ung wun midday

tee-wee TV

tén tent

ter you

těu carry

těung reach

tíng throw away

tíng wái leave behind

tôh! good heavens!

toh tahng glai long-distance call

toh-ra-lâyk telegram

toh-ra-sùp phone

toh-ra-sùp gèp ngern bplai tahng reverse-charge call, collect call

toh-ra-sùp săh-tah-ra-ná payphone

toh-ra-tút television

tong flag

too-a bus tour

tòo-a peanuts; peas; beans

tôo-a bpai everywhere

tôo-ay cup

tôo-ay chahm crockery

tóok every

tòok right, correct; cheap, inexpensive

tòok dàirt mâi sunburnt

tòok gòt-măi legal

tòok ka-moy-ee robbed; stolen

tóok kon everyone

tòok láir-o that's right

tóok yàhng everything

tòok-dtôrng accurate

... tôom ... p.m. (in the evening)

tŏong bag

tŏong bplah-sa-dtìk plastic bag

tŏong gra-dàht paper bag

tŏong meu gloves

tŏong norn sleeping bag

tŏong nôrng stocking(s)

tŏong táo sock(s)

tŏong yahng condom

tŏong yai boo-a tights, pantyhose

tóo-rá business

tóo-ra-gìt deal

tôr pipe

torng gold

tórng stomach

tórng pòok constipated

tórng sěe-a diarrhoea; upset stomach

tórp-fêe sweet(s), candy, candies

tôrt deep-fry

trah-wern ay-yen travel agency

tum make; do

tûm cave

tum dôo-ay meu handmade

tum hâi cause

tum hâi ôo-un fattening

tum kwahm sa-àht clean

tum lép manicure

tum ngahn work

tum têe bâhn home-made

tum-ma-châht nature; natural

tum-ma-dah normal; usually,

normally; ordinary; plain
tum-mai? why?
tûn you
tun sa-măi fashionable; modern
tŭng bucket
tŭng dtàirk broke
tŭng ka-yà dustbin, trashcan
túng mòt all; altogether; completely
tŭng núm mun petrol tank, gas tank
túng sŏrng both of them
tun-tee at once, immediately; suddenly
tun-wah-kom December

U

um-per amphoe (sub-division of province)
un thing
un năi? which one?
un née this one
un nún that one
un-dta-rai harm; danger; dangerous
ung-grìt English (adj); British
un-nóo-yâht allowed
ùt-dta-noh-mút automatic
ùt-dtrah rate
ùt-dtrah lâirk bplèe-un exchange rate
ùt-ta-noh-mút automatic
ùt-ti-bai explain

W

wâh say
wăhn sweet
wahn seun née the day before yesterday
wahng put
wâhng empty; deserted
wâhng bplào empty, vacant
wâhng ngahn unemployed
wâi náhm swim
wáir stopover
wăirn ring
wâirn dtah glasses, (US) eyeglasses
wăirn dtàirng ngahn wedding ring
wâirn gun dàirt sunglasses
wăirn mûn engagement ring
wai-yah-gorn grammar
wâo kite
way-lah time
way-lah sòo-un mâhk most of the time
way-lah-nún then, at that time
wĕe comb
wee-sah visa
wèet rórng scream
wew view
wí-nah-tee second (in time)
wîng run
wí-sàyt incredible, tremendous
wí-sàyt jung ler-ee fantastic
wít-ta-yah-lai college
wít-ta-yah-sàht science
wít-ta-yóo radio
wít-tee method

wong don-dtree orchestra
wong glom circle
woo-a cow
wun day
wun ah-tít Sunday
wun gèrt birthday
wun gòrn ... the day before ...
wun jun Monday
wun lŭng jàhk têe ... the day
  after ...
wun ma-reun née the day
  after tomorrow
wun née today
wun pa-réu-hùt Thursday
wun póot Wednesday
wun prá Buddhist holy day
wun săo Saturday
wun săo ah-tít weekend
wun seun née the day before
  yesterday
wun sîn bpee New Year's Eve
wun sòok Friday
wun têe date
wun ung-kahn Tuesday
wun yòot holiday, vacation
wun yòot râht-cha-gahn
  public holiday
wung palace
wŭng hope
wút temple; monastery
wùt cold (illness)
wút-ta-na-tum culture

Y

yah medicine
yâh grandmother (paternal);
  grass

yàh! don't!
yah dùp glìn dtoo-a
  deodorant
yah glông pipe tobacco
yàh gun láir-o divorced
yah gun ma-lairng insect
  repellent
yah kâh chéu-a antiseptic
yah kâh chéu-a rôhk
  disinfectant
yah koOm gum-nèrt
  contraceptive pill
yah kùt polish
yah kùt rorng táo shoe polish
yah kwin-neen quinine
yah láhng make-up remover
yah mét tablet
yah pít poison
yah ra-ngúp bpòo-ut
  painkiller
yah sà pŏm shampoo
yah sàyp-dtìt drug, narcotic
yah sĕe fun toothpaste
yah sòop tobacco
yah tah lotion; ointment
yah tah gun dàirt sunblock
yah tah lŭng àhp dàirt aftersun
  cream
yah tah lŭng gohn nòo-ut
  aftershave
yah tài laxative
yâhk hard, difficult
yàhk dâi want
yàhk (ja) I'd like to
yahng rubber
yahng a-lài spare tyre
yahng dtàirk puncture
yahng lóp rubber, eraser
yahng nai inner tube

yàhng née this way, like this
yàhng nóy at least
yahng rót tyre
yahng rút rubber band
yâht relatives
yai grandmother (maternal)
yài big, large
yài bêr-rêr enormous
yai sǔng-krór synthetic
yâir terrible, dreadful
yâir jung! too bad!
yâir long worse
yâir mâhk awful, terrible
yâir têe sòot worst
yâirk gun separate; separately
yao long
yêe hôr brand
yêe-bpòòn Japan; Japanese
yeen jeans
yêe-um excellent, brilliant; visit
yêe-um ler-ee lovely, excellent
yêe-um yôrt fantastic
yen cold; cool
yen née this afternoon
yen prôong née tomorrow evening
yép sew
yer-ra-mun Germany; German
yeun stand
yèu-uk jug
yím smile
yin dee glad
yǐng rúp chái maid, chambermaid
yók wáyn except
yòo live; still; in, at home
  káo mâi yòo he/she's not in

... yòo têe nǎi? where is ...?
yòo bon ... on top of ...; at the top of ...
yòo dtrong glahng in the middle
yòo dtrong nâh straight ahead
yòo glâi nearby
yòo kâhng bon at the top
yOOng mosquito
yOO-rohp Europe; European
yòot stop
yòot pôot ná! shut up!
yóot-dti-tum fair, just
yôrt smashing, fabulous
  yôrt! great!
yôrt yêe-um splendid, super
yung still; not yet
yung mâi sèt finish
yung-ngai? how?

Thai

→

English
Signs and
Notices

Abbreviations

ป.อ. bprùp ah-gàat air-
conditioned

อ. um-per Amphoe, district

ก.ท.ม. grOong-tâyp-ma-hăh-
na-korn Bangkok

พ.ศ. póot-ta-sùk-ga-ràht
Buddhist Era (BE) (543 years
ahead of AD)

ค.ศ. krít-dta-sùk-ga-ràht
Christian Era (AD)

ช.ม. chôo-a mohng hours

น. nah-li-gah hours

ก.ม. gi-loh-mét kilometre

ช. chai men

จ. jung-wùt province

ถ. ta-nŏn road

ต. dtum-bon Tambon, sub-
district

ญ. yĭng women

General signs

ระวัง ra-wung caution

อันตราย un-dta-rai danger

ห้าม ... hâhm ... ... forbidden

อย่า yàh ... do not ...

สอบถาม sòrp tăhm
enquiries

โรงพยาบาลห้ามใช้เสียง
rohng pa-yah-bahn: hâhm
chái sĕe-ung hospital: no
noise

ห้ามผ่าน hâhm pàhn no
admission

ห้ามเข้า hâhm kâo no entry

ห้ามทิ้งขยะ hâhm tíng ka-yà
no litter

ห้ามจอด hâhm jòrt no
parking

ห้ามถ่ายรูป hâhm tài rôop no
photographs

ห้ามสูบบุหรี่ hâhm sòop boo-
rèe no smoking

กรุณาอย่าส่งเสียงดัง ga-roo-
nah yàh sòng sĕe-ung dung
please don't make a noise

โปรดถอดรองเท้า bpròht tòrt
rorng táo please remove
shoes

ตำรวจ dtum-ròo-ut police

โปรดเงียบ bpròht ngêe-up
silence, please

Airport, planes

ที่ทำการบริษัทการบิน têe
tum gahn bor-ri-sùt gahn bin
airline company offices

ท่าอากาศยาน tâh ah-gàht-

249

sa-yahn airport

ถึง tĕung arrives

ประชาสัมพันธ์
ท่าอากาศยานกรุงเทพฯ
bpra-chah sŭm-pun tâh-ah-
gàht-sa-yăhn grOOng-tâyp
public relations, Bangkok
Airport

ศุลกากร sOOn-la-gah-gorn
Customs

สุขาชาย sòo-kăh chai gents'
toilets, men's room

ชาย chai gents

ตรวจคนเข้าเมือง dtròo-ut kon
kâo meu-ung immigration

ประชาสัมพันธ์ bpra-chah
sŭm-pun information

สุขาหญิง sòo-kăh yĭng ladies'
toilets, ladies' room

หญิง yĭng ladies

ออก òrk leaves

ฝากกระเป๋า fàhk gra-bpăo
left luggage, baggage
checkroom

ลิฟท์ lif lift, elevator

จุดนัดพบ jòot nút póp
meeting point

ห้ามสูบบุหรี่ hâhm sòop
bOO-rèe no smoking

จุดตรวจค้นผู้โดยสาร jòot
dtròo-ut kón pôo doy-ee
săhn passenger check-point

เฉพาะผู้โดยสารและลูกเรือเท่า
นั้น cha-pòr pôo-doy-ee săhn
láir lôok reu-a tâo-nún
passengers and crew only

ตรวจหนังสือเดินทาง dtròo-ut
núng-sĕu dern tahng
passport control

ภัตตาคาร pút-dtah-khan
restaurant

ตรวจสอบบัตรผู้โดยสารและ
กระเป๋า dtròo-ut sòrp bùt
pôo-doy-ee-săhn láir gra-
bpăo ticket and baggage
check

ที่จำหน่ายตั๋ว têe jum-nài
dtŏo-a ticket office

เวลา way-lah time

ผู้มาส่งผู้โดยสาร pôo mah
sòng pôo-doy-ee-săhn
visitors

ที่พักผู้มาส่งผู้โดยสาร têe púk
pôo mah sòng pôo-doy-ee-
sahn visitors' waiting area

ทางเข้า tahng kâo way in,
entrance

ทางออก tahng òrk way out

Banks, money

บาท bàht baht

ธนาคาร ta-nah-kahn bank

ฝากประจำ fàhk bpra-jum deposit account, savings account

ฝากเงิน fàhk ngern deposits

อัตราแลกเปลี่ยนเงิน ùt-dtrah lâirk bplèe-un ngern exchange rate

อัตราแลกเปลี่ยนเงินตราต่าง ประเทศ ùt-dtrah lâirk bplèe-un ngern dtrah dtàhng bpra-tâyt foreign exchange rate

สอบถาม sòrp tăhm enquiries

แลกเปลี่ยนเงินตราต่างประเท ศ lâirk bplèe-un ngern dtrah dtàhng bpra-tâyt bureau de change

เปิดบัญชีใหม่ bpèrt bun-chee mài new accounts

ถอนเงิน tŏrn ngern withdrawals

Bus travel

รถปรับอากาศ rót bprùp ah-gàht air-conditioned bus

ถึง tĕung arrives

ออก òrk departs

สุขาชาย sòo-kăh chai gents' toilets, men's room

ประชาสัมพันธ์ bpra-chah sŭm-pun information

สอบถาม sòrp tăhm information, enquiries

สุขาหญิง sòo-kăh yĭng ladies' toilets, ladies' room

รับฝากของ rúp fàhk kŏrng left luggage, baggage checkroom

ห้ามสูบบุหรี่ hâhm sòop boo-rèe no smoking

ห้องพักผู้โดยสาร hôrng púk pôo doy-ee săhn passengers' waiting room

ทางเข้าเฉพาะผู้ถือตั๋วโดยสาร tahng kâo cha-pòr pôo tĕu dtŏo-a doy-ee săhn passengers with tickets only

ที่จำหน่ายตั๋ว têe jum-nài dtŏo-a ticket office

กำหนดเวลาเดินรถ gum-nòt way-lah dern rót timetable, (US) schedule

รถทัวร์ rót too-a tour bus

Countries, nationalities

อาฟริกา ah-fri-gah Africa; African

อีก้อ ee-gôr Akha (hill tribe)

อเมริกา a-may-ri-gah America; American

เอเชีย ay-see-a Asia

251

ออสเตรเลีย òrt-sa-dtray-lee-a
Australia; Australian

พม่า pa-mâh Burma,
Myanmar; Burmese

กัมพูชา gum-poo-chah
Cambodia

แคนาดา kair-nah-dah
Canada; Canadian

จีน jeen China; Chinese

ประเทศ bpra-tâyt country

อังกฤษ ung-grìt England;
Britain; UK; English; British

ยุโรป yoo-rôhp Europe;
European

ฝรั่งเศส a-rùng-sàyt France;
French

ประเทศเยอรมัน bpra-tâyt
yer-ra-mun Germany;
German

ชาวเขา chao kǎo hill-tribe
person; hill-tribe people

แม้ว máy-o Hmong, Meo (hill
tribe)

ฮอลแลนด์ horn-lairn
Holland; Dutch

อินเดีย in-dee-a India; Indian

แขก kàirk Indian; Malaysian

อินโดนีเซีย in-doh-nee-see-a
Indonesia; Indonesian

ไอร์แลนด์ ai-lairn Ireland

ประเทศอิตาลี bpra-tâyt ì-
dtah-lee Italy

ญี่ปุ่น yêe-bpòon Japan;
Japanese

กะเหรี่ยง ga-rèe-ung Karen
(hill tribe)

เขมร ka-mǎyn Khmer;
Cambodian

เกาหลี gao-lěe Korea; Korean

ลาว lao Laos; Lao

มาเลเซีย mah-lay-see-a
Malaysia; Malaysian

นิวซีแลนด์ new see-lairn
New Zealand

ไอร์แลนด์เหนือ ai-lairn něu-a
Northern Ireland

ปากิสถาน bpah-gi-sa-tǎhn
Pakistan

ฟิลิปปินส์ fin-lip-bpin
Phillipines; Fillipino

สกอตแลนด์ sa-gort-lairn
Scotland

สิงคโปร์ sǐng-ka-bpoh
Singapore

ประเทศสเปน bpra-tâyt sa-
bpayn Spain

ไทย tai Thai

เมืองไทย meu-ung tai
Thailand (informal)

ประเทศไทย bpra-tâyt tai
Thailand (formal)

สหรัฐอเมริกา sa-hà-rút a-
may-ri-gah United States of
America

เวียดนาม wêe-ut-nahm
Vietnam;Vietnamese
เย้า yáo Yao (hill tribe)

Customs

ศุลกากร sŏon-la-gah-gorn
Customs
มีของต้องสำแดง mee kŏrng
dtôrng sǔm-dairng goods to
declare
ตรวจคนเข้าเมือง dtròo-ut
kon kâo meu-ung
immigration
ไม่มีของต้องสำแดง mâi mee
kŏrng dtôrng sǔm-dairng
nothing to declare
เฉพาะหนังสือเดินทางไทย
cha-pòr núng-sěu dern-tahng
tai Thai passport holders
only

Days

วัน wun day
อาทิตย์ ah-tít week
วันเสาร์อาทิตย์ wun sǎo ah-
tít weekend
วันจันทร์ wun jun Monday
วันอังคาร wun ung-kahn

Tuesday
วันพุธ wun póot Wednesday
วันพฤหัส wun pa-réu-hùt
Thursday
วันศุกร์ wun sòok Friday
วันเสาร์ wun sǎo Saturday
วันอาทิตย์ wun ah-tít Sunday

Entertainment

... บาท ... bàht ... baht
ถุงละ ... บาท toong la ... bàht
... baht per bag
ถ้วยละ ... บาท tôo-ay la ...
bàht ... baht per cup
ชิ้นละ ... บาท chín la ... bàht
... baht per piece
บริการ ๒๔ ช.ม. bor-ri-gahn
yêe-sìp sèe chôo-a mohng
24-hour service
รอบ ๑๗.๐๐ น. rôrp 17.00
n(ah-li-gah) 5 p.m. show
บาร์ bah bar
โบว์ลิ่ง bohn-lîng bowling
ที่จำหน่ายตั๋ว têe jum-nài
dtŏo-a box office
โรงภาพยนตร์ rohng pâhp-pa-
yon cinema, movie theater
เร็วๆนี้ ray-o ray-o née
coming soon
ดิสโก้ dít-sa-gôh disco

ทางเข้า tahng kâo entrance

ทางออก tahng òrk exit

เต็ม dtem full

อาบอบนวด àhp òp nôo-ut massage

รายการหน้า rai-gahn nâh next programme

อาทิตย์หน้า ah-tít nâh next week

ไนทคลับ náit klúp nightclub

ฉายวันนี้ chăi wun née now showing

ราคา rah-kah price

รอบ rôrp showing

Forms

ที่อยู่ têe yòo address

อายุ ah-yóo age

พ.ศ. por sŏr (year) ... BE (543 years later than AD)

สีตา sĕe dtah colour of eyes

สีผม sĕe pŏm colour of hair

เกิดวันที่ gèrt wun-têe date of birth

ชื่อ chêu first name

ตั้งแต่ ... ถึง ... dtûng-dtàir ... tĕung ... from ... until ...

ความสูง kwahm sŏong height

บ้านเลขที่ bâhn lâyk têe house number

ตรอก dtròrk lane

ซอย soy lane, soi

บันทึก bun-téuk memo

เดือน deu-un month

สัญชาติ sŭn-châht nationality

หมายเหตุ măi-hàyt note, n.b.

อาชีพ ah-chêep occupation

หนังสือเดินทางหมายเลข núng-sĕu dern tahng măi-lâyk passport number

จังหวัด jung-wùt province

เชื้อชาติ chéu-a châht race

อยู่ที่ yòo têe residing at

ถนน ta-nŏn road

เพศ pâyt sex

ลายเซ็น lai sen signature

ลงชื่อ long chêu signed

พักที่ púk têe staying at

นามสกุล nahm sa-goon surname

ตำบล dtum-bon Tambon, sub-district

หมู่บ้าน mòo-bâhn village

น้ำหนัก núm nùk weight

พยาน pa-yahn witness

Garages

บริการ ๒๔ ช.ม. bor-ri-gahn yêe-sìp sèe chôo-a mohng 24-hour service

บริการซ่อมรถ bor-ri-gahn sôrm rót car repairs
บริการล้างรถ bor-ri-gahn láhng rót car wash
ดีเซล dee-sen diesel
เปลี่ยนหม้อกรอง bplèe-un môr grorng filters changed
อู่ òo garage
ห้ามสูบบุหรี่ hâhm sòop boo-rèe no smoking
เปลี่ยนน้ำมันเครื่อง bplèe-un núm mun krêu-ung oil changed
บริการอัดฉีด bor-ri-gahn ùt chèet pressurized air
ปะยาง bpà yahng punctures repaired
เครื่องอะไหล่ krêu-ung a-lài spare parts

Geographical terms

คลอง klorng canal
เมืองหลวง meu-ung lŏo-ung capital city
ชนบท chon-na-bòt countryside
ป่าดงดิบ bpàh dong dìp forest, jungle
เขา kăo hill

เกาะ gòr island
ป่า bpàh jungle, forest
ที่ราบลุ่ม têe râhp lôom plain
แม่น้ำ mâir-náhm river
ทะเล ta-lay sea
ชายทะเล chai ta-lay seaside
เมือง meu-ung town; city; country
หมู่บ้าน mòo-bâhn village

Hairdresser's, beauty salons

เสริมสวย sěrm sŏo-ay beauty care
เครื่องสำอาง krêu-ung sŭm-ahng cosmetics
นวดหน้า nôo-ut nâh facial massage
ตัดผม dtùt pŏm hair cut
เป่าผม bpào pôm hair drying
ไดผม dai pŏm hair drying
สระผม sà pŏm wash
ตัดเล็บ dtùt lép manicure
ดัดผม dùt pŏm perm
เซทผม sét pŏm set
โกนหนวด gohn nòo-ut shave

Health

รถพยาบาล rót pa-yah-bahn
ambulance

คุมกำเนิด koom gum-nèrt
birth control

คลีนิค klee-ník clinic

ห้องคลอด hôrng klôrt
delivery room

ทันตแพทย์ tun-dta-pâirt
dentist

ทำฟัน tum fun dentist's

จำหน่ายยา jum-nài yah
dispensary

แพทย์หญิง pâirt yǐng doctor
(female)

พ.ญ. pâirt yǐng doctor (female)

น.พ. nai pâirt doctor (male)

นายแพทย์ nai pâirt doctor
(male)

ตรวจสายตา dtròo-ut sǎi dtah
eye test

ตรวจสายตา dtròo-ut sǎi dtah
dtròo-ut sǎi-dtah eye-testing

โรงพยาบาล rohng pa-yah-
bahn hospital

ฉีดยา chèet yah injections

นางพยาบาล nahng pa-yah-
bahn nurse

ห้างขายยา hâhng kǎi yah
pharmacy, drugstore

ตรวจปัสสาวะ dtròo-ut bpùt-
sǎh-wá urine test

เอ๊กซเรย์ X-ray X-ray

Hiring, renting

ชั่วโมงละ ... บาท chôo-a
mohng la ... bàht ... baht per
hour

เดือนละ ... บาท deu-un la ...
bàht ... baht per month

วันละ ... บาท wun la ... bàht
... baht per month

อพาร์ตเมนท์ให้เช่า ah-paht-
mén hâi châo apartment for
rent

บาท bàht baht (unit of currency)

รถให้เช่า rót hâi châo car for
hire, car to rent

เงินมัดจำ ngern mút-jum
deposit

แฟลทให้เช่า flàirt hâi châo
apartment for rent

ให้เช่า hâi châo for hire, to
let, to rent

บ้านให้เช่า bâhn hâi châo
house to let, house for rent

รถมอเตอร์ไซค์/รถจักรยานให้
เช่า rót mor-dter-sai/rót jùk-
ra-yahn hâi châo
motorcycle/bicycle for hire

จ่ายล่วงหน้า jài lôo-ung nâh pay in advance

ค่าเช่า kâh châo rental, fee

ห้องให้เช่า hôrng hâi châo room for rent

Hotels

คอฟฟี่ช้อบ kòrp-fêe chórp café serving coffees, alcoholic drinks, snacks and meals

ห้องคู่ hôrng kôo double room

ห้องคู่ปรับอากาศ hôrng kôo bprùp ah-gàht double room with air-conditioning

ทางออก tahng òrk exit

ชั้น chún floor

เกสท์เฮาส์ gàyt háot guesthouse

สอบถาม sòrp tăhm enquiries

ห้องน้ำสตรี hôrng náhm sa-dtree ladies' toilet, ladies' room

หญิง yĭng ladies

ลิฟท์ líf lift, elevator

บริการรถรับส่ง bor-ri-gahn rót rúp sòng limousine service

ห้องน้ำบุรุษ hôrng náhm boo-

ร็อต rôot men's toilet, men's room

ชาย chai men

ห้ามสูบบุหรี่ hâhm sòop boo-rèe no smoking

แผนกต้อนรับ pa-nàirk dtôrn rúp reception

ห้องอาหาร hôrng ah-hăhn restaurant

ห้อง hôrng room

ห้องให้เช่า hôrng hâi châo rooms to let

บริการนำเที่ยว bor-ri-gahn num têe-o sight-seeing tours

ห้องเดี่ยว hôrng dèe-o single room

ห้องเดี่ยวปรับอากาศ hôrng dèe-o bprùp ah-gàht single room with air-conditioning

สระว่ายน้ำ sà wâi náhm swimming pool

สุขา sòo-kăh toilet

ห้องน้ำ hôrng náhm toilets

ห้องว่าง hôrng wâhng vacancies

ยินดีต้อนรับ yin dee dtôrn rúp welcome

Lifts, elevators

ลง long down

ชั้น chún floor

ลิฟท์ **lif** lift, elevator

ไม่เกิน ... คน **mâi gern ... kon** maximum load ... people

ห้ามสูบบุหรี่ **hâhm sòop boo-rèe** no smoking

ขึ้น **kêun** up

Medicines

หลังอาหาร **lǔng ah-hǎhn** after meals

ทา **tah** apply (ointments)

ก่อนนอน **gòrn norn** before going to bed

ก่อนอาหาร **gòrn ah-hǎhn** before meals

ยาอันตราย **yah un-dta-rai** dangerous medicine

วิธีใช้ **wí-tee chái** instructions for use

กินเกินขนาดเป็นอันตราย **gin gern ka-nàht bpen un-dta-rai** it is dangerous to exceed the stated dose

ยา **yah** medicine

เม็ด **mét** tablet, pill

รับประทาน **rúp-bpra-tahn** take (orally)

ช้อนชา **chórn chah** teaspoon

วันละ ... ครั้ง **wun la ... krúng**

times ... times per day

วันละ ... เม็ด **wun la ... mét** tablets ... tablets per day

Months

เดือน **deu-un** month

มกราคม **mók-ga-rah-kom** January

กุมภาพันธ์ **goom-pah-pun** February

มีนาคม **mee-nah-kom** March

เมษายน **may-sǎh-yon** April

พฤษภาคม **préut-sa-pah-kom** May

มิถุนายน **mí-too-nah-yon** June

กรกฎาคม **ga-rúk-ga-dah-kom** July

สิงหาคม **sǐng-hǎh-kom** August

กันยายน **gun-yah-yon** September

ตุลาคม **dtoo-lah-kom** October

พฤศจิกายน **préut-sa-jik-gah-yon** November

ธันวาคม **tun-wah-kom** December

Notices on doors

เฉพาะเจ้าหน้าที่ cha-pór jâo-nâh-têe authorized personnel only
กริ่ง grìng bell
หมาดุ măh dòo beware of the dog
ปิด bpìt closed
ทางเข้า tahng kâo entry
ทางออก tahng òrk exit
ห้ามจอดรถขวางประตู hâhm jòrt rót kwăhng bpra-dtoo no parking in front of the gate
เข้า kâo in
ห้ามเข้า hâhm kâo no entry
ไม่มีกิจห้ามเข้า mâi mee gìt hâhm kâo no entry to unauthorized persons
ห้ามจอด hâhm jòrt no parking
ห้ามกลับรถ hâhm glùp rót no turning
เปิด bpèrt open
ออก òrk out
กรุณาถอดรองเท้า ga-roo-nah tòrt rorng táo please remove your shoes
กรุณากดกริ่ง ga-roo-nah gòt grìng please ring

กด gòt press
ถนนส่วนบุคคล ta-nŏn sòo-un bòok-kon private road
ดึง deung pull
ผลัก plùk push
ระวังสุนัขดุ ra-wung sŏo-núk dòo beware of the dog

Numbers

ศูนย์ sŏon zero
หนึ่ง nèung one
สอง sŏrng two
สาม săhm three
สี่ sèe four
ห้า hâh five
หก hòk six
เจ็ด jèt seven
แปด bpàirt eight
เก้า gâo nine
สิบ sìp ten
สิบเอ็ด sìp-èt eleven
สิบสอง sìp-sŏrng twelve
สิบสาม sìp-săhm thirteen
สิบสี่ sìp-sèe fourteen
สิบห้า sìp-hâh fifteen
สิบหก sìp-hòk sixteen
สิบเจ็ด sìp-jèt seventeen
สิบแปด sìp-bpàirt eighteen
สิบเก้า sìp-gâo nineteen
ยี่สิบ yêe-sìp twenty

ยี่สิบเอ็ด yêe-sip-èt twenty-one

สามสิบ săhm-sìp thirty

สามสิบเอ็ด săhm-sìp-èt thirty-one

สี่สิบ sèe-sìp forty

ห้าสิบ hâh-sìp fifty

หกสิบ hòk-sìp sixty

เจ็ดสิบ jèt-sìp seventy

แปดสิบ bpàirt-sìp eighty

เก้าสิบ gâo-sìp ninety

หนึ่งร้อย nèung róy one hundred

หนึ่งพัน nèung pun one thousand

สองพัน sŏrng pun two thousand

หนึ่งหมื่น nèung mèun ten thousand

สองหมื่น sŏrng mèun twenty thousand

หนึ่งแสน nèung săirn one hundred thousand

สองแสน sŏrng săirn two hundred thousand

หนึ่งล้าน nèung láhn one million

หนึ่งร้อยล้าน nèung róy láhn one hundred million

๐ sŏon 0

๑ nèung 1

๒ sŏrng 2

๓ săhm 3

๔ sèe 4

๕ hâh 5

๖ hòk 6

๗ jèt 7

๘ bpàirt 8

๙ gâo 9

๑๐ sìp 10

๑๑ sìp-èt 11

๑๒ sìp-sŏrng 12

๑๓ sìp-săhm 13

๑๔ sìp-sèe 14

๑๕ sìp-hâh 15

๑๖ sìp-hòk 16

๑๗ sìp-jèt 17

๑๘ sìp-bpàirt 18

๑๙ sìp-gâo 19

๒๐ yêe-sìp 20

๒๑ yêe-sìp-èt 21

๓๐ săhm-sìp 30

๓๑ săhm-sìp-èt 31

๔๐ sèe-sìp 40

๕๐ hâh-sìp 50

๖๐ hòk-sìp 60

๗๐ jèt-sìp 70

๘๐ bpàirt-sìp 80

๙๐ gâo-sìp 90

๑๐๐ nèung róy 100

๑๐๐๐ nèung pun 1,000

๒๐๐๐ sŏrng pun 2,000

๑๐๐๐๐ nèung mèun 10,000

๒๐๐๐๐ sŏrng mèun 20,000

๑๐๐๐๐๐ nèung săirn
100,000

๒๐๐๐๐๐ sŏrng săirn
200,000

๑๐๐๐๐๐๐ nèung láhn
1,000,000

๑๐๐๐๐๐๐๐๐ nèung róy láhn
100,000,000

Phones

บาท bàht baht (unit of currency)

รหัส ra-hùt code

เหรียญ rĕe-un coin

ต่อ dtòr extension

โทรศัพท์ทางไกล toh-ra-sùp tahng glai long distance telephone

เสีย sĕe-a out of order

ตำรวจ dtum-ròo-ut police

ตู้โทรศัพท์สาธารณะ dtôo toh-ra-sùp săh-tah-ra-ná public telephone box

โทร. toh tel.

โทรศัพท์ toh-ra-sùp telephone

สมุดเบอร์โทรศัพท์ sa-mòot ber toh-ra-sùp telephone directory

เบอร์โทรศัพท์ ber toh-ra-sùp telephone number

Place names

อยุธยา a-yóot-ta-yah Ayutthaya

บางปะอิน bahng-bpà-in Bang Pa-In

กรุงเทพฯ groong-tâyp Bangkok

บางลำภู bahng-lum-poo Banglamphu

เชียงใหม่ chêe-ung-mài Chiangmai

อนุสาวรีย์ประชาธิปไตย a-nóo-săh-wa-ree bpra-chah-típ-bpa-dtai Democracy Monument

หาดใหญ่ hàht yài Hat Yai

หัวหิน hŏo-a hin Hua Hin

หัวลำโพง hŏo-a lum-pohng Hua Lampong

กาญจนบุรี gahn-ja-na-boo-ree Kanjanaburi

ขอนแก่น kŏrn-gàirn Khonkaen

เกาะสมุย gòr sa-mŏo-ee Koh Samui

สวนลุมพินี sŏo-un loom-pi-nee Lumpini Park

นครปฐม na-korn bpa-tŏm Nakhorn Pathom

พัทยา pút-ta-yah Pattaya

261

ภูเก็ต poo-gèt Phuket
ประตูน้ำ bpra-dtoo náhm Pratu Nam
แม่น้ำแคว mâir-náhm kwair River Kwai
สนามหลวง sa-năhm lŏo-ung Sanam Luang
สยามแสควร์ sa-yăhm sa-kwair Siam Square
สงขลา sŏng-klăh Songkhla
สุโขทัย sòo-kŏh-tai Sukhothai
ธนบุรี ton-boo-ree Thonburi
อุบลราชธานี oo-bon râht-cha-tah-nee Ubonratchathani
อนุสาวรีย์ชัยสมรภูมิ a-nóo-săh-wa-ree chai sa-mŏr-ra-poom Victory Monument
เยาวราช yao-wa-râht Yaowarat (China Town area of Bangkok)

Post office

ผู้รับ pôo rúp addressee
ทางอากาศ tahng ah-gàht airmail
กรุงเทพฯ groong-tâyp Bangkok
ตู้จดหมาย dtôo jòt-măi letter box, mail box
ที่อื่น têe èun other places
พัสดุ pút-sa-dòo parcels
รหัสไปรษณีย์ ra-hùt bprai-sa-nee postcode
ที่ทำการไปรษณีย์ têe tum gahn bprai-sa-nee post office
ลงทะเบียน long ta-bee-un registered mail
ผู้ส่ง pôo sòng sender
ไปรษณียากร bprai-sa-nee-yah-gorn stamps
ทางเรือ tahng reu-a surface mail
โทรเลข toh-ra-lâyk telegrams
โทรศัพท์ toh-ra-sùp telephone

Public buildings

สนามบิน sa-năhm bin airport
ธนาคาร ta-nah-kahn bank
สนามมวย sa-năhm moo-ay boxing stadium
สถานีรถเมล์ sa-tăhn-nee rót may bus station
โรงภาพยนตร์ rohng pâhp-pa-yon cinema, movie theater
คลีนิค klee-ník clinic
วิทยาลัย wít-ta-yah-lai college

กรมศุลกากร grom sŏon-la-gah-gorn Customs Department

กรม grom department (government)

ที่ว่าการอำเภอ têe wâh gahn um-per district office

กอง gorng division (government)

สถานทูต sa-tăhn tôot embassy

โรงพยาบาล rohng pa-yah-bahn hospital

โรงแรม rohng rairm hotel

กองตรวจคนเข้าเมือง gorng dtròo-ut kon kâo meu-ung Immigration Department

กรมแรงงาน grom rairng ngahn Labour Department

ศาล săhn law court

ห้องสมุด hôrng sa-mòot library

ตลาด dta-làht market

กระทรวง gra-soo-ung ministry

พิพิธภัณฑ์ pí-pít-ta-pun museum

สนามกีฬาแห่งชาติ sa-năhm gee-lah hàirng châht National Stadium

ร้านขายยา ráhn kăi yah pharmacy

สถานีตำรวจ sa-tăhn-nee dtum-ròo-ut police station

ไปรษณีย์ bprai-sa-nee post office

โรงเรียน rohng ree-un school

ร้าน ráhn shop, store

ศูนย์การค้า sŏon gahn káh shopping centre

ห้าง hâhng store, shop

องค์การส่งเสริมการท่องเที่ยวแห่งประเทศไทย ong-gahn sòng sěrm gahn tôrng têe-o hàirng bpra-tâyt TAT – Tourist Organisation of Thailand

กรมสรรพากร grom sŭn-pah-gorn Tax Department

วัด wút temple

โรงละคร rohng la-korn theatre

สถานีรถไฟ sa-tăhn-nee rót fai train station

มหาวิทยาลัย ma-hăh-wít-ta-yah-lai university

Public holidays

วันพระ wun prá Buddhist holy day

วันหยุดราชการ wun yòot râht-cha-gahn official public

holiday

วันขึ้นปีใหม่ wun kêun bpee mài New Year's Day

วันสงกรานต์ wun sŏng-grahn Songkran Day (Thai New Year)

Rail travel

จองตั๋วล่วงหน้า jorng dtŏo-a lôo-ung nâh advance bookings

ถึง tĕung arrives

ออก òrk departs

แผนกสอบถาม pa-nàirk sòrp tăhm enquiries

สุขาชาย sŏo-kăh chai gents' toilets, men's room

สุขาหญิง sŏo-kăh yĭng ladies' toilets, ladies' room

รับฝากของ rúp fàhk kŏrng left luggage, baggage checkroom

ชานชาลา chahn-chah-lah platform, (US) track

ประชาสัมพันธ์ bpra-chah sŭm-pun public relations

สถานีรถไฟ sa-tăh-nee rót fai railway station, train station

ที่จำหน่ายตั๋ว têe jum-nài dtŏo-a ticket office

กำหนดเวลาเดินรถ gum-nòt way-lah dern ròt timetable,

(US) schedule

รถไฟ rót fai train

ห้องพักผู้โดยสาร hôrng púk pôo doy-ee săhn waiting room

Regions, provinces etc

ชายแดน chai dairn border

เขต kàyt boundary; area

ภาคกลาง pâhk glahng central region

แม่น้ำเจ้าพระยา mâir-náhm jâo pra-yah Chao Phraya River

ประเทศ bpra-tâyt country

อำเภอ um-per Amphoe, district

แม่โขง mâir-kŏhng Mekhong River

ภาคอีสาน pâhk ee-săhn north-eastern region

ภาคเหนือ pâhk nĕu-a northern region

จังหวัด jung-wùt province

ภาคใต้ pâhk dtâi southern region

ตำบล dtum-bon Tambon, sub-district

บ้านนอก bâhn-nôrk up-

country
ต่างจังหวัด dtàhng jung-wùt
up-country

Restaurants, bars

บริการ ๒๔ ชั่วโมง bor-ri-
gahn 24 chôo-a mohng
24-hour service
ห้องแอร์ hôrng-air air-
conditioned room
ร้านอาหารโต้รุ่ง ráhn ah-hăhn
dtôh rôong all-night
restaurant
บาร์ bah bar
ชาม chahm bowl, dish
อาหารเช้า ah-hăhn cháo
breakfast
คอฟฟี่ช็อบ kórp-fêe chórp
café serving coffees,
alcoholic drinks, snacks and
meals
อาหารจีน ah-hăhn jeen
Chinese food
อาหารเย็น ah-hăhn yen
evening meal
อาหาร ah-hăhn food
อาหารญี่ปุ่น ah-hăhn yêe-
bpòon Japanese food
อาหารกลางวัน ah-hăhn

glahng wun lunch
อาหารมุสลิม ah-hăhn
móo-sa-lim Muslim food
อาหารอีสาน ah-hăhn
ee-săhn North-Eastern
food
สวนอาหาร sŏo-un ah-hăhn
open-air restaurant
ชามละ ... chahm la ... ... per
bowl/dish
จานละ ... jahn la ... ... per
plate/dish
จาน jahn plate, dish
ราคา rah-kah price
ภัตตาคาร pút-dtah-kahn
restaurant
ร้านอาหาร ráhn ah-hăhn
restaurant
ห้องอาหาร hôrng ah-hăhn
restaurant
อาหารทะเล ah-hăhn ta-lay
seafood
เชลล์ชวนชิม chen choo-un
chim Shell® recommended,
seal of approval, equivalent
to Good Food Guide
อาหารปักษ์ใต้ ah-hăhn bpùk
dtâi Southern food
อาหารไทย ah-hăhn tai Thai
food
อาหารฝรั่ง ah-hăhn fa-rùng
Western food

Road signs

ทางโค้ง tahng kóhng bend
ระวังทางข้างหน้าเป็นทาง
เอก ra-wung tahng kâhng
nâh bpen tahng àyk caution:
major road ahead
ระวัง ra-wung caution
อันตราย un-dta-rai danger
ทางเบี่ยง tahng bèe-ung
diversion
ขับช้าๆ kùp cháh cháh drive
slowly
๔๐ ก.ม. sèe sìp gi-loh-mét
40 kilometres
๔ ตัน sìi dtun 4 tons
หยุด ตรวจ yòot - dtròo-ut
halt - checkpoint
โรงพยาบาลห้ามใช้เสียง
rohng pa-yah-bahn hâhm
chái sěe-ung hospital: no
sounding horns
ชิดซ้าย chít sái keep left
ห้ามเข้า hâhm kâo no entry
ห้ามแซง hâhm sairng no
overtaking, no passing
ห้ามจอดรถ hâhm jòrt rót no
parking
ห้ามเลี้ยว hâhm lée-o no
turning
ห้ามกลับรถ hâhm glùp rót no
U-turns
ห้ามรถทุกชนิด hâhm rót tóok
cha-nít no vehicles
ทางรถไฟ tahng rót fai railway
โรงเรียน rohng ree-un school
หยุด yòot stop
๓ ม. sahm mét 3 metres

Shopping

บาท bàht baht (unit of currency)
ลูกกละ ... บาท lôok la ... bàht
... baht each (e.g. for large fruit)
ใบละ ... บาท bai la ... bàht
... baht each (e.g. for eggs, fruit)
ตัวละ ... บาท dtoo-a la ...
bàht ... baht each (e.g. items of
clothing)
โลละ ... บาท loh la ... bàht
... baht per kilo
คู่ละ ... บาท kôo la ... baht
... baht per pair (e.g. shoes)
ชิ้นละ ... บาท chín la ... bàht
... baht per piece/portion
สุขภัณฑ์ sòok-ka-pun
bathroom accessories
ที่จ่ายเงิน têe jài ngern cash
desk, cashier
พนักงานเก็บเงิน pa-núk
ngahn gèp ngern cashier
แผนกเด็ก pa-nàirk dèk

children's department
แผนกไฟฟ้า pa-nàirk fai fáh
electrical goods
เครื่องเรือน krêu-ung reu-un
furniture
ราคา rah-kah price
วิทยุทีวี wít-ta-yóo - tee-wee
radio – TV
ลดราคา lót rah-kah sale;
reduced
รองเท้า rorng-táo shoes
ลดพิเศษ lót pi-sàyt special
reductions
อุปกรณ์กีฬา òo-bpa-gorn
gee-láh sports equipment
ของเล่น kŏrng lên toys
นาฬิกา nah-li-gah watches

Sport

กรีฑา gree-tah athletics
มวย moo-ay boxing
ฟุตบอล fóot-born football
ประตู bpra-dtoo goal
กอล์ฟ górp golf
สนามกอล์ฟ sa-nǎhm górp
golf course
สนามม้า sa-nǎhm máh race
course
กีฬา gee-láh sport
สนามกีฬา sa-nǎhm gee-láh
stadium
ว่ายน้ำ wâi náhm swimming
ทีม teem team
เทนนิส ten-nít tennis
สนามเทนนิส sa-nǎhm ten-nít
tennis court
มวยไทย moo-ay tai Thai
boxing

Streets and roads

ตรอก dtròrk lane (off a soi)
ซอย soy lane, soi
ถนน ta-nŏn road

Thai culture

เมืองโบราณ meu-ung boh-
rahn Ancient City
กรมศิลปากร grom sǐn-la-
bpa-korn Department of
Fine Arts
ตลาดน้ำ dta-làht náhm
Floating Market
พิพิธภัณฑ์ pi-pít-ta-pun
museum
พิพิธภัณฑ์สถานแห่งชาติ
pi-pít-ta-pun sa-tǎhn hàirng
châht National Museum

267

โรงละครแห่งชาติ rohng la-korn hàirng châht National Theatre

พระปฐมเจดีย์ prá-bpa-tŏm jay-dee Pra Pathom Jedi (Buddhist monument)

พระบรมมหาราชวัง prá-ba-rom-ma-hăh-râtch-a-wung Royal Palace

วังสวนผักกาด wung sŏo-un pùk-gàht Suan Pakkard Palace

วัด wút temple

วัดพระแก้ว wút pra-kâir-o Temple of the Emerald Buddha

มวยไทย moo-ay tai Thai boxing

รำไทย rum tai Thai dancing

วัดโพธิ์ wút poh Wat Po

Timetables

ถึง tĕung arrives

วันที่ wun-têe date

วัน wun day

ออก òrk departs

วันหยุด wun yòot holiday

นาฬิกา nah-li-gah hours

เวลา way-lah time

กำหนดเวลาเดินรถ gum-nòt way-lah dern rót timetable, (US) schedule

วันนี้ wun née today

พรุ่งนี้ prôong née tomorrow

วันเสาร์อาทิตย์ wun săo ah-tít weekend

เมื่อวานนี้ mêu-a wahn née yesterday

Toilets

ไม่ว่าง mâi wâhng engaged

บุรุษ boo-ròot gentlemen

ชาย chai gents

หญิง yĭng ladies

สตรี sa-dtree ladies

ผู้ชาย pôo-chai men

ช. chor men

ห้องน้ำ hôrng náhm toilet, rest room

สุขา sòo-kăh toilet, rest room

ว่าง wâhng vacant

ญ. yor women

ผู้หญิง pôo-yĭng women

Menu
Reader:
Food

Contents

Essential terms

bowl chahm ชาม
chopsticks dta-gèe-up ตะเกียบ
cup tôo-ay ถ้วย
dessert kŏrng wăhn ของหวาน
fish bplah ปลา
fork sôrm ส้อม
glass gâir-o แก้ว
knife mêet มีด
meat néu-a เนื้อ
menu may-noo เมนู
noodles gŏo-ay dtěe-o ก๋วยเตี๋ยว
pepper prík tai พริกไทย
plate jahn จาน
rice kâo ข้าว
salt gleu-a เกลือ
set menu ah-hăhn chóOt อาหารชุด
soup sóOp ซุป
spoon chórn ช้อน
table dtó โต๊ะ

another ... èek ... nèung อีก ... หนึ่ง
excuse me! (to call waiter/waitress) kOOn krúp (kâ)! คุณครับ(ค่ะ)
could I have the bill, please? chék bin เช็คบิล

272

Basic foods

เนยสด ner-ee sòt butter
เนยแข็ง ner-ee kăirng cheese
น้ำพริก núm prík chilli paste
กะทิ ga-tí coconut milk
น้ำปลา núm bplah fish sauce
แป้งสาลี bpâirng săh-lee flour
น้ำผึ้ง núm pêung honey
แยม yairm jam; marmalade
น้ำมันพืช núm mun pêut oil
น้ำมันมะกอก núm mun ma-gòrk olive oil
น้ำมันหอย núm mun hŏy oyster sauce
น้ำจิ้ม núm jîm sauce
น้ำซีอิ๊ว núm see éw soy sauce
น้ำตาล núm dtahn sugar
น้ำส้ม núm sôm vinegar
โยกัด yoh-gut yoghurt

Basic main meals

ข้าวผัดไก่ kâo pùt gài chicken fried rice
ข้าวมันไก่ kâo mun gài chicken rice
ข้าวผัดปู kâo pùt bpoo crab fried rice

บะหมี่แห้ง ba-mèe hâirng 'dry' egg noodles, served without soup
ก๋วยเตี๋ยวแห้ง gŏo-ay dtĕe-o hâirng 'dry' noodles, served without soup
ข้าวหน้าเป็ด kâo nâh bpèt duck rice
บะหมี่น้ำ ba-mèe náhm egg noodle soup
ก๋วยเตี๋ยวผัดซีอิ๊ว gŏo-ay dtĕe-o pùt see éw noodles fried in soy sauce
ก๋วยเตี๋ยวผัดราดหน้า gŏo-ay dtĕe-o pùt râht nâh noodles with fried meat, vegetables and thick gravy
ก๋วยเตี๋ยวน้ำ gŏo-ay dtĕe-o náhm noodle soup
ข้าวผัดหมู kâo pùt mŏo pork fried rice
ข้าวหมูแดง kâo mŏo dairng 'red' pork rice (pork soaked in a red marinade)
ข้าวคลุกกะปิ kâo klóok ga-bpì rice and shrimp paste fried together and served with pork and shredded omelette
ข้าวผัดกุ้ง kâo pùt gôong shrimp fried rice
ผัดไทย pùt tai Thai-style fried

noodles

ขนมจีนแกงไก่ ka-nŏm jeen gairng gài Thai vermicelli with chicken curry

Beef and beef dishes

เนื้อผัดน้ำมันหอย néu-a pùt núm mun hŏy beef fried in oyster sauce

เนื้อผัดพริก néu-a pùt prík beef fried with chillies

เนื้อผัดกระเทียมพริกไทย néu-a pùt gra-tee-um prík tai beef fried with garlic and pepper

เนื้อผัดขิง néu-a pùt kĭng beef fried with ginger

เนื้อสับผัดพริกกระเพรา néu-a sùp pùt prík gra-prao minced beef fried with chillies and basil

เนื้อเสต็ก néu-a sa-dték steak

Bread

ขนมปัง ka-nŏm-bpung bread; roll

ปอนด์ bporn loaf

ขนมปังปิ้ง ka-nŏm bpung bpîng toast

Cakes and biscuits, sweet pastries

คุกกี้ kóok-gêe biscuit, cookie

ขนมเค้ก ka-nŏm káyk cake

แป้งขนม bpâirng ka-nŏm pastry (dough)

ขนม ka-nŏm pastry, small cake

Condiments and seasonings, herbs and spices

ใบกระเพรา bai gra-prao basil

พริก prík chilli

ผักชี pùk chee coriander

ข่า kàh galangal (similar to ginger)

ขิง kĭng ginger

เครื่องเทศ krêu-ung tâyt herbs

ตะไคร้ dta-krái lemon grass

พริกไทย prík tai pepper

เกลือ gleu-a salt

Cooking methods and typical combinations

... ต้ม ... dtôm boiled ...

... ย่าง ... yâhng charcoal-grilled ...

... ทอด ... tôrt deep-fried ...

... ผัดหน่อไม้ ... pùt nòr-mái ... fried with bamboo shoots

... ผัดใบกระเพรา ... pùt bai gra-prao ... fried with basil leaves

... ผัดพริก ... pùt prík ... fried with chillies

... ทอดกระเทียมพริกไทย ... tôrt gra-tee-um prík tai ... fried with garlic and pepper

... ผัดขิง ... pùt kǐng ... fried with ginger

... อบ ... òp oven-cooked ...

... ผัด ... pùt stir-fried ...

... เปรี้ยวหวาน ... bprêe-o wǎhn sweet and sour ...

ปิ้ง bpîng toasted

Curries

แกงเนื้อ gairng néu-a beef curry

แกงเขียวหวาน gairng kěe-o wǎhn beef curry made using green curry paste, made from green chilli peppers

ข้าวแกง kâo gairng curry and rice

แกงไก่ gairng gài chicken curry

พะแนง pa-nairng 'dry' curry (in thick curry sauce)

พะแนงเนื้อ pa-nairng néu-a 'dry' beef curry (in thick curry sauce)

พะแนงไก่ pa-nairng gài 'dry' chicken curry (in thick curry sauce)

พะแนงหมู pa-nairng mǒo 'dry' pork curry (in thick curry sauce)

แกงกาหรี่ gairng ga-rèe Indian-style curry made with beef and potatoes cooked in coconut milk with yellow curry paste

แกงมัสหมั่น gairng mút-sa-mùn 'Muslim' curry containing beef, potatoes and peanuts

แกงเผ็ด gairng pèt spicy curry

แกงจืด gairng jèut vegetable soup or stock (an accompaniment to curries)

แกง gairng 'wet' curry – meat cooked in coconut milk and served in a bowl full of liquid

Desserts

กล้วยบวชชี glôo-ay bòo-ut chee banana in sweet coconut-milk sauce

ของหวาน kŏrng wăhn dessert

ไอศครีม ai-sa- kreem ice cream

ข้าวเหนียวมะม่วง kăo něe-o ma-môo-ung sweet sticky rice, mango and coconut cream

ตะโก้ dta-gôh Thai-style jelly with coconut cream

Eggs and egg dishes

ไข่ต้ม kài dtôm boiled egg

ไข่ kài egg

ไข่พะโล้ kài pa-lóh egg stewed

in soy sauce and spices

ไข่ยัดไส้ kài yút sâi filled omelette

ไข่ดาว kài dao fried egg

ไข่เจียว kài jee-o omelette

ไข่ลูกเขย kài lôok kěr-ee 'son-in-law' eggs – hard-boiled eggs with various condiments

ไข่ลวก kài lôo-uk very soft boiled egg (eaten, or rather 'drunk' almost raw)

Fish and seafood

ปู bpoo crab

ปลา bplah fish

กุ้งใหญ่ gôong yài lobster

หอยแมงภู่ hŏy mairng pôo mussels

ปลาหมึกยักษ์ bplah-mèuk yúk octopus

หอยนางรม hŏy nahng rom oyster

อาหารทะเล ah-hăhn ta-lay seafood

หอย hŏy shellfish

กุ้ง gôong shrimp, prawn

ปลาหมึก bplah-mèuk squid

Fish and seafood dishes

กุ้งเผา gôong păo barbecued prawns

กุ้งทอดกระเทียมพริกไทย gôong tôrt gra-tee-um prík tai prawns fried with garlic and pepper

กุ้งผัดใบกระเพรา gôong pùt bai gra-prao shrimps fried with basil leaves

กุ้งผัดพริก gôong pùt prík shrimps fried with chillies

ทอดมันกุ้ง tôrt mun gôong shrimp 'tort mun', finely minced shrimps, fried in batter with spices

ปลาหมึกผัดพริก bplah-mèuk pùt prík squid fried with chillies

ปลาหมึกทอดกระเทียม พริกไทย bplah-mèuk tôrt gra-tee-um prík tai squid fried with garlic and pepper

ปลาเปรี้ยวหวาน bplah bprêe-o wăhn sweet and sour fish

Fruit

แอปเปิ้ล air-bpêrn apple

กล้วย glôo-ay banana

มะพร้าว ma-práo coconut

น้อยหน่า nóy-nàh custard apple – green heart-shaped fruit with white flesh

อินทผาลัม in-ta-păh-lum dates

ทุเรียน too-ree-un durian – large green fruit with spiny skin, yellow flesh and a pungent smell

ผลไม้ pŏn-la-mái fruit

องุ่น a-ngòon grapes

ฝรั่ง fa-rùng guava – green-skinned fruit with white flesh

ขนุน ka-nŏon jackfruit – large melon-shaped fruit with thick, green skin and yellow flesh

มะนาว ma-nao lemon; lime

ลำใย lum-yai longan – like a lychee

ลิ้นจี่ lín-jèe lychee

มะม่วง ma-môo-ung mango

มังคุด mung-kóot mangosteen – round fruit

with a thick, purplish-brown skin and white flesh

แตงไทย dtairng tai melon

ส้ม sôm orange

มะละกอ ma-la-gor papaya – green or yellow-skinned oblong-shaped fruit with reddish-orange flesh

ลูกพีช lôok pêech peach

ลูกแพร์ lôok pair pear

สับปะรด sùp-bpa-rót pine-apple

ลูกพลัม lôok plum plum

ส้มโอ sôm oh pomelo – similar to grapefruit

เงาะ ngór rambutan – small fruit with reddish prickly skin and white flesh

ชมพู่ chom-pôo rose apple – red, pink or white strawberry-shaped fruit

ละมุด la-móot sapodilla – small brown-skinned fruit, similar in taste and texture to a pear

สตรอเบอรี่ sa-dtror-ber-rêe strawberry

แตงโม dtairng moh water melon

Meat

เนื้อ néu-a beef; meat

ไก่ gài chicken

เป็ด bpèt duck

เครื่องใน krêu-ung nai kidneys

ไต tai kidneys

เนื้อแกะ néu-a gàir lamb

ตับ dtùp liver

หมู mŏo pork

เนื้อหมู néu-a mŏo pork

Menu terms

อาหารจีน ah-hăhn jeen Chinese food

อาหาร ah-hăhn cuisine, cooking; meal; food

กับข้าว gùp kâo dish, meal

เมนู may-noo menu

รายการอาหาร rai gahn ah-hăhn menu

ราคา rah-kah price

Miscellaneous dishes

ทอดมัน tôrt mun deep-fried fish-cakes

ขนมจีบ ka-nŏm jèep 'dim-sum' – steamed balls of minced pork in dough

ปอเปี๊ยะทอด bpor bpêe-a tôrt Thai spring roll

Pork and pork dishes

หมูสับผัดพริกกระเพรา mŏo sùp pùt prík gra-prao minced pork fried with chillies and basil

หมู mŏo pork

เนื้อหมู néu-a mŏo pork

หมูผัดใบกระเพรา mŏo pùt bai gra-prao pork fried with basil leaves

หมูผัดพริก mŏo pùt prík pork fried with chillies

หมูทอดกระเทียมพริกไทย mŏo tôrt gra-tee-um prík tai pork fried with garlic and pepper

หมูผัดขิง mŏo pùt kĭng pork fried with ginger

หมูพะโล้ môo pa-lóh pork stewed in soy sauce

ซี่โครง sêe krohng mŏo spare ribs

หมูเปรี้ยวหวาน mŏo bprêe-o

wăhn sweet and sour pork

หมูสะเต๊ะ mŏo sa-dtáy thin strips of charcoal-grilled pork

Poultry and poultry dishes

ไก่ย่าง gài yâhng barbecued or roast chicken

ไก่ gài chicken

ไก่ต้มข่า gài dtôm kàh chicken boiled in spicy stock

ไก่ผัดหน่อไม้ gài pùt nòr-mái chicken fried with bamboo shoots

ไก่ผัดใบกระเพรา gài pùt bai gra-prao chicken fried with basil leaves

ไก่ผัดเม็ดมะม่วงหิมพานต์ gài pùt mét ma-môo-ung hĭm-ma-pahn chicken fried with cashew nuts

ไก่ผัดพริก gài pùt prík chicken fried with chillies

ไก่ทอดกระเทียมพริกไทย gài tôrt gra-tee-um prík tai chicken fried with garlic and pepper

ไก่ผัดขิง gài pùt kĭng chicken

fried with ginger

ไก่ผัดหน่อไม้ฝรั่ง gài pùt nòr-mái fa-rùng chicken with asparagus

เป็ด bpèt duck

เป็ดย่าง bpèt yâhng roast duck

ไก่ผัดเปรี้ยวหวาน gài pùt brêe-o wǎhn sweet and sour chicken

Rice and noodles

ข้าวสวย kâo sǒo-ay boiled rice

หมี่กรอบ mèe gròrp crispy noodles

บะหมี่ ba-mèe egg noodles

ข้าวผัด kâo pùt fried rice

เส้นใหญ่ sên yài large (width of noodles)

ผัดราดหน้า pùt râht nâh noodles with fried vegetables and meat, served with a thick gravy

ก๋วยเตี๋ยว gǒo-ay dtěe-o rice-flour noodles

ข้าว kâo rice

ข้าวต้ม kâo dtôm rice porridge

เส้นเล็ก sên lék small (width of noodles)

ข้าวเหนียว kâo něe-o sticky rice

ขนมจีน ka-nǒm jeen Thai vermicelli

วุ้นเส้น wóon-sên transparent noodles

เส้นหมี่ sên mèe very small (width of noodles)

Salads

ส้มตำ sôm dtum papaya salad made with unripe green papaya, chillies, lime juice, fish sauce and dried shrimps

สลัด sa-lùt salad

ยำ yum Thai salad

Snacks and sweets

ช็อกโกเลต chórk-goh-let chocolate

มันฝรั่งทอด mun fa-rùng tôrt crisps, (US) potato chips

ไอศครีม ai-sa-kreem ice cream

ไอศครีมแท่ง ai-sa-kreem

tâirng ice lolly

อมยิ้ม om-yím lollipop

ถั่ว tòo-a nuts; peanuts

ถั่วลิสง tòo-a li-sŏng
  peanuts

ทอฟฟี่ tórp-fêe sweets,
  candies

ลูกกวาด lôok gwàht sweets,
  candies

Soups

ต้มยำไก่ dtôm yum gài
  chicken 'tom yam' spicy
  soup

บะหมี่น้ำ ba-mèe náhm egg
  noodle soup

ต้มยำปลา dtôm yum bplah
  fish 'tom yam' spicy soup

ต้มยำโป๊ะแตก dtôm yum bpó
  dtàirk mixed seafood 'tom
  yam' spicy soup

ก๋วยเตี๋ยวน้ำ gŏo-ay dtĕe-o
  náhm noodle soup

ต้มยำกุ้ง dtôm yum gôong
  shrimp 'tom yam' spicy
  soup

แกงส้ม gairng sôm spicy
  vegetable soup

Vegetables and vegetable dishes

หน่อไม้ฝรั่ง nòr-mái fa-rùng
  asparagus

มะเขือ ma-kěu-a aubergine,
  eggplant

หน่อไม้ nòr mái bamboo
  shoots

ถั่วงอก tòo-a ngôrk bean
  sprouts

กะหล่ำปลี ga-lùm-bplee
  cabbage

หัวผักกาดแดง hŏo-a pùk-
  gàht dairng carrot

ดอกกะหล่ำปลี dòrk ga-lùm-
  bplee cauliflower

พริก prík chilli

มันฝรั่งทอด mun fa-rùng tôrt
  chips, French fries

แตงกวา dtairng-gwah
  cucumber

ผัดผักบุ้งไฟแดง pùt pùk
  bôong fai dairng fried
  morning-glory (type of greens)

กระเทียม gra-tee-um garlic

ขิง kĭng ginger

พริกหยวก prík yòo-uk green
  pepper

ผักกาด pùk-gàht lettuce

281

ถั่วลันเตา tòo-a lun-dtao
  mange-tout

ผักบุ้ง pùk bôong morning-
  glory (type of greens)

เห็ด hèt mushrooms

หัวหอม hŏo-a hŏrm onion

ถั่ว tòo-a peas; beans; lentils

มันฝรั่ง mun fa-rùng potato

พริกหยวกแดง prík yôo-uk
  dairng red pepper

ผักคะน้า pùk ka-náh spring
  greens

ต้นหอม dtôn hŏrm spring
  onions

ข้าวโพด kâo pôht sweet corn,
  maize

มะเขือเทศ ma-kĕu-a tâyt
  tomato

ผัก pùk vegetables

Menu Reader:
Drink

Contents

Essential terms

beer bee-a เบียร์
bottle kòo-ut ขวด
  another bottle of ..., please kŏr ... èek kòo-ut nèung ขอ ... อีกขวดหนึ่ง
coconut juice núm ma-práo น้ำมะพร้าว
coffee gah-fair กาแฟ
cup tôo-ay ถ้วย
  a cup of ..., please kŏr ... tôo-ay nèung ขอ ... ถ้วยหนึ่ง
fruit juice núm pŏn-la-mái น้ำผลไม้
gin lâo yin เหล้ายิน
  a gin and tonic, please kŏr yin toh-nik ขอยินโทนิค
glass gâir-o แก้ว
milk nom นม
mineral water núm râir น้ำแร่
soda (water) núm soh-dah น้ำโซดา
soft drink náhm kòo-ut น้ำขวด
sugar núm dtahn น้ำตาล
tea núm chah น้ำชา
tonic (water) núm toh-nik น้ำโทนิค
water náhm น้ำ
whisky lâo wit-sa-gêe เหล้าวิสกี้
wine lâo wai เหล้าไวน์
wine list rai-gahn lâo wai รายการเหล้าไวน์

Beer, spirits, wine etc

เหล้า lâo alcohol, liquor
เบียร์ bee-a beer
ขวด kòo-ut bottle
เหล้าบรั่นดี lâo brùn-dee brandy
ค็อกเทล kórk-tayn cocktail
แก้ว gâir-o glass
เหล้ายิน lâo yin gin
ยินโทนิค yin toh-nik gin and tonic
น้ำแข็ง núm kǎirng ice
แม่โขง mâir-kǒhng Mekhong® whisky
เบียร์สิงห์ bee-a sǐng Singha® beer
วอดก้า word-gâh vodka
เหล้าวิสกี้ lâo wít-sa-gêe whisky, scotch
เหล้าไวน์ lâo wai wine

Coffee, tea etc

คาฟีน kah-feen caffeine
เย็น yen chilled
โกโก้ goh-gôh cocoa
กาแฟ gah-fair coffee
โอเลี้ยง oh-lée-ung iced black coffee
กาแฟเย็น gah-fair yen iced coffee
ชาใส่มะนาว chah sài ma-nao lemon tea
กาแฟผง gah-fair pǒng instant coffee
น้ำชา núm chah tea
ไม่ใส่นม mái sài nom without milk
ไม่ใส่น้ำตาล mái sài núm dtahn without sugar

Soft drinks

น้ำมะพร้าว núm ma-práo coconut juice
โค้ก kóhk Coke®
เครื่องดื่ม krêu-ung dèum drinks
ซ่า sâh fizzy, carbonated
น้ำส้มคั้น núm sôm kún fresh orange juice
น้ำแข็ง núm kǎirng ice
น้ำผลไม้ náhm pǒn-la-mái juice
นม nom milk
น้ำมะนาว núm ma-nao lemonade
น้ำแร่ núm râir mineral water
น้ำส้ม núm sôm orange juice

(bottled)

น้ำสับปะรด **núm sùp-bpa-rót**
pineapple juice

น้ำโซดา **núm soh-dah** soda
water

น้ำขวด **náhm kòo-ut** soft
drink

นมกระป๋อง **nom gra-bpŏrng**
tinned milk

น้ำมะเขือเทศ **núm ma-kĕu-a**
tâyt tomato juice

น้ำ **náhm** water